MALTHUS AND HIS WORK

Truly Yours
T R Malthus.

MALTHUS
AND HIS WORK

JAMES BONAR

Routledge
Taylor & Francis Group
LONDON AND NEW YORK

First published in 1885 by Frank Cass & Co. Ltd.

Second Edition	**1924**
New Impression	**1966**

This edition published 2013 by Routledge
2 Park Square, Milton Park, Abingdon, Oxfordshire OX14 4RN
711 Third Avenue, New York, NY 10017

First issued in paperback 2014

Routledge is an imprint of the Taylor & Francis Group, an informa business

ISBN 13: 978-0-714-61273-7 (hbk)
ISBN 13: 978-0-415-76038-6 (pbk)

INTRODUCTION.

Of the three English writers whose work has become a portion of all Political Economy, Malthus is the second in time and in honour. His services to general theory are at least equal to Ricardo's; and his full illustration of one particular detail will rank with the best work of Adam Smith.

In the following pages the detail will be the main subject, and general theory the episode. The *Political Economy* and minor writings of Malthus (which are not few) will be noticed only in relation to the *Essay on Population.*

Accordingly, the First of these Five Books will deal with the genesis, history, and contents of the Essay, plunging the reader *in medias res* and keeping him there, till the facts force him, in the Second Book, to recur with the author to Economical theory. The Third will show the mind of Malthus more clearly by adding to his economics his Ethics and Political

Philosophy; and the Fourth, with the case now fully stated, will criticize the Critics of the Essay, and try to determine how much of its doctrine remains still valuable. The Fifth Book, with its Biography, may help the reader to associate the living personality of the man with his writings.

London, June 1885.

1924.

In this Reprint, the biography (Book V.) has been expanded. There are Notes added to Book I. ch. ii. **44**; ch. v. **152**; ch. vi. **169**; Book II. ch. ii. **281**; ch iv. **318**; and Book IV. **398**.

The critic of page **344** was the late Prof. Edward Caird, to whom the book was dedicated.

Some obvious mistakes have been corrected. Otherwise the book remains as it was in 1885. It is not a treatise on population, or else after thirty-nine years (forty-five for the first two chapters) it would need to be entirely rewritten in view of new evidence and discussion, not to say of political changes before and after the Great War.

It is an account of one writer on population, generally ranked above his rivals.

The biography is placed last, for it was thought that interest in Malthus could not be assumed till something was known of his Work.

There are signs that the twentieth century will give him a fair hearing. This book will serve its purpose if it leads its readers to study the Essay for themselves.

Hampstead, 1st January, **1924.**

CONTENTS.

MALTHUS AND HIS WORK

MALTHUS AND HIS WORK.

BOOK I. THE ESSAY.

CHAPTER I.

FIRST THOUGHTS, 1798.

The Common Caricature—The Essay an Inquiry into the Poverty of Nations—Godwin's *Political Justice* and *Enquirer*—The Two Postulates and Conclusions from them—Condorcet's *Sketch of the Progress of the Human Mind*—Organic Perfectibility of Man and its Obstacles—Historical Context of the Essay—*The Crisis*—Pitt's Poor Bill—Malthus and his Teachers—Success explained—Theology and Metaphysics—Faults of the Essay—Immediate aim secured.

HE was the "best-abused man of the age." Bonaparte himself was not a greater enemy of his species. Here was a man who defended small-pox, slavery, and child-murder; who denounced soup-kitchens, early marriage, and parish allowances; who "had the impudence to marry after preaching against the evils of a family;" who thought the world so badly governed that the best actions do the most harm; who, in short, took all romance out of life and preached a dull sermon on the threadbare text—"Vanity of vanities, all is vanity." Such was the character of Malthus as described by his opponents.

If an angry man is probably in the wrong, an abusive man is certainly so; and, when not one or two, but one or two thousand are engaged in the abuse, the certainty amounts to a demonstration. We may measure the soundness of the victim's logic by the violence of the personal attacks made upon him. For most worldly purposes, to be ignored and to be refuted are the same thing.

Malthus from the first was not ignored. For thirty years it rained refutations. The question, as he stated it, was thoroughly threshed out. The *Essay on Population* passed in the author's lifetime through six editions (1798, 1803, 1806, 1807, 1817, and 1826); even between the first edition, in 1798, and the second, in 1803, there were more than a score of 'Replies'; and the discussion was carried on in private correspondence, as well as in public journals and parliamentary speeches. The case was fully argued; and no one who fairly considers the extent of the discussion, and the ability of the disputants, can fail to believe that we have, in the records of this controversy, ample materials for forming our own judgment on the whole question in dispute.

Such a privilege is seldom used. The world has no time to consult authorities, though it likes them to be within reach of consultation. When an author becomes an authority, he too often ceases to be read, and his doctrines, like current coin, are worn by use till they lose the clear image and superscription of the issuer. In this way an author's name may come to suggest, not his own book, but the current version of his doctrines. Malthus becomes Malthusianism, — Darwin, Darwinism; and if Adam Smith's name were more flexible he too would become an epithet.[1] As it is, Adam Smith has left a book which "every one praises and nobody reads," Malthus a book which no one reads and all abuse. The abuse is, fortunately, not quite unanimous; but it is certain that Malthus for a long time had an experience worse than Cassandra's, for his warnings were disbelieved without being heard or understood. Miss Martineau, in her girlhood, heard him denounced "very eloquently and forcibly by persons who never saw so much as the outside"[2] of his book. This was in 1816; and when at a later time she inquired about him for herself, she could never find any one who had read his book, but scores who could "make great argument about it and about," or write sentimental pamphlets on supposed Malthusian subjects. This carelessness was not confined to the general public; it infected the savants. Nothing more clearly shows how political economy, or at least one question of it, had descended into the streets and become a common recreation. Even Nassau William Senior, perhaps the most distinguished professor of political economy in his day, confessed with penitence that he had trusted more to his ears than to his eyes for a knowledge of Malthusian doctrine, and had written a learned criticism, not of the opinion of Mr. Malthus, but of that which

[1] The Germans talk of 'Smithianismus.' [2] *Autobiogr.*, vol. i. p. 71.

"the multitudes who have followed and the few who have endeavoured to oppose" Mr. Malthus, have assumed to be his opinion.[1]

The "opinion" so imagined by Senior and the multitude is still the current Malthusianism. A Malthusian is supposed to forbid all marriage. Mr. Malthus was supposed to believe that "the desire of marriage, which tends to increase population, is a stronger principle than the desire of bettering our condition, which tends to increase subsistence."[2] This meant, as Southey said, that "God makes men and women faster than He can feed them." The old adage was wrong then: Providence does not send meat where He sends mouths; on the contrary, He sends mouths wherever He sends meat, so that the poor can never cease out of the land, for, however abundant the food, marriage will soon make the people equally abundant. It is a question of simple division. A fortune that is wealth for one will not give comfort to ten, or bare life to twenty. The moral is, for all about to marry, "Don't," and for all statesmen, "Don't encourage them."

This caricature had enough truth in it to save it from instant detection, and its vitality is due to the superior ease in understanding, and therefore greater pleasure in hearing, a blank denial or a blank affirmation as compared with the necessary qualifications of a scientific statement. The truth must be told, however, that Malthus and the rest of the learned world

[1] Senior, *Two Lectures on Population*, 1829, Appendix, pp. 56, 57.

[2] Senior, *l. c.*, p. 56.

were by no means at utter discord. He always treated a hostile economist as a possible ally. He was carrying on the work of their common Founder. In the *Essay on Population* he was inquiring into the nature and causes of poverty, as Adam Smith had inquired into the nature and causes of wealth. But Malthus himself did not intend the one to be a mere supplement to the other. He did not approach the subject from a purely scientific side. He had not devoted long years of travel and reflection to the preparation of an economical treatise. Adam Smith had written his *Moral Sentiments* seventeen years before his greater work. When he wrote the latter he had behind him an academical and literary reputation; and he satisfied the just expectations of the public by giving them, in the two quarto volumes of the *Wealth of Nations*, his full-formed and completely digested conclusions and reasonings definitively expressed (1776). Malthus, on the contrary, gained his reputation by a bold and sudden stroke, well followed up. His *Essay* was an anonymous pamphlet in a political controversy, and was meant to turn the light of political economy upon the political philosophy of the day. Whatever the essay contained over and above politics, and however far afield the author eventually travelled in the later editions, there is no doubt about the first origin of the essay itself. It was not, as we are sometimes told, that, being a kind-hearted clergyman, he set himself to work to inquire whether after all it was right to increase the numbers of the population without caring for the quality of it. In 1798 Malthus was no doubt in holy orders and held a curacy at Albury; but he seems never to have been more than a curate. The Whigs offered him a living in his later years, but he passed it to his son;[1] and we should be far astray if we supposed his book no more than the "recreations of a country parson." "Parson" was in his case a title without a *rôle* and Cobbett's immortal nickname is very unhappy.[2] He had hardly more of the parson than Condillac of the abbé. In 1798 Pitt's Bill for extending relief to large families, and thereby encouraging population, was no doubt before the country; but we owe the essay not to William Pitt, but to William Godwin. The changed aspect of the book in its later editions need not blind us to the efficient cause of its first appearance.

Thomas Robert Malthus had graduated at Cambridge as ninth wrangler in the year 1788, in the twenty-second year of his age. In 1797, after gaining a fellowship at Jesus College, he happened to spend some time at his father's house at Albury in Surrey. Father and son discussed the questions of the day, the younger man attacking Jacobinism, the elder

[1] Macvey Napier's *Correspondence*, p. 187. Cf. *Pol. Econ.*, 2nd ed., pp. xxxv, liv.

[2] "Why," said I, "how many children do you reckon to have at last?" "I do not care how many," said the man, "God never sends mouths without sending meat." "Did you ever hear," said I, "of one Parson Malthus? he wants an act of parliament to prevent poor people from marrying young, and from having such lots of children." "Oh, the brute!" exclaimed the wife; while the husband laughed, thinking I was joking."—Cobbett's *Advice to Young Men*, Letter 3, p. 83. The references to Cobbett in the Essay are probably, 7th ed., pp. 310 and 318, cf. p. 313; but his name is not mentioned.

defending it. Daniel Malthus had been a friend and executor of Rousseau, and was an ardent believer in human progress. Robert had written a Whig tract, which he called *The Crisis*, in the year of Pitt's new loan and Napoleon's Italian campaign (1797); but he did not publish it, and his views were yet in solution. We may be sure the two men did not spare each other in debate. In the words of the elder Malthus, Robert then, if at no other time, "threw little stones" into his garden. An old man must have the patience of Job if he can look with calmness on a young man breaking his ideals. But in this case he at least recognized the strength of the slinger, and he bore him no grudge, though he did not live to be won by the concessions of the second essay (1803). That Robert, on his part, was not wanting in respect, is shown by an indignant letter, written in February, 1800, on his father's death, in reply to the supposed slight of a newspaper paragraph.[1]

The fireside debates had in that year (1797) received new matter. William Godwin, quondam parson, journalist, politician, and novelist, whose *Political Justice* was avowedly a "child of the Revolution,"[2] had written a new book, the *Enquirer*, in which many of his old positions were set in a new light. The father made it a point of honour to defend the *Enquirer*; the son played devil's advocate, partly from conviction, partly for the sake of

[1] Namely, in the *Monthly Magazine* for Jan. 1800. But see below, Book V.

[2] *Thoughts on Parr's Sermon*, p. 2, and *Pol. Justice*, Pref. p. x.

argument; and, as often happens in such a case, Robert found his case stronger than he had thought. Hard pressed by an able opponent, he was led, on the spur of the moment, to use arguments which had not occurred to him before, and of which *The Crisis* knows nothing. In calmer moments he followed them up to their conclusions. "The discussion," he tells us,[1] "started the general question of the future improvement of society, and the author at first sat down with an intention of merely stating his thoughts to his friend upon paper in a clearer manner than he thought he could do in conversation." But the subject opened upon him, and he determined to publish. This is the plain story of the publication of the *Essay on Population*, reduced to its simplest terms. At the very time when the best men in both worlds were talking only of progress, Malthus saw rocks ahead. French and English reformers were looking forward to a golden age of perfect equality and happiness; Malthus saw an irremovable difficulty in the way, and he refused to put the telescope to his blind eye.

There had been Cassandras before Malthus, and even in the same century. Dr. John Bruckner of Norwich had written in the same strain in his *Théorie du Système Animal*, in 1767;[2] and a few years earlier (in 1761) Dr. Robert Wallace, writing of the *Various Prospects of Mankind, Nature, and Providence*, had

[1] Preface to first edition of Essay, 1798.

[2] Leyden, 1767, translated under the title *Philosophical Survey of the Animal Creation*, Lond., 1768. See especially chs. vii. and x.

talked of community of goods as a cure for the ills of humanity, and then had found, very reluctantly, one fatal objection—the excessive population that would ensue. Men are always inclined to marry and multiply their numbers till the food is barely enough to support them all. This objection had since Wallace's time become a stock objection, to be answered by every maker of Utopias. It was left for Malthus to show the near approach which this difficulty makes to absolute hopelessness, and to throw the burden of proof on the other side. As the *Wealth of Nations* altered the standing presumption in favour of interference to one in favour of liberty in matters of trade, so the *Essay on Population* altered the presumption in favour of the advocates of progress to a presumption against them. This may not describe the final result of the essay, but it is a true account of its immediate effect. People had heard of the objection before; it was only now that they began to look on it as conclusive.

How had Godwin tried to meet it, when it was still in the hands of weaker men, and therefore not at all conclusive? He could not ignore it. In his *Political Justice* (1793) he had given the outlines of a "simple form of society, without government," on the principle of Tom Paine, which was also a received Jacobin motto, "Society is produced by our wants, government by our wickedness."[1] He says, with the ruling philosophy, that man is born a blank, and his outward circumstances make him good or evil.

[1] *Common Sense*, p. 1, quoted in *Pol. Justice*, Bk. II. ch. i. p. 124 (3rd ed.).

Thanks to human institutions, especially lawyers, sovereigns, and statesmen, the outward circumstances, he says, are as bad as they can be. Everywhere there is inequality. There is great poverty alongside of great riches, and great tyranny with great slavery. In the same way the best of his novels, *Caleb Williams* (1794), tells us how "things as they are" enable the rich sinner to persecute the poor righteous man. But he is no pessimist. The *Political Justice* does not end with a statement of evils. It goes on to show that in the end truth will conquer; men will listen to reason, they will abandon their present laws, and they will form a society without law or government or any kind of force; no such things will be needed when every man listens to reason, and contents himself with plain living and high thinking. There will be no king in Israel; every man will do that which is right in his own eyes. In our present society, says Godwin, it is distribution and not production that is at fault. There is more than enough of wealth for all, but it is not shared amongst all. One man has too much, another little or nothing. In the new society reason will change all that. Reason tells us that, if we make an equal division, not only of the good things of this life, but of the labour of making them, then we shall secure a production quite sufficient for the needs of plain livers, at the cost of perhaps half-an-hour's labour in a day from each of them.[1] Each of them will, therefore,

[1] *Pol. Justice*, Bk. VIII. ch. vi. p. 484. On the other hand, Franklin, in his *Letter on Luxury, Idleness, and Industry* (1784), had estimated the

have leisure, which is the true riches, and he will use the time for his own moral and intellectual improvement. In this way, by the omnipotence of truth and the power of persuasion, not by any violence or power of the sword, perfection and happiness will in time be established on the earth.

Godwin made no essential change in these views in the later editions of the *Political Justice* (1796 and 1798), or in the *Enquirer* (1797). "Among the faithless, faithful only he," when the excesses of the Terror made even Sir James Mackintosh (not to say Bishop Watson, Southey, and Wordsworth) a lukewarm reformer. Nothing in Godwin's life is more admirable than the perfect confidence with which he holds fast to his old faith in democratic principles and the perfectibility of man. If it is obstinacy, it is very like devotion; and perhaps the only author who shows an equal constancy is Condorcet, the Girondist, marked out for death, and writing in his hiding-place, almost under the eyes of the Convention, his eager book on the *Progress of the Species*. Nothing but intense sincerity and sheer depth of conviction could have enabled these men to continue the defence of a dishonoured cause. They had not the martyr's greatest trial, the doubt whether he is right. The great impression made by their works was a sign that, as they felt strongly, they wrote powerfully. Malthus, who refuted both of them, apologized for giving serious

necessary labour more moderately at four hours. Sir Thos. More suggested nine. Owen recurred to the half-hour. *New Moral World*, 1836, pp. x, xi.

criticism to Condorcet's palpable extravagances by saying that Condorcet has many followers who will hold him unanswerable unless he is specially answered.[1] Of Godwin, Mr. Sumner, writing in 1816, says that though his book (the *Political Justice*) was becoming out of date, it was still "the ablest and best known statement" of the doctrines of equality that had ever appeared in England.[2] It has been justly called the "first text-book of the philosophical radicals." The actual effect of it cannot be measured by the number of copies sold on its first appearance. Godwin had placed it far beyond the reach of ordinary democrats by fixing the price at three guineas. In 1793 many who would have been his keenest readers could not have paid three shillings for it. But the event proved him wise in his generation. The Privy Council decided they might safely tolerate so dear a book; and a small audience even of the rich was better to Godwin than prosecution, which might mean exile and no audience at all.[3] Few writers of our own day have so good an excuse for making themselves inaccessible to the poor. Godwin, however, like Ruskin, reached the poor in spite of his arrangements for avoiding them. He filtered down among the masses; and his writings became a political as well as a literary power in England,

[1] *Essay*, 1st ed., pp. 161-2, footnote.

[2] *Records of the Creation*, vol. i. p. 54, note.

[3] Life by Kegan Paul, vol. i. p. 80. Cf. a curious passage in the *Edinburgh Review*, about Godwin's *Population*: "As the book was dear, and not likely to fall into the hands of the labouring classes, we had no thoughts of noticing it," July 1821, p. 363.

long before he had a poetic son-in-law to give him reflected glory. If a species is to be judged by its best individual, then Godwin represents better than Paine the class of political writers to which they both belong; and many fell down with Godwin when he fell down before Malthus.

The *Enquirer* was less popular than the *Political Justice.* Part of the charm of the latter undoubtedly lay in the elaborate completeness and systematic order of the whole discussion. The foundations were laid in the psychology of Locke ; and then the building was raised, stone by stone, until the whole was finished. But in the *Enquirer* Godwin's dislike of law had extended even to the form of composition. He had been wrong, he said, in trying to write a systematic treatise on society, and he would now confine himself to detached essays, wholly experimental, and not necessarily in harmony with one another. "He (the author) has carried this principle so far that he has not been severely anxious relative to inconsistency that may be discovered between the speculations of one essay and the speculations of another."[1] The contrast between these two styles is the contrast between a whole oratorio and a miscellaneous concert, or between a complete poem and a volume of extracts.

The thoughts were the same, though they had lost their attractive expression. The essay on *Avarice and Profusion*[2] tells us, among other things, that "a state of cultivated equality is that state which, in

[1] *Enquirer* (1797), Pref., p. 7. [2] Part II., Essay II.

speculation and theory, appears most consonant to the nature of man, and most conducive to the extensive diffusion of felicity." This was the essay which led Malthus and his father into their fruitful argument. The essay on *Riches and Poverty*, and the one on *Beggars*,[1] contain other applications of the same idea, with many moralizing digressions. Godwin has not lost his sweet Utopian vision; he has not yielded to the objections that baffled Dr. Robert Wallace; he thinks he has removed all objections.

He meets them[2] by saying first of all: "There is a principle in the nature of human society by means of which everything seems to tend to its level," when not interfered with; and the population of a country when left to itself does not seem to increase beyond the food. But in the second place, supposing things not to find their level in this way, the earth is wide and the evil day is far off. It may take myriads of centuries to till the untilled acres and to replenish the empty earth wi·h people, and much may happen before then. In fact, he views the subject as many of us view the question of our coal supply. Before it is exhausted we may be beyond the need of it.[3] The earth itself may have collapsed with all its inhabitants. Don't let us refuse a present blessing from fear of a remote future danger. Besides, it is not very hard to imagine a safeguard. Franklin says that "mind will one day become omnipotent over matter;"[4] why

[1] Part II., Essays I. and III.

[2] *Political Justice*, Book VIII. ch. ix. pp. 515-19 (3rd ed.).

[3] Cf. Rich. Jones, *Pol. Econ.* (1859), p. 596.

[4] Quoted, *Political Justice*, Book VIII. ch. viii. pp. 503, 520, on the authority of Price.

not over the matter of our own bodies? Does not the bodily health depend largely on the mind?

"A merry heart goes all the day;
Your sad tires in a mile, O!"

The time may come when we shall be so full of liveliness that we shall not sleep, and so full of life that we shall not die. The *need* for marriage will be superseded by earthly immortality, and the *desire* for it by the development of intellect. On the renewed earth of the future there will be neither marrying nor giving in marriage, but we shall be as the angels. "The whole will be a people of men, and not of children. Generation will not succeed generation, nor truth have, in a certain degree, to recommence her career every thirty years. Other improvements may be expected to keep pace with those of health and longevity. There will be no war, no crimes, no administration of justice as it is called, and no government. Besides this, there will be neither disease, anguish, melancholy, nor resentment. Every man will seek with ineffable ardour the good of all."[1]

This sweet strain had been enchanting the public for four or five years, when Malthus ventured to interrupt it with his modest anonymous *Essay on the Principle of Population as it affects the Future Improvement of Society.* The writer claims to be as hearty a philanthropist as Mr. Godwin, but he cannot allow the wish to be father to the thought, and believe in future perfection against evidence.

[1] *l. c.*, Book VIII. ch. ix. p. 528.

To prove a theory true, he says, it is not enough to show that you cannot prove its contradiction, or that you can prove its usefulness. It would be very useful to have eyes in both sides of our head; but that does not prove that we are going to have them. If you told me that man was becoming a winged creature like the ostrich, I should not doubt that he would find wings very useful, but I could hardly believe your prophecy without some kind of proof beyond the mere praises of flying. I should ask you to show palpable signs in his body and habits that such a change was going on, that his neck has been lengthening, his lips hardening, and his hair becoming feathery. In the same way, when you tell me that man is becoming a purely intellectual being, content with plain living and high thinking, I see there might be advantage in the change, but I ask for signs that it is in progress. I see none; but, on the contrary, I see strong reasons for believing in its impossibility. Grant me two postulates, and I disprove your millennium. The first is, that food is necessary; the second, that the instinct for marriage is permanent. No one denies the first, and Godwin's denial of the second is purely dogmatic. He has given us no proofs. Men have no doubt made progress in other respects; they have passed from barbarism to civilization. But in respect of the second postulate they are the same now as they were 4000 years ago. Individual exceptions are individual exceptions still. I am bound, therefore, to believe in the truth of my postulates, and I infer from them the impossibility of your millennium.

You speak of a society, he continues, where the members are all equally comfortable and at leisure. Suppose it established, it could not last; it would go to pieces through the principle of population alone. The seven years of plenty would be at once devoured by seven years of want. The proof of this is short and decisive:—Population, when unchecked, increases in a geometrical ratio; subsistence only in an arithmetical. "A slight acquaintance with numbers will show the immensity of the first power in comparison with the second."[1] "The race of plants and animals shrinks under this great restrictive law, and the race of man cannot by any efforts of reason escape from it. Among plants and animals its effects are waste of seed, sickness, and premature death, among men misery and vice," the former necessary, the latter probable. Now, in the old countries of Europe, population never is unchecked. It is checked by want of room and food. Vice and misery, and the fear of them, are always "equalizing" the numbers of the people with the food of the people. In the New World, "the cynosure of neighbouring eyes," there are fewer hindrances to early marriage; there is more room and there is more food; hard work is the only condition of a happy life. But, even there, population is not entirely unchecked; the hard work will at least interfere with the rearing of children; and the

[1] *Essay*, 1st ed., p. 14.

people, however comfortable, are not at the very highest pitch of comfort, or at the highest pitch of purity and simplicity of life; whereas, by assumption, Godwin's imaginary society is all these. If, therefore, the people of old Europe double their numbers once a century, and the people of new America (at least in the United States) once in twenty-five years, we may be sure that in the millennial society of Godwin,

> "Where all are proper and well-behaved,
> And all are free from sorrow and pain,"

the increase would be much faster. The "leisure" he talks of would soon disappear, and the old scramble for bread, the old inequality of rank and property, would again become the order of the day. We should have our own kind of society back again, with its masters and servants, landlords and tenants, rich and poor.[1]

Therefore (argues the writer of the essay) if Godwin's society were once made it could not last. But we grant too much in supposing it could ever be made. We cannot believe this and believe in the second postulate at the same time; and the second postulate is so certain that we can predict by it. The same causes, then, that would have destroyed Godwin's newly-formed society will prevent it from ever being formed at all. "The passion between the sexes has appeared in every age to be so nearly the same that it may always be considered, in

[1] 1st ed., pp. 20, 173, &c., 7th ed., Book III. ch. ii.

algebraic language, as a given quantity."[1] In spite of the whimpering of old men and *roués*, "the pleasures of pure love will bear the contemplation of the most improved reason and the most exalted virtue."[2] Godwin views the matter in a dry, intellectual light, and asks us to abstract from all accessories before we form an estimate of the passion in question. One man or one woman will then be as good as another. But he might as well tell us to strip off all the leaves before we estimate our liking for trees. We do not admire the bare pole, but the whole tree, the tree with all the "attendant circumstances" of branches and foliage. As well deprive a magnet of its chief powers of attraction, and then ask us to confess it as weak as other minerals.[3] The fact is, that man's large discourse, which marks him out from the brutes, makes him hide the marriage instinct under a mass of "attendant circumstances" before he lets himself be drawn by it. He will not obey the instinct simply *more feræ*, or in animal fashion, because he feels it. But it is not destroyed, only disguised. The love is not purely intellectual. Reason, with its calculation of consequences, can save a man from the abuse of a passion, but cannot destroy the passion itself;[4] and (he might have added) its "looking before and after" includes fancy as well as thought. Take this passion then as it is, an adoration it may be of an assemblage of accessories; it can never die out of the world.

[1] 1st ed., p. 128; cf. p. 210.
[2] *Ibid.* p. 211.
[3] *Ibid.* p. 215.
[4] *Ibid.* p. 215.

From this cheerful premise, what conclusion follows? One not altogether cheerful: Wherever Providence sends meat He will send mouths. Wherever the people have room and food, they will marry and multiply their numbers, till they press against the limits of both, and begin a fierce struggle for existence, in which death is the punishment of defeat. Godwin and the whole French school are sadly wrong in attributing all inequality to human institutions; human nature is to blame, and, without any artificial aid, this one passion of human nature will be the standing cause of inequality, the most serious obstacle to the removal of it.[1] Dr. Robert Wallace had more wisdom than he wot of.

Examine the meaning of this argument and its conclusion. It involves an answer to Godwin's first defence against Wallace. Here is something very like a law of nature, a truth past, present, and future, or, in other words, a truth which, being scientific, ought not to be stated in terms of time at all: "Where goods increase, they are increased that eat them." The "struggle for existence" (Malthus uses the very phrase) is a present fact, as it has been a past fact, and will be a future. No good is gained by rhetorical references to the wideness of the world and the possibilities of the ages.[2] In our own day and land we see people multiplying up to the limit of the food, and a "great restrictive law" preventing

[1] 1st ed., p. 17; cf. pp. 47-8.

[2] Even Comte, who reproves economists for saying that difficulties right themselves in the "long run," thinks that this particular difficulty will only occur *there*. (*Pos. Phil.*, ii. 128 (tr.); cf. p. 54.)

them, as it prevents all other animals, from multiplying beyond that limit.[1] In our own day and country, men marry when they cannot support a family; the children whom they cannot support die of hunger or sickness, if the charity of the public does not interfere; —or else the fear of misery makes men avoid a marriage for which they have not the means, and their celibacy, whether pure or impure, keeps the numbers of the people on a level with the food.[2] Godwin himself had written in so many words: "There is a principle in human society by which population is perpetually kept down to the level of the means of subsistence."[3] Why did he not take one step more, and discover what that principle is?[4]

The fact is that Godwin was at once intellectually sanguine and emotionally cold. His ideal would have been a man "of large brain and no affections;" and when he wrote the *Political Justice* he was not aware of his own defect. At a later time he was not only aware of it, but anxious to remove it. In his Memoir of his wife, Mary Wollstonecraft (1798), and in the story of *St. Leon* (1799), the man who found the philosopher's stone, and became, to his own sorrow, immortal on earth, he confesses that he has hitherto taken too little thought of feeling as an element in human action. If Mary had been too much of a Werther, her husband had been too little.

[1] 1st ed., pp. 15, 16. [2] *Ibid.* pp. 19, 62—66.

[3] *Pol. Just.*, VIII. iii. 466.

[4] *Essay*, 1st ed., pp. 175-6, 193; 7th ed., pp. 272, 277. Cf. Gibbon, ch. L., quoted in *Essay*, 2nd ed., p. 94; 7th ed., p. 65: "The measure of population is regulated by the means of subsistence."

Like Condorcet (and like Buckle), he had believed civilization to be a purely intellectual movement. He had dogmatized on the omnipotence of truth and reason, and inferred the growth of a perfect society. He had dogmatized on the development of intellect, and inferred an earthly immortality. Moreover, in the *Memoir*, and in *St. Leon*, if he had added a little to his doctrines, he had recanted little or nothing, even in regard to immortality.

St. Leon is miserable only because his gift is peculiar to himself; an immortality that is common to all would be acceptable to all. A Methuselah would not be melancholy among antediluvians. Such was probably Godwin's position. The mere belief in the possibility of earthly immortality was not uncommon; Godwin is careful to number Bacon among its supporters.[1] Malthus was probably right in tracing it to the unconscious influence of Christianity,[2] though the progress in Godwin's days of the new science of chemistry had perhaps more to do with it, and Godwin's religion was never more than a bare Theism.[3] It was held by Holcroft, one of Godwin's most intimate friends,[4] and it was an important part of Condorcet's *Sketch of the Progress of the Human Spirit*.

In the days of the Terror (1794) Condorcet, from his hiding-place in the Rue Servandoni, had written of the "organic perfectibility of man." He looked

[1] *Pol. Just.*, Book VIII. ch. ix. p. 520 n. (3rd ed.).
[2] *Essay*, 1st ed., pp. 240-1.
[3] Due to Coleridge. See Godwin's *Life*, i. 357. [4] *Ibid.* i. 25.

to medicine, and to the arts and sciences in general, to banish disease and prolong human life "indefinitely."[1] Godwin trusted to the inward development of the mind, not to outward appliances.[2] But by different ways they arrive at the same terminus, and receive from their great critic very much the same reception there. Malthus points out to Godwin that there is no sign that the body is becoming subjugated to the mind. Even philosophers, said he (and he wrote feelingly, as he had the malady at the time of writing), cannot endure the toothache patiently,[3] and even a merry heart will not enable a weak man to walk as fast and as far as a strong man. There is no change in the human body, and little or no change in the relation of the mind to it. To Condorcet he simply points out that, while the arts have made the lengthening of life "indefinite," that does not mean "infinite." Gardeners can grow carnations "indefinitely" large; no man can ever say that he has seen the largest carnation that will ever be grown; but this he can say, that a carnation will never be as large as a cabbage. The limit is there, though it is undefined, and there is a limit also to the lengthening of human life, though no one can fix it to a year. Condorcet therefore has proved an earthly immortality only by a misuse of the word "indefinite." He has shown no organic change in man which would prove the possibility of perfection

[1] *Esquisse d'un tableau historique des progrès de l'esprit humain* (3rd ed., 1797), pp. 384 *seq.*

[2] *Political Justice*, VIII. ix. 520 n.

[3] *Essay*, 1st ed., p. 227.

in this world. Neither has Condorcet repelled the objection which troubled Dr. Wallace. It is true that, like Godwin, he faces the difficulty and admits the importance of it.[1] The growth of population will always, he says, cause inequality; there will always be a rich leisured class and a poor industrial class; and to lighten the hardships of the latter there ought to be a State Insurance fund, which will make all the poorest citizens sure of support. But one cannot help thinking, if all are sure of support, all will marry, and if all marry, will not the difficulty be increased?[2] Yes, Condorcet grants this; the numbers will soon be too great, and so throughout the ages there will be an "oscillation" between the blessings of progress and the evils of overcrowding, now the one predominating, now the other. In despair he clutches at the old fallacy, "the day is distant," but he feels it fail him, and must needs add a new and startling solution of his own which Malthus freely denounces.[3] This is not the place to discuss the questions associated in our own times with Neo-Malthusianism.[4] But it is probable that the Neo-Malthusians are the children not of Robert Malthus, but of Robert Owen. Malthus was not Malthus because he said, "The people are too many; thin them down"—any more than Darwin was Darwin because he said, "Species

[1] *Esquisse*, pp. 362 *seq.*
[2] *Essay*, 1st ed., pp. 146, 150.
[3] *Ibid.* p. 154; Condorcet, *Esquisse*, pp. 364—373.
[4] The *locus classicus* in Malthus is *Essay*, Append. (of 1817), p. 512; cf. III. iii. 286, IV. xiii. 474. The pages are those of the 7th edition (Reeves and Turner), a reprint of the 6th.

are not made, but grow." If Darwinians are to be judged by Darwin, Malthusians must be judged by Malthus; and the originality of neither Malthus nor Darwin can be explained by a single phrase. We cannot understand the meaning of an author's words, far less of his work, till we know the context in which they are set. Once know the context and we understand the text. The devil, citing Scripture for his purpose, only succeeds because he never quotes in full.

It follows that, to understand the full meaning of the essay, we must go beyond its efficient cause, and take a view of its material cause, or the whole circumstances in which it was written. If the text of the sermon was Godwin and Condorcet, the application was to the poor of England and the philanthropists who were trying to relieve them.

The early life of Malthus, coinciding, as it largely does, with the latter half of the eighteenth century, coincides with England's greatest industrial revolution. Malthus was born in 1766, three years after the Peace of Paris. There was an end, for the time, to foreign wars, and trade was making a brave start. The discoveries of coal and iron in Northern England, going hand in hand with the inventions of cotton-spinning and weaving, were beginning to convert the poorest counties into the richest, upsetting the political balance. The new science of chemistry had begun to prove its usefulness. Wedgwood was perfecting his earthenware, Brindley cutting his canals, Metcalf laying out his roads, Watt building his steam-engines. England in Roman days had been a granary;

in later ages she had been a pasture-ground; she was now becoming the land of machinery and manufacture, as well as the centre of foreign trade. In other words, she had begun an industrial change, which was the greatest till then in her history, and rich in the most magical improvements. But in the early stages of the change, the evils of it were nearly as much felt as the blessings. The sufferings of displaced workmen, and the anarchy of the new factory system, supplanting home labour, and making the word "manufacturer" forget its etymology,[1] were real evils, however transient. Combined with the general democratic influence of an expansive manufacturing industry, they might easily have caused a social convulsion in these days of no extraordinary virtue; and the country owed its escape in some degree to the evangelical movement under Whitefield and the Wesleys, which was fatal at once to religious torpor and to political excitement.[2] The annoyances of a meddlesome tariff and the futile attempts to exclude foreign food were to vanish away before a hundred years had passed; but in the boyhood of Malthus the voice of Adam Smith raised against them in the *Wealth of Nations* (1776) was a cry in the wilderness. There was a general agreement that, whether the high prices prevailing after the Peace of Paris were caused by the growth of the population, or by the lessened value of silver, or by the troubles in Poland, the

[1] Malthus sometimes uses the word in the earlier sense, and Adam Smith seldom in the later.

[2] Lecky, *Hist. of Eighteenth Century*, vol. ii. p. 638.

remedy was not to lie in a free corn trade. The poor were not to have cheap corn, they were to have large allowances. Legislation had gone backwards in this matter. In 1723 a new law had introduced a wise workhouse test of destitution, which might have prevented wilful poverty by reducing out-door relief; but the clause was repealed by Gilbert's Act in 1782; the poor were to be "set on work" at their own houses; and the new stringency gave place to the old laxity, with the usual results. The close of the century saw the troubles of a European war added to the list, and the tide of political reform ebbed for forty years (1792—1832). Because the French reform had gone too far, the English reform was not allowed to take its first steps.

It is a commonplace with historians that the French Revolution would have been very different without Voltaire and Rousseau to prepare the way for it. Hunger and new ideas are two advocates of change which always plead best in each other's company; hunger makes men willing to act, and the new ideas give them matter for enactment. In France, when the crisis came in 1789, the new ideas were not far to seek. Writers of Utopias, from Plato to More, and from Rousseau to Ruskin, have always adopted one simple plan: they have struck out the salient enormities of their own time and inserted the opposite, as when men imagine heaven they think of their dear native country with its discomforts left out. Inequality at home had made Frenchmen ready to dote on a vision of equality when Rousseau presented it to them, and the state of Nature was the state of France reversed. Philosophically, the theorists of the Revolution traced their descent to Locke, and their ideas were not long in recrossing the Channel to visit their birthplace.

Even if Englishmen had not had in America a visible Utopia, or, at least, Arcadia, there was hunger enough in England to recommend the new ideas to every rank in society. This is the reason why, in 1793, Godwin's book was so successful. It was not only a good English statement of the French doctrines of equality, and therefore a book for the times, but it had a vigour of its own, and was no mere translation. Rousseau and Raynal had thought it necessary to sacrifice universal improvement to universal equality; they saw (or thought they saw) that the two could not go together, and they counted equality so desirable that they were willing to purchase it at the expense of barbarism. Now, they were perhaps more logical than Godwin; equality may mean barbarism. But Godwin's ideal was at least higher than theirs; he thought of civilization and equality as quite compatible, for he thought that when all men were truly civilized they would of their own accord restore equality. As he left everything to reason and nothing to force, his book was in theory quite harmless; but the tendency of it seemed dangerous, for it criticized the British constitution in a free way to which the British nation was not accustomed. In England, moreover, the people have always confounded ideas with persons. They were not in love with liberty when it took the form of an American "War of Independence" against England, and, even if equality had pleased them in 1789, they would have nothing of it after the Terror. They forsook Fox for Burke, and went to war for a sentiment. At the time when Malthus wrote, the bulk of the English people had lost their enthusiasm for the new ideas. It needed some fortitude to call oneself a Reformer, or even a Whig, when Napoleon had overrun Italy and was facing us in Egypt. Pitt held all persons seditious who did not believe in the wisdom of the war.

But even Pitt, though he now ignored the need of reform, could not overlook the existence of distress. In 1795 there had been a serious scarcity; war prices had become famine prices. It was the year when "the lower orders" were held down by special coercion acts;[1] it was the year when the king's carriage was stopped by a mob crying "Bread, bread!" Mr. Whitbread and the rest thought Parliament ought to "do something"; and Pitt proposed (1796) to meet the difficulty by amending the Poor Laws. His bill proposed "to restore the original purity of the Poor Laws" by modifying the law of settlement in the direction of greater freedom, and by assisting the working man in other ways. One of these other ways was an attempt of a harmless kind to found schools of industry, another to attach every labourer to a friendly society. But another less innocently proposed to encourage the growth of population by making the poor relief greater where the family was

[1] Cf. Godwin, pref. to *Pol. Just.*

larger. "Let us make relief," in such cases, "a matter of right and honour, instead of a ground for opprobrium and contempt. This will make a large family a blessing and not a curse; and this will draw a proper line of distinction between those who are to provide for themselves by their labour, and those who, after enriching their country with a number of children, have a claim upon its assistance for their support."[1]

Malthus in 1797 did not doubt the infallibility of Pitt in such a matter; *The Crisis* gives no hint of objection. But in 1798, with his new light, he could no longer take the recruiting officer's view of population. If he had had a good case against Godwin and Condorcet, who had simply failed to show how population could be kept from growing too fast, he had still a better case against Pitt, who proposed to make it grow faster. Besides, their schemes were merely on paper; they had no chance of realizing them, whereas Pitt's majority would carry any measure on which he had set his heart. The danger from this third quarter was therefore the most imminent. But Malthus needed no new argument for it; he needed simply to shift round his old argument, and point the muzzle of it at his new enemy. There is no need, he said, to encourage marriage; there is no need for Government to make population grow faster. Wherever Providence has sent meat, He will soon send

[1] Hansard, *Parl. Hist.*, vol. xxxiii. pp. 703 *seq.*, Feb 12, 1796; cf. vol. xxxii. pp. 687 *seq.* The "Speenhamland Act of Parliament" was really an act of the Berkshire magistrates (1795), but had been widely imitated, and had certainly prepared the way for Pitt's bill.

mouths to eat it; and, if by your artificial encouragements you increase the mouths without increasing the meat, you will only bring the people one step nearer starvation, you will only multiply the nation without increasing the joy. If stalwart numbers are strength, starving numbers are weakness.[1]

These commonplaces were then a paradox. Even at the end of the eighteenth century there was no party in the English House of Commons identified with enlightened views on the position of the British workman. Whitbread had always some measure on hand for helping the labourer out of the rates, or by some other State interference; it was in opposing one of Whitbread's bills that the Prime Minister promised to introduce his own memorable measure. Fox was free to follow either, not professing to understand the new economical doctrines. Pitt, who admired Adam Smith,—Fox, Condorcet, and Godwin, who owed Smith no allegiance,[2]—all were equally purblind in this matter. All Pitt's study of the fourth book of the *Wealth of Nations*, chapter fifth, had not shown him the fallacy of a bounty on children. Yet Malthus had got his light from no obscure sources, but from "Hume, Wallace, Adam Smith, and Dr. Price,"[3] who were all well-known and widely-read authors of the day. "The populousness of ancient nations" had been a happy hunting-ground for learned antiquarian essay writers over half a

[1] Cf. *Essay*, 7th ed., I. vii. p. 65; 1st ed., pp. 94, 95, &c.
[2] Godwin, *Pol. Just.*, VIII. viii. 508 (3rd ed.).
[3] Preface to *Essay*, 2nd ed.

century. Montesquieu, Wallace, and Price[1] claimed the advantage for the ancients. David Hume, with his usual acute divination, decides for the moderns, though with his usual irony he professes to adopt a sceptical conclusion, and makes several concessions to Wallace.[2] This controversy itself might have been expected to bring men nearer to the truth on the subject of population than it actually did. It was left to Malthus to convert Hume's probability into a certainty from a higher vantage-ground; but the sifting of the arguments by the various writers before him must have simplified his task.[3] Other aids and anticipations were not wanting. As early as 1786, Joseph Townsend, the Wiltshire rector, had written a *Dissertation on the Poor Laws*, which gives an admirable statement of those wise views of charity and poor relief that are only in these latter days becoming current among us. Malthus records his opinion of Townsend's work in the best of all possible ways. From his careful inquiry (in the second edition of the *Essay*) into the population of European countries, he omits Spain on the ground that Mr. Townsend's *Travels in Spain* has already done the work for him.[4]

The *Essay on Population* was therefore not original in the sense of being a creation out of nothing, but in the same way as the *Wealth of Nations*. In both

[1] By implication. See below, Book I. ch. vii. p. 175.

[2] *Moral and Political Essays*, Vol. I., Essay XI., Of the Populousness of Ancient Nations (ed. 1768), written in 1752.

[3] So even Sir James Steuart, Vol. I. *Pol. Econ.*, ch. iii. p. 22 (ed. 1805), might have helped him. Steuart wrote in 1767.

[4] *Essay*, Book II. ch. vi.; 7th ed., p. 184.

cases the author got most of his phrases, and even many of his thoughts, from his predecessors; but he treated them as his predecessors were unable to do; he saw them in their connection, perspective, and wide bearings. We must not assume anticipation where there is mere identity of language or partial identity of thought; the words of an earlier writer are not unfrequently quoted by a later away from their logical context, and therefore not as part of an argument of which the writer sees the consecutive premises. This is true of Adam Smith when he is compared with Sir Dudley North, Josiah Tucker, or the other prophets of free trade[1] catalogued by MacCulloch or Blanqui. They talked free trade almost as Monsieur Jourdain talked prose, without knowing it. Precisely the same is true of Adam Smith himself in relation to Malthus. Of his own generalizations he is complete master. Having reasoned up to them, he can reason down from them. But, when he says, "Every species of animals naturally multiplies in proportion to the means of their subsistence," "The demand for men necessarily regulates the production of men,"[2] he has not anticipated Malthus. His phrases are touching a principle of which he does not see the most important bearings; and not having reasoned up to it, he makes hardly any attempt to reason down from it. Malthus, on the other hand,

[1] Buckle would include Voltaire. See *Civil. in Europe*, ii. 304 n.

[2] *Wealth of Nations*, I. viii. 36, 2 (MacCulloch's ed.). These passages are said to have suggested to Malthus the idea of his essay. The article on Population in *Edin. Review*, Aug. 1810, possibly written by Malthus himself, bears out this view.

has taken fast hold of a general principle, and is able to solve a number of dependent questions in the way of simple corollaries. Others may have given right answers to the special questions about the Poor Law and the populousness of ancient nations. Malthus is the first to show one comprehensive reason why all these answers must be right.

This was the secret of his success. As Godwin's *Political Justice* was successful because systematic, the *Essay on Population* was successful because it seemed to put chaos in order. The very sadness of his conclusion had a charm for some minds; but the bulk of his readers did not love him for taking their hopes away, they loved him for giving them new light. Pestilence and famine begin to lose their vague terrors when we know whence they come and what they do for the world. Even if the desire of marriage is itself an evil, it is well to know the truth about it. Ignorance can only be blissful where it is total; and wilful ignorance, being of necessity partial, is a perpetual unrest, not even a fool's paradise.[1]

The truth in this case was not all sadness. In the last portion of the essay of 1798 Malthus expounds an argument which he afterwards reproduced in later editions with a more terrestrial application. He uses the style of Paley and the Apologists, and he tries to discover the final cause of the principle of population, on metaphysical lines that were followed by Mr. Sumner nearly twenty years afterwards, when the discussion had taken a new

[1] Compare *Essay*, Appendix (to 3rd ed., 1806), 7th ed., p. 507.

turn.[1] The question is how to reconcile the suffering produced by the principle of population with the goodness of God. Malthus answers that the difficulty is only one part of the general problem of evil, the difference between this part and the rest being that in this case we see farther into the causes; and it is therefore the easier for us to justify the ways of God to man. "Evil exists not to create despair but activity."[2] We ought not to reason from God to nature, but from nature to God; to know how God works, let us observe how nature works. We shall then find that nature sends all sentient creatures through a long and painful process, by which they gain new qualities and powers, presumably fitting them for a better place than they have in this world. This world and this life are therefore in all probability "the mighty process of God," not indeed for the mere "probation" of man (for that would imply that his Maker was suspicious of him, or ignorant of what was in him), but for the "creation and formation" of the human mind out of the torpor and corruption of dead matter,[3] "to sublimate the dust of the earth into soul, to elicit an ethereal spark from the clod of clay." The varied influences of life are the forming hand of the Creator, and they are infinitely diverse, for (in spite of Solomon) there is nothing old under the sun.[4] Difficulties generate talents.[5] "The first

[1] *Records of Creation*, 1816. [2] 1st ed., p. 395.

[3] *Ibid.* p. 353. This and much else were probably suggested by Tucker, *Light of Nature*, Theology, ch. xix. (especially § 20). Cf. below, Book III.

[4] *Essay*, 1st ed., p. 381. [5] *Ibid.* p. 371.

awakeners of the mind are the wants of the body;" it is these that rouse the intellect of the infant and sharpen the wits of the savage. Not leisure but necessity is the mother of invention:

ἁ πενία, Διόφαντε, μόνα τὰς τέχνας ἐγείρει.

Locke was right; the desire to avoid pain is even stronger than the desire to find pleasure. In this way evil leads to good; for pain, which is a kind of evil, creates effort, and effort creates mind. This is the general rule. A particular example of it is, that want of food, which is one of the most serious of evils, leads to good. By contriving that the earth shall produce food only in small quantities, and in reward of labour, God has provided a perpetual spur to human progress. This is the key to the puzzle of population. By nature man is a lotos-eater till hunger makes him a Ulysses. Why should he toil, the roof and crown of things? Mainly because, if he does not toil, neither can he live; the lotos country will soon be overpeopled, and he must push off his bark again. "The first awakeners of the mind are the wants of the body," though, once awakened, the mind soon finds out wants beyond the body, and the development of intellect and civilization goes on indefinitely.[1] The people "tend to increase" more quickly than their food, not in order that men may suffer, but in order that they may be roused to save

[1] Cf. *Essay*, 2nd ed., p. 65; later editions, I. vi. (beginning), where he says that sloth is the natural state of man, and his activity is due in the first instance to the "strong goad of necessity," though it may be kept up afterwards by habit, the spirit of enterprise, and the thirst for glory.

themselves from suffering. The partial ill of all such general laws is swallowed up in the general good; and the general good is secured in two ways: humanity is developed; the resources of the world are developed. In the first place, the intellect of individual men is developed, for the constancy of nature is the foundation of reasoning, and human reason would never be drawn out unless men were absolutely unable to depend on miracles, and were obliged as well as able to make calculations on the basis of a constant law. To this constancy of nature we owe "the immortal mind of a Newton." In the second place, the world must be peopled. If savages could have got all their food from one central spot of fertile ground, the earth at large would have remained a wilderness; but, as it is, no one settlement can support an indefinite increase of numbers; the numbers must spread out over the earth till they find room and food. If there were no law of increase, a few such careers as Alexander's or Tamerlain's might unpeople the whole world; but the law exists, and the gaps made by any conqueror, or by any pestilence, are soon filled to overflowing, while the overflowing flood passes on to reclaim new countries.[1]

This is the cosmology of Malthus. "Life is, generally speaking, a blessing independent of a future state."[2] "The impressions and excitements of this world are the instruments with which the Supreme

[1] 1st ed., pp. 360—366. For the replenishment of the gap made by the Great Plague of 1348, see Prof. Rogers, *Six Centuries of Work and Wages* (1884), p. 226.

[2] 1st ed., p. 391.

Being forms matter into mind." The necessity of constant exertion, to avoid evil and pursue good, is the principal spring of these impressions, and is therefore a sufficient reason for the existence of natural and moral evil, including the difficulties which arise from the principle of population. All these are present difficulties, but they are not beyond remedy. They do not serve their purpose unless human exertion succeeds in diminishing them. Absolute removal Malthus does not promise; but, while believing in science and reason as strongly as Condorcet or Godwin, declines to regard an earthly immortality as a reasonable hope, and points us instead to a future life and to another world for perfection and happiness.[1]

Perhaps the great economist went beyond his province in attacking the problem of evil. In the controversy that followed the essay there are few references to this part of it, and after the appearance of the second edition, where this part is omitted altogether, people forgot the existence of the first edition. From the way in which Sumner speaks of the difference between his point of view and that of Malthus, it might fairly be suspected that he knew nothing of the first edition; and yet the second of his two learned volumes is simply an expansion of its ideas.[2] The metaphysic itself might

[1] 1st ed., pp. 394-6; cf. pp. 241-6. Compare Mr. Henry George's epilogue to *Progress and Poverty*. It is right to remember that this passage of Malthus was written two years before Paley's *Natural Theology*, though four years after his *Evidences of Christianity*, and many more after the *Moral and Political Philosophy*.

[2] *R. of Cr.*, vol. ii. 103.

be deep or shallow; it would be impossible to tell till we heard the sense in which the metaphysical phrases were used, and that we have hardly any means of doing. They point at least to the "monistic" view, that there is no gulf between mind and matter. We might believe them idealistic in a German sense; but we cannot forget how closely the ethical views of Malthus are connected with those of the English moralists of his century. He cannot be said to have a place in the history of philosophy; and it is mainly of a curious personal interest to discover that, although he is nominally a utilitarian, he separates himself from Paley by refusing to allow moral value to action done from either fear of punishment or hope of reward.[1] There is no indication that he was a metaphysical genius. His researches in the heavier German literature did not perhaps extend much farther than to the quaint optimist Johann Peter Süssmilch,[2] from whose *Göttliche Ordnung* he freely drew his statistics.

Malthus at one time intended to expound his metaphysical views at greater length.[3] In other words, he meant to write a book in the manner of Price's essays, half economical and half literary. We need not deeply regret the "particular business," whatever it was, that nipped this intention in the bud, besides delaying the publication of the essay as we now have it.[4] The metaphysical and theological

[1] *Essay*, 1st ed., p. 387.

[2] See below, Book I. ch. v.

[3] *Ibid.* p. 356 note.

[4] *l. c.* He is ready with a similar excuse in the tract on the *Measure of Value*, p. 61. Where there is no will there is no way.

passages, as they stand, have the look of an episode, though the thought of them is logically enough connected with the tenor of the book. The views of the author on the other world, the punishment of the wicked, and the use of miracles, have, like the philosophy, mainly a personal interest. Adam Smith, in the later edition of his *Moral Sentiments*, had omitted at least one very marked expression of theological opinion (on the Atonement) that had appeared in the first edition,[1] and perhaps his disciple did well to follow suit. At the same time, omission is not recantation, and we get light on an author's mind and character by discovering any views in which he once professed to believe. A writer who reached absolute truth at a very early stage of study, has patronized Adam Smith[2] by editing his chief work, and honoured the other economists by tabulating their conclusions in an historical introduction. He extends this favour to Malthus. The reasonings of Malthus he finds, though valuable, are not free from error; he has "all but entirely overlooked" the beneficial effects of the principle of population as a stimulus to invention and progress.[3] This charge is refuted by the essay even in its later form; but, placed alongside of the cosmology of the first edition,

[1] Part II. sect. ii. pp. 204-6.

[2] MacCulloch (J. R.), editor of the *Commercial Dictionary*, and probably the original of Carlyle's Macrowdy. No one could have a proper reverence for the Fathers of Political Economy who perpetually referred to the greatest of them without his distinctive prænomen.

[3] Introduction to *W. of N.*, p. lii. So the writer of *Progress and Poverty* tells us "the doctrine of Malthus did not originally and does not necessarily involve the idea of progression" (Bk. II. ch. i. p. 89, ed. 1881).

it seems merely grotesque. Malthus is accused of ignoring the very phenomena which Malthus glorifies as the "final cause" of the principle of population. He thought he had explained not only one of the chief causes of poverty, but one of the chief effects; if Adam Smith had shown the power of labour as a cause of wealth, Malthus thought he had shown the power of poverty as a cause of labour. No doubt the mistake was a common one; and (to say nothing of the encyclopædias and biographical dictionaries) there are few economical text-books which do justice to Malthus in this matter.[1] But one who speaks with authority should not be content with a borrowed knowledge. The same authority tells us that "the work of Mr. Malthus is valuable rather for having awakened public attention to the subject than for its giving anything like a complete view of the department of the science of which it treats."[2] Malthus for his part lays no claim to infallibility; like most pioneers, he is sure of little beyond his leading principles, and he is never ashamed to change his views.[3] But, if his *Essay on Population*, gradually amended and expanded as it was, to keep pace with the searching criticisms of thirty years, has not reached the heart of the matter, surely there is no profit in discussion.

[1] Bagehot (*Econ. Studies*, p. 136 *seq.*), W. R. Greg (*Enigmas of Life*), and Held (*Sociale Geschichte Englands*) may be acquitted, but they are not writers of text-books.

[2] *Wealth of Nations*, Introduction, p. lii.

[3] See *e. g.* the tract on the *Measure of Value*, p. 23, and cf. *Pol. Ec.* (2nd ed.), p. 234.

The fact is, that though the anonymous small 8vo of 1798 was a mere draught of the completed work of later years, its main fault was not incompleteness, but wrongness of emphasis. When a man is writing a controversial pamphlet, he does not try to bring all truths into the front equally; he sets the neglected ones in the foreground, and allows the familiar to fall behind, not as denied or ignored, but simply as not emphasized. It is always possible, in such cases, that the neglected truths, though unworthy of the old neglect, did not deserve the new pre-eminence, and must not be allowed to retain it. Science, seeking answers to its own questions, and not to questions of the eighteenth century, has no toleration for the false emphasis of passing controversy. It puts the real beginning first, the middle next, and the end last, not the end in the middle, or the last first. Accordingly it takes up the first essay of Malthus on population, and requires the author to amend it. He must be less critical and more creative, if he is to give a satisfactory answer to the general problem which he has chosen to take in hand. The times and the subject, both, demand a change of attitude,—the times, because political theories have now become less important than social difficulties, and the subject, because he has hitherto, while clearly explaining the difficulties, done little more than hint at the expedients for overcoming them. True, no critic or iconoclast can ever fully vanquish an opponent except by a truth of his own which goes beyond the opponent's falsity; and it is to this he owes the enthusiasm of his followers. But he does not always expound the truth so fully as the error; and so, beyond the point of negation, his friends often follow him rather by faith than by sight. This, then, was what Malthus had yet to do; to state what were the trustworthy as well as the delusive methods of raising modern society, and what were the right as well as the wrong ways of relieving the poor.

The success of the essay, so far, had been very remarkable. It had provoked replies by the dozen, and an unwilling witness tells us it had converted friends of progress by the hundred.[1] We find Godwin writing to the author in August 1798,[2] and we may conclude that the veil of anonymousness was not very thick, though Malthus used it again in 1800 in the tract on High Price. In a debate in the House of Commons on the 11th February, 1800, Pitt took occasion to say that, though he still believed his new Poor Bill a good one, he had dropped it in deference to the objections of "those whose opinions he was bound to respect."[3] He meant Bentham and Malthus. We cannot tell which had the greater share of the credit, but we know that Malthus regarded Pitt and Paley as his most brilliant converts.[4] Pitt's declaration that he still believed his bill to be a good

[1] Godwin's *Thoughts on Parr's Sermon*, 1801, p. 54; cf. Godwin's *Population* (1820), Bk. i. 27.

[2] Godwin's *Life*, by Kegan Paul, vol. i. 321.

[3] Hansard, *sub dato*, p. 1429.

[4] Empson in *Edinburgh Review*, Jan. 1837, p. 483; cf. *Essay on Population*, 7th ed. p. 473 n. Empson's authorship of that article appears from Macvey Napier's *Correspondence*, p. 187. See below, Book V.

one could only mean that he still wished to believe it so. It must have been peculiarly galling to a statesman who affected the political economist to find that not only the solemn criticisms of Malthus, but the jocose "Observations" of Bentham,[1] which threshed the chaff out of the bill clause by clause, had turned his favourite science against himself.

[1] *Works*, vol. viii. p. 440.

Note.—ROBERT OWEN (above, p. 24).

In the passage cited (from the Appendix of 1817) Malthus speaks of Owen as "fully sensible" that under his plan of equality and communism there will be no check on population from the felt difficulty of supporting a family; he is unable to suggest any others that are not "unnatural, immoral, and cruel." But Malthus mentions in this place only the just published *New View of Society*, 1816, which contains no such matter. There, Owen rises above checks of any kind, holding that when rightly trained, men produce far more than the means of their support, and accordingly the whole population of the earth for many thousand years "may continue to live in abundance and happiness, without one check of vice or of misery" (2nd ed., 1816, pp. 174–5). Malthus, however, knew Owen's views by personal intercourse. We are told he once visited New Lanark (Sargant, *Life of Owen*, p. 85, on authority of G. J. Holyoake). Owen writes (in his own Life by himself, 1857, Vol. I. pp. 103–4) that he had "frequent discussions" with the economists, Malthus expressly included. Malthus must have known his mind very well. Still, without *litera scripta*, Owen must have the benefit of the doubt. Prof. J. A. Field of Chicago has probed the matter further in his address (on Neomalthusianism) to the American Economic Association, St. Louis, December 1910.

CHAPTER II.

SECOND THOUGHTS, 1803.

Exaggerations of the First Essay—Its two Postulates not co-ordinate—Distinctive feature of the Second Essay—Its moderate Optimism—Rough Classification of Checks—Moral Restraint and Mixed Motives—Freedom as understood by Godwin and by Malthus—The two men contrasted.

WHILE Malthus was making such converts as Pitt, Paley, and Parr, and when even Godwin acknowledged the "writer of the essay" to have made a "valuable addition to political economy,"[1] the essay was not beyond criticism. There were some familiar facts of which the writer had taken too little account, and they were impressed on him by his critics from all sides. To use the language of philosophy, he had not been sufficiently concrete; he had gone far to commit Godwin's fault, and consider one feature of human nature apart by itself, instead of seeing it in its place with the rest. The position and prospects of civilized society in our own day depend on a combination of political, intellectual, physical, and moral causes, of which the growth or decrease of population may be only an effect. If we are part

[1] *Thoughts on Parr's Sermon*, p. 56.

man, part lion, and part hog, it is not fair to assume the predominance of the hog any more than the predominance of the man. In a herd of animals, as distinguished from a society of men, the units are simply the fittest who have survived in the struggle for existence. The principle of population is in the foreground there; there is no check to it but famine, disease, and death. We can therefore understand how the study of the *Essay on Population* led Charles Darwin to explain the origin of species by a generalization which Malthus had known and named, though he did not pursue it beyond man.[1] The "general struggle" among animals "for room and food" means among civilized men something very like free trade, the old orthodox economical panacea for economic evils; and the essayist agrees with Adam Smith in a general resistance to legislative interference. Bad as are the effects of the irremovable causes of poverty, interference makes them still worse. But at least, when we come to man, the struggle is not so cruel. "Plague take the hindmost" is not the only or the supreme rule. If the fear of starvation, the most earthly and least intellectual of all motives, is needed to force us to work at first, it need not therefore be necessary ever afterwards. The baser considerations are by their definition the lowest layers of our pile; we rise by means of them, but we tread them down, and the higher the pile the less their importance. Within civilized countries, in proportion to their

[1] *Essay*, 1st ed., pp. 17, 47, 48; *Origin of Species*, ch. iii. p. 50. Hence Sir Chas. Lyell even denies the originality of Darwin and Wallace (*Antiquity of Man*, ch. xxi. p. 456).

civilization, the struggle in the lowest stages is abolished; the weakest are often saved, and the lowest raised, in spite of unfitness.[1] View man not as an animal, but as a citizen; view the principle of population as checked not only by vice, misery, and the fear of them, but by all the mixed motives of human society, and we recognize that Malthus, with the best intentions, had treated the matter too abstractly. Godwin had over-rated the power of reason, Malthus the power of passion. "It is probable," he wrote at a later time, "that, having found the bow bent too much one way, I was induced to bend it too much the other, in order to make it straight."[2] The abstract principle of increase getting more, and concrete humanity less, than justice, the next step was, naturally, to deny the possibility of permanent improvement in this world, and to regard every partial improvement as a labour of Sisyphus.[3]

It could hardly be otherwise, if we began, like Malthus, by setting down the desire of food and the desire of marriage as two co-ordinate principles.[4] They are not really co-ordinate. It is true not merely

[1] Cf. A. R. Wallace, *Contributions to Theory of Natural Selection*, and the discussions raised thereupon, 1868. See also *Essays in Philosophical Criticism* (1883), Essay VIII., *The Struggle for Existence*, in which some of the mixed motives are further described.

[2] Appendix to 5th ed., 1817; 7th ed., p. 526. Cf. Bacon (Essay XXXVIII.), "to bend nature like a wand to a contrary extreme whereby to set it aright." Adam Smith had used the simile of a bent stick to describe the reaction of the French Economists against the Mercantile theorists (*Wealth of Nations*, IV. ix. 300).

[3] *Essay*, 1st ed., p. 367. Cf. Senior's *Lectures on Population*, p. 79, and p. 75, where he compares such progress to the exploits of the snail which every day climbed up a wall four feet and fell back three.

[4] *Essay*, 1st ed., p. 10.

of most men, but of all men without a single exception, that they cannot live without food. Even if a man survive an abstinence from solid food for forty days, he cannot deny himself water, and he is for all useful purposes dead to the world during his fast. The second postulate of the first essay is, on the contrary, true only of most men, and even then under qualifications. It is not true of any till manhood, and it is not true of all men equally. Some are beyond its scope by an accident of birth, and a still larger number, whether priests or laymen, put themselves beyond its scope for moral reasons.[1] Coleridge puts the case pertinently enough: "The whole case is this: Are they both alike passions of physical necessity, and the one equally with the other independent of the reason and the will? Shame upon our race that there lives the individual who dares even ask the question."[2]

Malthus saw that he had been hasty, and he did not republish the essay till he had given it five years of revision, and added to it the results of foreign travel and wider reading. In 1799 he went abroad with some college friends, Otter, Clarke the antiquarian and naturalist, and Clarke's pupil Cripps,[3] and visited Germany, Sweden, Norway, Finland, and part of Russia, these being the only countries at that time open to English travellers. After his return he

[1] Cf. St. Matth. xix. 12.

[2] MS. notes on p. vii of S. T. Coleridge's copy of the 2nd ed. of the *Essay*, in Brit. Museum (from the library of his executor, Dr. Joseph H. Green).

[3] See Otter's biographical preface to Malthus' *Pol. Ec.* (1836), p. xxxvi, and Otter's *Life of Clarke* (1825), i. 437, &c.

published his tract on the *High Price of Provisions* (1800),[1] and at the conclusion of it he promised a new edition of the *Essay on Population.* Some people, he says, have thought the essay "a specious argument inapplicable to the present state of society," because it contradicts preconceived opinions; but two years of reflection have strengthened his conviction that he has discovered "the real cause of the continued depression and poverty of the lower classes;" and he will not recant his essay: "I have deferred giving another edition of it in the hope of being able to make it more worthy of the public attention, by applying the principle directly and exclusively to the existing state of society, and endeavouring to illustrate the power and universality of its operation from the best authenticated accounts that we have of the state of other countries." But he was not satisfied with the accounts of other people. When the Peace of Amiens let loose thousands of pleasure-seekers on the Continent, Malthus went to France and Switzerland on no errand of mere pleasure; and he was luckily at home again, and passing his proof-sheets through the press, before Napoleon's unpleasant interference with English travellers.

It was a happy coincidence that in the dark fighting days of 1798, Malthus should write only of vice and misery, while in the short gleam of peace in 1802 and 1803, when the tramp of armed men had ceased for the moment, he should recollect himself, and write of a less ghastly restraint on

[1] See below, Book II. chap. iv.

population, a restraint which might perhaps, like the truce of Amiens, hold out some faint hope for the future. For the sake of the world let us hope that the parallel goes no further. The wonder is not that he forgot there was such a thing as civilization, but that amidst wars and rumours of wars he should ever have remembered it.

In the preface to the new edition (June 1803), he says he has "so far differed in principle" from the old edition "as to suppose the action of another check to population which does not come under the head either of vice or misery," and he has "tried to soften some of the harshest conclusions of the first essay." There was really more change than this. The first essay contained much of the imperfection of the sudden magazine-article; and if the writer had lived half a century later he would probably, instead of writing a small book, have contributed a long article to a monthly or quarterly magazine, giving a review of Godwin's political writings, with incidental remarks on the Poor Bill of Mr. Pitt. This was evidently the light in which he himself regarded his first work, or he would not have handled it so freely in republication. The new edition had new facts, new arrangement, and new emphasis. He had not written a book once for all, leaving the world to fight over it after his death. He took the public into partnership with him, and made every discussion a means of improving his book. This gives the *Essay on Population* a unique character among economical writings. It leads the author to interpret his thoughts to us from many various points of view, leaving us, unhappily, often in doubt whether an alteration of language is or is not an alteration of thought. Malthus adds to the difficulty by omitting and inserting instead of re-writing in full. His chapters cease to be old without becoming new.

The very face of the book revealed a change. In 1798 it was *An Essay on the Principle of Population as it affects the Future Improvement of Society;* in 1803, *An Essay on the Principle of Population, or a View of its Past and Present Effects on Human Happiness.* The dreams of the future are now in the background, and the facts of the present in the foreground. In 1798 Malthus had given Godwin the lie:—

> "Colouring he, dilating, magniloquent, glorying in picture,
> He to a matter of fact still softening, paring, abating,
> He to the great might-have-been upsoaring, sublime and ideal,
> He to the merest it-was restricting, diminishing, dwarfing."

He must do more now, or his political economy is a dismal science. He must show how we can cling to the matter of fact without losing our ideal. It is not enough to refer us to the other world. How far may we have hope in this world? Let Malthus answer.

The second essay is his answer; and if second thoughts are the best, then we may rejoice over the second essay, for it lifts the cloud from the first. It tells us that on the whole the power of civilization is greater than the power of population; the pressure of the people on the food is therefore less in modern than it was in ancient times or the middle ages; there are now less disorder, more knowledge, and more temperance.[1] The merely physical checks are falling into a subordinate position. There are two kinds of checks on population. A check is (*a*) positive, when it cuts down an existing population, (*b*) preventive, when it keeps a new population from growing up. Among animals the check is only misery, among savage men vice as well as misery, and, in civilized society, moral restraint as well as, till now, both vice and misery. Even in civilized society there are strata which moral restraint hardly reaches, for there are strata which are not civilized. On the whole, however, it is true that among animals there is no sign of any other check than the positive, while among men the positive is gradually subordinated to the preventive. Among men misery may act both positively and preventively. In the form of war or disease it may slay its tens of thousands, and cut down an existing population. By the fear of its own coming it may prevent many a marriage, and keep a new population from growing up. Vice may also act in both ways: positively as in child murder, preventively as in the scheme of Condorcet. But in civilized society the forces of both order and progress are arrayed against their two common enemies; and, if we recognized no third check, surely the argument that was used against Godwin's society holds against all society; its very purification will ruin it, by

[1] 2nd ed., Book IV. chap. xii.; 7th ed., p. 477.

forbidding vice and misery to check the growth of population, and by thereby permitting the people to increase to excess. There is, however, a third check, which Malthus knows under the title of moral restraint.

Moral restraint is a distinct form of preventive check. It is not to be confused with an impure celibacy, which falls under the head of vice; and yet the adjective "moral" does not imply that the motives are the highest possible.[1] The adjective is applied not so much to the motive of the action as to the action itself, from whatever motives proceeding; and in the mouth of a Utilitarian this language is not unphilosophical. Moral restraint, in the pages of Malthus, means simply continence; it is an abstinence from marriage followed by no irregularities.[2] He speaks of the "moral stimulus" of the bounty on corn, meaning the expectations it produced in the minds of men, as distinguished from the variations it produced in the prices of grain;[3] and the word "moral" is often, like "morale," used in military matters to denote mental disposition, as distinguished from material resources. The vagueness of the word is perhaps not accidental, for nothing is vaguer than the mixed motives which it denotes; but continence, which is unambiguous, would seem the better word.

[1] 2nd ed., I. ii. 10, 11; cf. xiv. 180; 7th ed., pp. 8 note, 262, &c.

[2] 2nd ed., p. 11.

[3] 7th ed., p. 351; so I. ix. 82, "moral impossibility" of increase, in a case where there is plenty of food, but bad distribution makes it unattainable. The impossibility is due not to physical law but to human institutions (*mores*).

With the enunciation of the third check the theory of Malthus entered definitively on a new phase; and in sketching the outlines of his work we shall no longer need to treat it as paradoxical and overstrained, but as a sober argument from the ground of accepted facts. The author's analysis of human nature has been brought into harmony with common sense. He confesses that it had hitherto been too abstract, and had separated the inseparable.

The mind of man cannot be sawed into quantities; and, even if it is possible to distinguish the mixed motives that guide human action, the fact remains that they only operate when together. It is probable that no good man's motives were ever absolutely noble, and no bad man's ever absolutely bestial. Even the good man is strongest when he can make his very circumstances war against his power to do evil. Mixed from the first of time, human motives will, in this world, remain mixed unto the last, whether in saint, sage, or savage. But civilization, involving, as it does, a progressive change in the dominant ideas of society, will alter the character of the mixture and the proportion of the elements. The laws of Malthus will be obeyed, though the name of Malthus be not mentioned, and the checks, physical or moral, be never brought to mind. Society, moving all together, if it move at all, cannot cure its evils by one single heroic remedy; but as little can it be content with self-denying ordinances, prohibitions, or refutations. It needs a positive truth, and an ideal, that is to say, a religion, to give new life to the bodily members by giving new hope to the heart. "The fear of the Lord is the beginning of wisdom, but the end of wisdom is the love of the Lord and the admiration of moral good."[1] It follows that an economist, if he knows nothing but his economy, does not know even that.

No economists are more reproached with their want of idealism than Malthus and his brethren. As the French Revolutionists were said to believe that the death of their old rulers would of itself bring happiness and good government, so these writers were said to teach that the mere removal of hindrances would lead to the best possible production and distribution of the good things of this life. The ideal state then, as far as wealth was concerned, would be anarchy *plus* the police constable. Godwin would have dispensed with the constable. "Give a state liberty enough," he says, "and vice cannot exist in it."[2] But neither he nor the economists desired a merely negative change or removal of hindrances. Their political reformation was to be, like the Protestant, only successful as it went beyond image-breaking. Malthus, it will be seen,[3] is far from being an unqualified advocate of *laissez faire;* and, in all cases where he did desire it, he wished to make the state small only to make public opinion great. Godwin was not far away from him here. If he was wrong in attributing too much evil to

[1] Malthus, *Essay*, 1st ed., p. 387.

[2] In an unpublished MS. quoted in his *Life*, i. 76. His published writings contain nothing quite so strong.

[3] See below, Book III.

institutions, and too little to human nature, he has furnished his own correction. The *Political Justice* disclaimed all sympathy with violence; it taught that a political reform was worthless unless effected peacefully by reason; and Malthus[1] has the same cure for social evils—argument and instruction. The difference between them is, that Malthus takes more into account the unreasonableness as well as the reasonableness of men. In essentials they are agreed. The thorough enlightenment of the people, which includes their moral purification as well as their intellectual instruction, is to complete the work of mending all, in which men are to be fellow-workers with God—so runs the teaching of Malthus and all the greatest economists of the last hundred years. Whether the evils of competition are many or few, serious or trifling, depends largely on the character of the competitors; and the more free we make the competition, the more thoroughly we must educate the competitors. Adam Smith was well aware of this; he recommended school-boards a hundred years before the Acts of 1870 and 1872;[2] and Malthus was not behind him.[3] They are aware that the more completely we exclude the interference of Government, the more actively we must employ every other moral and social agency. Whether Malthus was prepared to exclude the interference of Government entirely, even under this condition, we shall see by-and-by.

[1] *Essay*, 7th ed., B. IV. chap. vi. and ix.
[2] *Wealth of Nations*, B. V. ch. i. Pt. iii. Art. 2.
[3] *Essay*, Book IV. ch. ix. of 7th ed., esp. p. 439.

The characters of the two men, Malthus and Godwin, are a striking contrast. Malthus was the student, of quiet settled life, sharing his little wealth with his friends in unobtrusive hospitality, and constantly using his pen for the good, as he believed, of the English poor, that in these wretched times they might have domestic happiness like his own. There never was a more singular delusion than the common belief in the hard-heartedness of Malthus. Besides the unanimous voice of private friends, he has left testimony enough in his own books to absolve him. While Adam Smith and others owe their errors to intellectual fallibility, Malthus owes many of his to his tender heart. His motive for studying political economy was no doubt a mixed motive ; it was partly the interest of an intelligent man in abstract questions ; but it was chiefly the desire to advance the greatest happiness of the greatest number. In his eyes the elevation of human life was much more important than the solution of a scientific problem. Even when in 1820 he wrote a book on the "*Principles of Political Economy*," he took care to add on the title-page, "*considered with a view to their practical application*," refusing to consider in abstractness what always exists in the concrete. His keen sympathy for the sufferings of displaced workmen led him to fight a losing battle with Say and Ricardo in favour of something like an embargo on inventions, and in protest against a fancied over-production.[1] His private

[1] Cf. even *Essay*, 1st ed., pp. 33, 34, and 324. But see later, B. II. chaps. ii. and iii.

life showed the power of gentleness; Miss Martineau could hear his mild, sonorous vowels without her ear-trumpet, and his few sentences were as welcome at her dinner-table as the endless babble of cleverer tongues. He felt the pain of a thousand slanders "only just at first," and never let them trouble his dreams after the first fortnight, saying, with a higher than stoical calmness, that they passed by him like the idle wind which he respected not.[1] He outlived obloquy, and saw the fruit of his labours in a wiser legislation and improved public feeling.

With Godwin all was otherwise. There were fightings within and fears without. With an immovable devotion to ideas he combined a fickleness of affection towards human beings. He heeded emotion too little in his books and too much in his own life, yielding to the fancy of the moment, quarrelling with his best friends twice a week, and quickly knitting up the broken ties again. He loved his wife well, but hardly allowed her to share the same house with him, lest they should weary of one another.[2] He was the sworn enemy of superstition, and himself the arch-dreamer of dreams.

Yet when we contrast the haphazard literary life of the one, ending his days ingloriously[3] in a Government sinecure, unsuccessful and almost forgotten, with the academical ease of the other, centred in

[1] 7th ed., Append., p. 495. Cf. Miss Martineau's *Autob.*, vol. i. p. 211; cf. pp. 209, 210.

[2] *Life*, vol. i. ch. ix. p. 233.

[3] Ingloriously, because of the severe chapter he wrote in the *Political Justice*, 'Of Pensions and Salaries' (ch. ix. of Bk. VI.).

the sphere of common duties, and passing from the world with a fair consciousness of success, we feel a sympathy for Godwin that is of a better sort than the mere liking for a loser. It is a sympathy not sad enough for pity. It is not wholly sad to find Godwin in his old age a lonely man, his friends dropping off one by one into the darkness and leaving him solitary in a world that does not know him. The world that had begun to realize the ideas of Malthus had begun to realize the ideas of Godwin also. It was a world far more in harmony with political justice than that into which Godwin had sent his book forty years before. It was good that Malthus had lived to see the new Poor Law, but still better that both had lived to see the Reform of '32.

They passed away within two years of each other, Malthus in the winter of 1834, Godwin in the spring of 1836, the year of the first league of the people against the Corn Laws. In their death they were still divided, but, "si quis piorum manibus locus," they are divided no longer, and they think no hard thoughts of each other any more.

CHAPTER III.

THESES.

Position stated in the Essay—Tendency of Life to increase beyond Food—Problem not the same for Humanity as for the lower forms of Life—Man's Dilemma—Tendency to increase not predicable of Food in same sense as of Life—The Geometrical and Arithmetical Ratios—Position stated in *Encyclopædia Britannica*—Milne's Confirmation of the Geometrical Ratio—Arithmetical Ratio proved differently—Private Property a condition of great Production—Fallacy of confusing possible with actual Production.—Laws of Man as well as of Nature responsible for necessity of Checks—Position stated in "Summary View"—The Checks on Population classified (*a*) objectively and (*b*) subjectively—Relation to previous Classification—Cycle in the movement of Population.

THE second essay applies the theory of the first to new facts and with a new purpose. The author, having gained his case against Godwin, ceases to be the critic and becomes the social reformer. Despairing to master all the forms of evil, he confines his study to one of them in particular, the tendency of living beings to increase beyond their means of nourishment. This phenomenon is important both from its cause and from its effects. Its cause is not the action of Governments, but the constitution of man; and its effects are not of to-day or yesterday, but constant and perpetual;[1] it frequently hinders the moral

[1] Cf. *Essay*, 7th ed., II. xiii. p. 259.

goodness and general happiness of a nation as well as the equal distribution of its wealth.

This is the general position, which the several chapters of the essay are to expound in detail. It is not by itself quite simple. "The constant tendency in all animated life [*sic*][1] to increase beyond the nourishment prepared for it" is in one sense common to humanity with plants and animals, but in another sense is not common to any two of the three. It is certainly true of all of them that the seeds of their life, whencesoever at first derived, are now infinitely numerous on our planet, while the means of rearing them are strictly limited. In the case of plants and animals the strong instinct of reproduction is "interrupted by no reasoning or doubts about providing for offspring,"[2] and they crowd fresh lives into the world only to have them at once shorn away by starvation. With the exception of certain plants which ape their superiors, like the drosera, and certain men who ape their inferiors, like the cannibals, the lines of difference between the three classes of living things are tolerably distinct. The first class, in the struggle for room and food, can only forestall each other and leave each other to die; the second deliberately prey on the first and on each other; while the third prey on both the rest. But with man this "tendency to increase beyond the food" differs from the same instinct in the other two cases by more than the fact that man has larger resources and is longer in reaching his limit. The instinct is equally strong in him, but

[1] *Essay*, 2nd ed., p. 2. [2] 2nd ed., p. 3.

he does not unquestioningly follow it. "Reason interrupts his career," and asks him whether he may not be bringing into the world beings for whom he cannot provide the means of support.[1] If he brushes reason aside, then he shares the fate of plants and animals; he tends to multiply his numbers beyond the room and food accessible to them, and the result is that his numbers are cut down to these limits by suffering and starvation. There is nothing in this either more or less contrary to the notion of a benevolent Providence than in the general power given to man of acting rationally or irrationally according to his own choice in any other instance. On the other hand, if he listens to reason, he can no doubt defeat the tendency, but too often he does it at the expense of moral purity. The dilemma makes the desire for marriage almost an "origin of evil." If man obeys his instincts he falls into misery, and, if he resists them, into vice. Though the dilemma is not perfect, its plausibility demands that we should test it by details, and to this test Malthus may be said to have given his whole life. His other economical works are subordinate to the essay, and may be said to grow out of it. Though we cannot omit them if we would fully understand and illustrate the central work, still the latter must come first; and its matured form requires more than the brief summary which has been given in the two preceding chapters.

The body of the book consists of historical details, and particular examples showing the checks to popu-

[1] *Essay*, 2nd ed., p. 3.

lation in uncivilized and in civilized places, in present and in past times. The writer means to bring his conclusions home to his readers by the "longer way" of induction. As this, however, was not the way in which he himself reached them, or even stated them at first, he will ask us first of all to look at the terms of the dilemma in the light of his two original postulates[1]—(*a*) food is necessary, (*b*) the desire of marriage is permanent. What is the quickest possible increase of numbers in obedience to the second, and of food in obedience to the first? In the most crucial of the known instances, the actual rapidity of the increase of population seems to be in direct proportion to the easy possession of food; and we can infer that the ideally rapid increase would take place where all obstacles (whether material or moral) to the getting of food and rearing of a family were removed, so that nature never needed to remonstrate with instinct. "In no state that we have yet known has the power of population been left to exert itself with perfect freedom."[2] We can guess what it would be from the animal and vegetable world, where reason does not as a matter of fact interfere with instinct in any circumstances, so far as we can judge. Benjamin Franklin, in a passage quoted by Malthus in this connection,[3] supposes that if the earth were bared of other plants it might be replenished in a few years

[1] 1st ed.; see p. 16, above. "Food" in such propositions includes all the outward conditions necessary to life.

[2] 2nd ed., p. 4; 7th ed., p. 3.

[3] *l. c.* Franklin's *Observations concerning the Increase of Mankind*, 1751.

with fennel alone. Even as things are now, fennel would fill the whole earth if the other plants would only allow it; and the same is true of each of the others. Townsend's goats and greyhounds on Juan Fernandez are a better instance, because not hypothetical.[1] Juan Fernando, the first discoverer, had covered the island with goats from one pair.[2] The Spaniards resolved to clear it of goats, in order to make it useless to the English for provisioning. They put on shore a couple of greyhounds, whose offspring soon caused the goats to disappear. But without some few goats to eat all the dogs must have died; and the few were saved to them by their inaccessible refuges in the rocks, from which they descended at risk of their lives. In this way only the strongest and fleetest dogs and the hardiest and fleetest goats survived; and a balance was kept up between goat food and hound population. Townsend thereupon remarks that human populations are kept down by want of food precisely in the same way.

There is nothing to prevent the increase of human numbers if we suppose reason to have no need (as in the lower creatures it has no opportunity) to interfere. To understand the situation, however, it is best not to assume the truth of this parallelism, but to take the actually recorded instances of human increase under the nearest known approaches to absolute plenty combined with moral goodness, that is to

[1] *Dissertation on the Poor Laws by a well-wisher to Mankind* (1786), pp. 42—45, 53. He is quoting Dampier's *Voyages*, vol. i. pt. ii. p. 88.

[2] It is fair to say that Ulloa, B. II. ch. iv., says "two or three goats."

say, with a state of society in which vice is at a minimum. "In the northern states of America, where the means of subsistence have been more ample, the manners of the people more pure, and the checks to early marriages fewer than in any of the modern states of Europe, the population was found to double itself for some successive periods every twenty-five years."[1] From this near approach to an unchecked increase, we infer that the unchecked would mean a doubling in less than twenty-five years (say twenty, or perhaps fifteen), and that all population, in proportion as it is unchecked, tends towards that rate of increase.

If it is difficult to find an unchecked increase of population, it is still harder to find an unchecked increase of food; for what is meant is not that a people should find their food in one fertile country with as much ease as in another, but that, for a new people, new supplies should always be found with the same ease as the old ones. Now it is not necessary to suppose that the most fertile land is always used first;[2] very often it might only be used late after the rest, through political insecurity, imperfect agriculture, incomplete explorations, or the want of capital; but, when it is once occupied, the question is, will it supply new food to new comers without any limit at all? This would be an ideally fertile land corresponding to the ideally expanding population. And on some such inexhaustible increase

[1] 2nd ed., p. 4; cf. 7th ed., p. 3.

[2] Carey (H. C.) has certainly made a good case for the reverse. See *Princ. of Social Science*, vol. i. ch. iv. (1858).

of food an unchecked increase of population would depend, unless men became able to live without food altogether.

Malthus afterwards pointed out, in the course of controversy,[1] that there is strictly speaking no question here of the comparison of two tendencies, for we cannot speak of a tendency to increase food in the same sense as a tendency to increase population. Population is increased by itself; food is increased not by food itself, but by an agency external to it, the human beings that want it; and, while the former increase is due to an instinct, the latter is (in a sense) acquired. Eating is instinctive, but not the getting of the food. We have, therefore, to compare an increase due to an instinctive desire with an increase due to labour, and "a slight comparison will show the immensity of the first power over the second." Malthus allows that it is difficult to determine this relation with exactness;[2] but, with the natural liking of a Cambridge man for a mathematical simile,[3] he says that the one is to the other as an arithmetical to a geometrical ratio,—that is to say, in any given time (say a century) the one will have increased by multiplication, the other only by addition. If we represent both the population and the food at the beginning of that century by ten, then the population

[1] Letter to Senior, Appendix to Senior's *Lectures on Population*, pp. 60—72.

[2] *Essay*, 2nd ed., p. 5.

[3] He might have been warned from such by "οὐ γεωμετρικαῖς ἀλλ' ἐρωτικαῖς ἀνάγκαις" (Plato, *Republic*, v. 458). But Bacon had applied the same figure still more widely: "Custom goes in arithmetical, Nature in geometrical progression" (*Advancement of L.*, VI. iii. 259).

will double itself in twenty-five years; the ten will become twenty in the first twenty-five years, forty in the second, eighty in the third, one hundred and sixty in the last, while the food will only become twenty in the first, thirty in the second, forty in the third, fifty in the fourth. If this is true, it shows the tendency of population to outrun subsistence. But of course it needs to be shown from experience that, while the strength of the desire remains the same in the later stages of the growth of population as in the earlier, the laboriousness of the labour is greater in the later stages of the increase of food than in the earlier. It is the plain truth, says Malthus, that nature is niggardly in her gifts to man, and by no means keeps pace with his desires. If men would satisfy their desire of food at the old rate of speed, they must exert their mind or their body much more than at first.[1] An obvious objection presents itself. Since man's food consists after all of the lower forms of life, animal and vegetable, and since these admittedly tend to increase, unchecked by themselves, in a geometrical ratio, it might be thought that the increase of human population and the increase of its food could proceed together, with equal ease. But the answer is that this unchecked geometrical increase of the first could go on only so long as there was room for it. It could only be true, for example, of wheat in the corn-field at the time when the seed of it was sown, and the field was all before it. The equality of the two ratios would only be true of the first

[1] Cf. what is said of the cosmology of Malthus above, pp. 34 *seq.*

crop.[1] At first there might be five or sixfold the seed; but in after years, though the geometrical increase from the seed would tend to be the same, there could be no geometrical increase of the total crop by unassisted nature. The earth has no tendency to increase its surface. There is a tendency of animals and vegetables to increase geometrically, in their quality of living things, but not in their quality of being food for man. The same amount of produce might no doubt be gained on a fresh field, from the seed yielded by the first, and at the same geometrical rate; but this assumes that there is a fresh field, and we should not then be at the proper stage to contrast the two ratios. The contrast begins to show itself as soon as the given quantity of land has grown its crop, and its animal and human population have used all its food. The question is then how any increase of the said population, if they are confined to their own supplies, is at all to be made possible; the answer is, only by greater ingenuity and greater labour in the getting of food; and, however possible this may be, it can hardly be so easy as the increase of living beings by their own act.

The degree of disparity between the two will of course depend on the degree of rapidity with which an unchecked population is supposed to double itself. Sir William Petty,[2] with few trustworthy statistics,

[1] Or, keeping in view Carey's exception, we should say not perhaps the first crop, but the earliest in which the farmer did justice to the known resources of the best land.

[2] *Political Arithmetic—Essay on the Multiplication of Mankind*, 1682, pp. 7, 13 *seq.*, especially p. 21 (ed. 1755).

had supposed ten years; Euler, with somewhat better, twelve and four-fifths; but Malthus prefers to go by the safe figures of the American colonies, which he always regarded as a crucial proof that the period was not more than twenty-five. He admits the risk of his own mathematical simile when he grants that it is more easy to determine the rate of the natural increase of population than the rate of the increase of food which is in a much less degree natural (or spontaneous); and he argues from what had been done in England in his own time that the increase would not even be in an arithmetical ratio, though agricultural improvement (thanks to Arthur Young and the Board of Agriculture, and the long reign of high prices) was raising the average produce very sensibly. If the Napoleonic times were the times of a forced population in England, they were also the times of a forced agricultural production. Yet we ourselves, long after this stimulus, and after much high farming unknown to our fathers, have reached only an average produce of twenty-eight bushels per acre of arable land as compared with twenty-three in 1770,[1] while the population has risen from about six millions to twenty-five. It may be said, that applies only to wheat. But until lately wheat-growing was the chief object of all our scientific agriculture; and this is the result of a century's improvements. It is far from an arithmetical increase; and, even had the produce been multiplied sevenfold, along with the population, this would not overthrow the contention

[1] Sir James Caird, *Landed Interest*, 4th ed., 1880, p. 177.

of Malthus, for he is not speaking of any and every increase of food, but of such an increase made by the same methods and by the same kind of labour as raised the old supplies.[1] Once it is acknowledged that to raise new food requires greater labour and new inventions, while to bring new men into the world requires nothing more than in all times past, the disparity of the two is already admitted. The fact that the two processes are both dependent on the action of man, and both practically illimitable, does not prevent them from being essentially unlike.[2] Objectors often suppose that the tendency of population to outrun subsistence is contradicted by the existence of unpeopled or thinly-peopled countries, just as if the tendency of bodies to attract each other were contradicted by the incompressibility of matter. The important point to notice is that the one power is greater than the other. The one is to the other as the hare is to the tortoise in the fable. To make the slow tortoise win the race, we must send the hare to sleep.[3]

Carey (*Social Science*, vol. i. ch. iii. § 5) represents the view of Malthus by the following propositions :— 1. "Matter tends to take upon itself higher forms," passing from inorganic to vegetable and animal life, and from these to man. 2. Matter tends to take on itself the vegetable and animal forms in an arithmetic ratio only. 3. It tends to take its highest form, man, in a geometrical ratio, so that the highest outstrips

[1] But see below, Bk. II. ch. i. [2] 2nd ed., I. i. p. 8 ; 7th ed., p. 6.
[3] *Essay*, IV. iii., 7th ed., p. 407.

the lowest. In short he believes that Malthus holds the geometrical increase to be true of man alone, and only the arithmetical to be true of animals and vegetables. But Malthus really attributed the tendency to geometrical increase to all life whatsoever, and arithmetical to all food, as such.

In Macvey Napier's Supplement to the *Encyclopædia Britannica* (1824) Malthus has left his mature statement of his cardinal principles, and, at the risk of repetition, that account may be added here. The main difference from the essay is in arrangement of the leading ideas; and we may learn at least what he conceived to be their relative importance towards the end of his life.

He begins by observing (1) that *all living things*, of whatever kind, when furnished with their proper nourishment tend to increase in a geometrical ratio, whether (as wheat) by multiplying sixfold in one year, or (as sheep) by doubling their numbers in two years, tending to fill the earth, the one in fourteen, the other in seventy-six years. But (2) as a matter of fact they do not so increase, and the reason is either man's want of will or man's want of power to provide them their proper soil or pasture. The actual rate of increase is extremely slow, while the power of increase is prodigious. (3) Physically man is as the rest; and if we ask what is the factor of his geometrical increase, we can only tell it, as in the case of wheat and sheep, by experience. (4) In the case of other living beings, where there are most room and food there is greatest increase. These conditions are best fulfilled for man in the United States, where the distribution of wealth is better than in other equally fertile places, and the greater number share the advantages. The American census shows for the three decades between 1790 and 1820 a rate of increase that would double the numbers in $22\frac{1}{5}$, $22\frac{1}{2}$, and $23\frac{7}{13}$ years respectively, after we deduct as immigrants ten thousand on an average every year.

A striking indirect confirmation of this view of the American increase was supplied to Malthus[1] by Joshua Milne, the author of the *Treatise on Annuities.* His calculations were founded on the new Swedish table of mortality. This table had been drawn up from the registers of the first five years of the century, years of unusual healthiness; and might therefore be presumed to represent the normal condition of a new and healthy country like the United States better than the old table drawn up from the years before sanitary reform and vaccination. Milne took the Swedish table as his guide, and one million of people as his unit of measurement; he calculated in what proportions the component individuals of the million must belong to childhood, youth, mature life, and old age, in order that by the principles of the Swedish table the million might double itself by natural increase in twenty-five years; and he arrived at a distribution so like that given by the American census, that he was bound to conclude the American rate of increase to be at the least very like one that doubles a population in twenty-five years. But the

[1] *Encycl. Brit.*, *art. Population.* Cf. *Essay*, 7th ed., p. 236 n.

Swedish law of mortality could not be exactly true of the United States, which are healthier as a whole than Sweden even in Sweden's best years.[1] The United States themselves are not the very healthiest and wealthiest and happiest country conceivable; and their increase is therefore not the fastest conceivable. If the observed fact of increase is the best proof of the capacity for increase, the observed presence of checks leads to an *a fortiori* reasoning, whereby we infer the capacity for a greater increase than any actually observed. To sum up the whole of this first branch of the argument,—"taking into consideration the actual rate of increase which appears from the best documents to have taken place over a very large extent of country in the United States of America, very variously circumstanced as to healthiness and rapidity of progress,—considering further the rate of increase which has taken place in New Spain and also in many countries of Europe, where the means of supporting a family, and other circumstances favourable to increase, bear no comparison with those of the United States,—and adverting particularly to the actual increase of population which has taken place in this country during the last twenty years[2] under the formidable obstacles which must press themselves upon the attention of the most

[1] Sweden was a favourite with statisticians because Sweden alone at that time furnished sound statistics. For an account of the American population down to 1880, and its probable future, see Mr. Giffen's Address on the Utility of Common Statistics (Stat. Soc., Dec. 1882).

[2] 1804-24, or simply from the first census, 1801, to the third, 1821. The increase was such as would double the population of England in fifty-one years at the least (*Essay*, II. ix., 7th ed., p. 217).

careless observer, it must appear that the assumption of a rate of increase such as would double the population in twenty-five years, as representing the natural progress of population when not checked by the difficulty of procuring the means of subsistence or other peculiar causes of premature mortality, must be decidedly within the truth. It may be safely asserted, therefore, that population when unchecked increases in a geometrical ratio of such a nature as to double itself every twenty-five years." [1]

The problem is only half stated; it is still to be shown what is the rate of the increase of Food. The case does not admit the same kind of proof. We can suppose an unchecked increase of men going on without any change in human nature; we have only to suppose for the future the same encouragement to marriage and the same habits of life, together with the same law of mortality. But with the increase of food the causes do not remain the same. If good land could be got in abundance, the increase of food from it would be in a geometrical ratio far greater than that of the men; that of wheat, for example, would be sixfold, as we have seen. But good lands are comparatively few; they will in the nature of things soon be occupied; and then the increase of the food will be a laborious process at a rate rather resembling a decreasing than an increasing geometrical ratio. "The yearly increment of food, at least, would have a constant tendency to diminish;" and the amount of the increase in each successive ten

[1] *Encycl. Brit.*, l. c.

years would probably be less and less. In practice, the inequalities of distribution may check the increase of food with precisely the same efficacy as an actual arrival at the physical limits to the getting of the food. "A man who is locked up in a room may fairly be said to be confined by the walls of it, though he may never touch them."[1] But the main point is, that, inequalities or no inequalities, there is a tendency to diminished productiveness. Under either condition the quantity yielded this year will not be doubled or trebled for an indefinite period with the same ease as it was yielded this year. In a tolerably well-peopled country such as England or Germany the utmost might be an increase every twenty-five years equal to the present produce. But the continuance of this would mean that in the next two hundred years every farm should produce eight times what it does now, or, in five hundred years, twenty times as much; and even this is incredible, though it would be only an arithmetical progression. No doubt almost all parts of the earth are now more thinly peopled than their capacities might allow; but the difficulty is to use the capacities. That this view of Malthus need not imply any ignorance or any disregard of the resources of high farming may be judged from the fact that our highest agricultural authority, who recognizes the power of English farming to provide on emergency even for our entire annual wants, admits at the same time that, "where full employment and the means of subsistence are abundant,

[1] *Essay*, III. xiv., 7th ed., p. 387.

population increases in geometrical progression, and therefore in a far more rapid proportion than the increased productiveness of the soil, which after a certain point is stationary."[1] "It follows necessarily" (sums up Malthus) "that the average rate of the actual increase of population over the greatest part of the globe, obeying the same law as the increase of food, must be totally of a different character from the rate at which it would increase if unchecked." On no single farm could the produce be so increased as to keep pace with the geometrical increase of population; and what is true of a single farm is true in this case of the whole earth. Machinery and invention can do less in agriculture than in manufacture, and they can never do so much as to make preventive checks unnecessary.[2]

This is the argument of the *Encyclopædia* so far as it relates to the theses of the essay. Malthus follows it up by a remark on the institution of property. The alternatives to his mind are always private property as we now have it, and common property as desired by Godwin. He upholds the first because, "according to all past experience and the best observation which can be made on the motives which operate upon the human mind," the largest produce from the soil is got by that system, and because (what is socially much more important), by making a man feel his responsibility and his dependence on his own efforts, it tends to cause prudence in marriage as well as industry in work. Common property has not

[1] Caird, *Landed Interest*, pp. 18, 46. [2] *Encycl. Brit.*, l. c.

been successful, historically; and the widest extension of popular education would not make men the fitter for it. There is indeed a sense in which common property might tend to carry production farther than private property; cultivation, not being for profit but for mere living, would not, like the present, stop at the point where production ceased to be a good investment. But this would mean[1] that the whole energies of the society were directed to the mere getting of food; neither the whole society nor any part of it would have leisure, for intellectual labour or enjoyment. Whereas private property not only secures the leisure, but, by stopping at the point of profitableness, it keeps an unused reserve, on which society may fall back in case of need. Malthus therefore would stand by private property, though he thinks that private proprietors may damage the national wealth by game-preserving, and injure the poorer classes by not spending enough on what they make.[2]

The actual increase of population (he goes on) and the necessity of checks to it depend on the difficulty of getting food, from whatever cause, whether the exhaustion of the earth or the bad structure of society; and the difficulty is not for the remote future but for the present.

It is chiefly the contrast between the actual and the possible supplies that makes men incredulous about the necessity of checks; and we may grant that

[1] Apart, he ought to have said, from prudence in marriage, which would allow each man's share to be much more than a bare living. But see below, Bk. II. ch. ii.

[2] See below, Bk. II. ch. iii.

under an ideal government, a perfect people, and faultless social system the produce would at first be so great that the necessity for checks on population would be very much reduced; but, as the earth's productiveness does not expand with population, it would be a very short time before the pressure of the checks would reassert itself—this time from no fault of man, but from the mere nature of the soil.[1] The bad government of our ancestors left much produce unused, and in consequence we have for the present a large margin to draw on. But, "if merely since the time of William the Conqueror all the nations of the earth had been well governed, and if the distribution of property and the habits both of the rich and the poor had been the most favourable to the demand for produce and labour, though the amount of food and population would have been prodigiously greater than at present, the means of diminishing the checks to population would unquestionably be less."

But, though the laws of nature are responsible for the necessity of checks to population,[2] "a vast mass of responsibility remains behind, on man and the institutions of society." To them in the first place is due the scantiness of the present population of the earth, there being few parts of it that would not with better government and better morals support twice, ten times, or even one hundred times as many inhabitants as now. In the second place, though man cannot

[1] By the "law" of decreasing returns. See below, Bk. II. ch. i.

[2] Mr. Giffen, in the Address above quoted, speaks as if Malthus considered the positive checks as the "natural checks" (p. 531). This, however, is against his distinct statement in *Essay*, 7th ed., App. p. 480.

remove the necessity of checks, or even make them press much more lightly in any given place,[1] he is responsible for their precise character and particular mode of operation. A good government and good institutions can so direct them that they shall be least hurtful to the general virtue and happiness, vice and misery disappearing before moral restraint, though after all the influence of government and institutions is indirect, and everything depends on the conduct of the individual citizens.

The rest of the article contains little that is not in the *Essay on Population* (5th ed., 1817) and the treatise on *Political Economy* (1st ed., 1820). It gives the historical sketches of the former, some small part of the economical discussions (*e.g.* on wages) of the latter, and a short answer to current objections, together with some tables of mortality and other figures, of more special interest to the professional actuary than to the general reader. The article is an authoritative summary of the author's doctrines in their final form. It was not his last work. From the fact that he undertook the paper in Sept. 1821,[2] we may perhaps infer that he placed it in Macvey Napier's hands in the year 1822.[3] But it was his last attempt to re-state the subject of the essay in an independent form with anything approaching to fulness of detail, and it shows he had made no change

[1] This is probably the meaning of the author's phrase, "alter the *proportionate amount* of the checks to population, or the degree in which they press upon the actual numbers" (*Encyclop.*, l. c., p. 415).

[2] See his letter of that date in Macvey Napier's *Correspondence*, p. 29.

[3] It was not published till 1824. It was certainly written after the results of the Census of 1821 had been published.

in his position. The *Summary View of the Principle of Population* (1830) was avowedly an abridgment of the article in the *Encyclopædia*, and is in fact that article with a few paragraphs omitted and a few pronouns altered.

The clear statement of the two tendencies was, in his own eyes, the least original part of his work. It had been often perceived distinctly by other writers that population must always be kept down to the level of the means of subsistence. "Yet few inquiries have been made into the various modes by which this level is effected, and the principle has never been sufficiently pursued to its consequences, nor those practical inferences drawn from it which a strict examination of its effects on society appears to suggest."[1] What some people would count the more interesting question remained to be considered—the question that touches individuals and familiar circumstances more nearly, and is not to be answered by a generality, from which we easily in thought except our own individual selves. Since, at any given time, in any given place, among any given people, there is (1) a tendency of population to outrun subsistence, and there is (2) no such excess as a matter of fact, in what way or ways is the tendency prevented from carrying itself out? As was said above,[2] this is effected in two kinds of ways—(1) by the way of a positive, (2) by the way of a preventive check, the former cutting down an actual population to the level of its food, the second forbidding a population to

[1] Pref. to 2nd ed., pp. iv, v ; 7th ed., p. vi. [2] p. 52.

need to be cut down, and being, so far as it is voluntary, peculiar to man among living creatures. Of the positive, all those that come from the laws of nature may be called misery pure and simple; and all those that men bring on themselves by wars, excesses, and avoidable troubles of all kinds are of a mixed character, their causes being vice and their consequences misery. Of the preventive, that restraint from marriage which is not accompanied by any immoral conduct on the part of the person restraining himself or herself is called moral restraint. Any restraint which is prudential and preventive, but immoral, comes under the head of vice, for every action may be so called which has "a general tendency to produce misery," however innocuous its immediate effects.[1] We find, therefore, that the positive and the preventive checks are all resolvable into vice, misery, and moral restraint, or sin, pain, and self-control, a threefold division that makes the second essay "differ in principle" from the first.[2]

We have here a twofold alongside of a threefold division of the checks to population. The one is made from an objective, the other from a subjective point of view. The division of checks (1) into positive and preventive has regard simply to the outward facts; a population is in those two ways kept down to the food. The division of them (2) into vice, misery, and moral restraint has regard to the human agent and his inward condition, the state of his feelings and of his will. For example, the positive

[1] *Essay*, 2nd ed., p. 11 n.; 7th ed., p. 9 n. [2] 2nd ed., Pref. p. vii.

check viewed subjectively, or from the human being's point of view, is the feeling of pain; the will is not directly concerned with it. The preventive, from the same point of view, is of a less simple character. First of all, moral restraint involves a temporary misery or pain in the thwarting of a desire; "considered as a restraint upon an inclination otherwise innocent and always natural, it must be allowed to produce a certain degree of temporary unhappiness, but evidently slight compared with the evils which result from any of the other checks to population,"[1] and "merely[2] of the same nature as many other sacrifices of temporary to permanent gratification which it is the business of a moral agent continually to make." The reverse is true of vicious excesses and passions; in their immediate gratification they are pleasant, but their permanent effects are misery. From the point of view of the will the case is clear, for the state of the will would be described by Malthus, if he ever used such terms, as in the one case good, and in the other case evil, pure and simple. Of course in treating the matter historically we may neglect the subjective point of view, not because it is not necessary for proper knowledge of the facts, but because it leads to a psychological inquiry, the results of which are independent of dates.

Malthus goes on to say that, in all cases where there is the need for checks at all, it is the sum-total of all the preventive and positive checks that forms the check to population in any given country at any

[1] 2nd ed., Bk. I. ch. ii. p. 10. [2] Adds the 3rd ed.

given time,[1] and his endeavour will be to show in what relative proportions and in what degree they prevail in various countries known to us. He assumes further that the preventive and the positive checks will "vary inversely as each other." In countries where the mortality is great the influence of the preventive check will be small; and, where the preventive check prevails much, the positive check, or in brief the mortality, will be small.[2]

In society, as it was in the first years of the nineteenth century, Malthus thinks he can trace out even by his own observation an "oscillation," or what it is the fashion to call a "cycle," in the movement of population. History does not show it well, simply because "the histories of mankind which we possess are in general only of the higher classes," [3] and it is the labouring classes to which the observation applies. Their painful experience of the ruder checks has not prevented a "constant effort" in the labouring population to have larger families than they can well support. The consequence is that their numbers are increased; they must divide amongst eleven and a half millions the food that was formerly divided among eleven millions; they must have lower wages and dearer provisions. But this state of distress will so check population that in process of time the numbers will be almost at a standstill, while at the same time, since the demand for food has been greater

[1] 3rd ed., p. 21; 7th ed., p. 9. [2] 3rd ed. *l. c.*

[3] 2nd ed., p. 13; 7th ed., p. 10. His own book has helped to make this less true.

and labour has been cheaper, the application of capital to agriculture will have increased the available food. The result will be the same tolerable degree of comfort as at the beginning of the cycle, and the same relapse from it as at the second stage. He conceives the two stages to follow each other as naturally as sunshine rain and rain sunshine. The existence of such a cycle may remain concealed from the ordinary historian, if he looks merely to the money-wages of the labourer, for it frequently happens that the labourer gets the same sums of money for his wages during a long series of years when the real value of the sums has not remained the same,—the price of bread in what we have called the second stage of the cycle being much dearer than it was in the first, and than it will be in the third.[1] Though Malthus expressly qualifies his statements by showing that civilization tends to counteract these fluctuations, it certainly seemed to be his belief in 1803 that on the whole the working classes of Europe, and especially of England, were powerless to escape from them. How far this view is justified will be seen presently.

[1] 2nd ed., pp. 14, 15. With this description of the "cycle" compare the view of Marx as given below in Book IV.

CHAPTER IV.

THE SAVAGE, BARBARIAN, AND ORIENTAL.

Simile supplanted by Fact—Savage Life—Population dependent not on possible but on actual Food—Indirect Action of Positive Checks—Hunger not a Principle of Progress—Otaheite a Crux for Common Sense—Cycle in the Movement of Population—Pitcairn Island—Barbarian and Oriental—Nomad Shepherds—Abram and Lot—Cimbri and Teutones—Gibbon *versus* Montesquieu—" At bay on the limits of the Universe "—Misgovernment an indirect Check on Population—Ancient Europe less populous than Modern—Civilization the gradual Victory of the third Check.

THE main position of the essay was so incontrovertible, that when the critics despaired to convict Malthus of a paradox, they charged him with a truism. To the friendly Hallam[1] the mathematical basis of the argument appeared as certain as the multiplication table, and the unfriendly Hazlitt " did not see what there was to discover after reading the tables of Noah's descendants, and knowing that the world is round."[2] If the essayist had done nothing more than put half-truths together into a whole, he would have " entrenched himself in an impregnable fortress " and given his work a great " air of mastery."[3] But he would have convinced the understanding

[1] Miss Martineau, *Autob.*, vol. i. p. 210.
[2] Reply to Malthus, p. 20. Cf. below, Book IV.
[3] Pref. to 2nd ed., p. vi.

without convincing the imagination. Adam Smith himself would have done no more than half his work, if he had been content to prove the reasonableness of free trade without showing, in detail, the effect of it and its opposites. Even the most competent reader has seldom all the relevant facts marshalled in his memory, ready to command; and he will always be thankful for illustrations. The *Essay on Population* in its second form certainly excelled all economical works, save one, in its pertinent examples from life and history.

Imagination in the narrower sense of the word is to be out of court. Malthus, like Adam Smith, not only leaves little to his reader's fancy, but makes little use of his own. His own had misled his readers in the first essay, though it had certainly given that little book much of its piquancy; and he resolves for the sake of truth to chain it up, as Coleridge chained up his understanding. The self-denying ordinance is only too fully executed. The style of his essay is truly described by himself[1] as having gradually "lost all pretensions to merit." Edition follows edition, each with its footnotes, supplements, re-arrangements, and corrections, till the reader feels that this writer "would be clearer if he were not so clear."

But the title-page supplies a guiding thread. From the second edition onwards to the last, "Past" and "Present" appear in large letters, "Future" in small. The entire work may therefore be divided according to the three tenses, with the emphasis on the two former.

[1] 2nd ed., Pref. p. vi. True even then, and much more afterwards.

The first book is devoted to the past, the second to the present, and the third and fourth to the future.

The First deals with the less civilized parts of the world as it now is, and the uncivilized past times; the Second with the different states of modern Europe; the Third criticizes popular schemes of future improvement; while the Fourth gives the author's own views of the possible progress of humanity.

After explaining his principles, Malthus takes a survey of human progress, if not from brute to savage, at least from savage to citizen. He shows us how the rude and simple positive checks become complicated with the preventive; and he leads us up from barbarism to civilization till we find ourselves in a society where the citizens think less of check than of chief end, and less of self-sacrifice than of self-devotion, to some cause or person, and even the inferior members act, at worst, from mixed motives, containing good as well as evil. These are the two extreme ends of his line. It would be useless to deny that he lingers longest over the less pleasing, and gives Godwin some excuse for questioning his logical right to believe in the more pleasing at all.[1] At the same time it would have been (even logically) impossible for him to have attacked Godwin for taking abstract views of human nature, and then to have persisted in an abstraction of his own, after all his own European travel and historical studies. His fault had lain in defective premises, not in false reasoning; and he remedies the fault.

[1] Godwin, *On Population*, I. iv. 31, 32.

Let us take his account in his own order. Beginning with present savagery, which with some qualifications is a picture of our own past, he sifts out the descriptions of Cook, Vancouver, and other travellers, to see what checks to population operate in different grades of savage humanity. At the very bottom of the scale comes Tierra del Fuego, by general consent the abode of pure misery, and therefore naturally the home of a sparse population. Next come the natives of the Andaman Islands and of Van Diemen's Land. "Their whole time is spent in search of food," which consists of the raw products of the soil and sea; the whole time of every individual is devoted to this one labour, and there is neither room nor inducement for any other industries. Vice is hardly needed; misery in the shape of perpetual scarcity and famine keeps down the people to the food. Third in the scale of human beings are the New Hollanders, the original inhabitants of North-West Australia, among whom can be traced not only the check of misery, but the check of vice. The women are so cruelly treated at all times, and the children have so harsh an upbringing, that there is no difficulty in understanding how population does not even reach the full limit of the scanty food. War and pestilence make the assurance doubly sure. As savages are entirely innocent of sanitary science, the dirt of their persons and their houses deprives them of "the advantage which usually attends a thinly-peopled country," comparative exemption from pestilence.[1]

[1] 2nd ed., p. 31; 7th ed., p. 23.

Even the North American Indians, who are one step higher than the New Hollanders, come under the same condemnation for overcrowding, and for much else besides. The account which Malthus gives of them may be compared with that of De Tocqueville half a century later. Romance has clung to them only because they were the nearest and best-known savages of their kind, and their necessary labours were in Europe rich men's pleasures. But hunting and river-fishing cannot yield much food unless pursued over a wide area. A hunter is so far like the beast of prey which he pursues, that he must go long distances for his food, and must either fly from or overcome every rival. The North American Indian must therefore either go West after his old food, or else he must stay where he is, to beat off the Europeans, or to adopt their food and their habits. "The Indians have only two ways of saving themselves, war and civilization. They must either destroy the Europeans or become their equals."[1] As the civilization of a nation of hunters is almost impossible, their extinction seems inevitable. The question remains, How is this population cut down to the level of its food?

In Malthus' answer to the question occur three remarks of great general importance. First, what limits the numbers of a people is not the possible but the actual food.[2] Second, want destroys a

[1] *Démocratie en Amérique*, Pt. II. ch. x. p. 278. The author is in thorough agreement with Malthus.

[2] 2nd ed., p. 39 ; 7th ed., p. 28.

population less often directly by starvation than indirectly through the medium of manners and customs.[1] Third, the mere pressure of impending starvation does not lead to progress.[2]

Malthus is never tired of insisting on the first of these remarks; and a proper understanding of it is essential to a fair judgment on his doctrine. He never says that it is the tendency of a population to increase up to the limits of the greatest possible amount of food that can be produced in a given country. The valley of the Mississippi when highly cultivated may possibly support a hundred millions; but the question is not what it would do when highly cultivated, but what it can do when cultivated as it now is and as men now are. "In a general view of the American continent as described by historians, the population seems to have been spread over the surface very nearly in proportion to the quantity of food which the inhabitants of the different parts in the actual state of their industry and improvements could as a matter of fact obtain; and that with few exceptions it pressed hard against this limit, rather than fell short of it, appears from the frequent recurrence of distress for want of food in all parts of America."[3] What is said here of the Indians a hundred years ago applies to the Colonists now. "The actual state of industry" is of course a much more improved one; but the population the land will bear is still in proportion to it, and the amount could not have been

[1] 2nd ed., p. 25; 7th ed., p. 18. [2] *Ibid.* p. 43; 7th ed., p. 31.
[3] *Ibid.* p. 39; 7th ed., p. 28.

increased till the actual state of the industry had first been bettered. One cause of the decay of the numbers of the Indians was that their method of industry, so far from becoming better, became worse by their contact with Europeans, and therefore the limit of population was actually contracted instead of being extended.[1] This explains how it is that their diminishing numbers do not bring them greater comfort. Whether the numbers in any given case are too great or too small depends always on the quantity of the food that is divided among them; and, where the food decreases faster than the population, a population that has become smaller numerically becomes actually larger in proportion to the food. The statement that England or any other country could bear millions more than it does now is a mere reference to unexplored possibilities, landing us in the infinite. It may be answered in the same way as the Eleatic puzzles about motion; land infinitely improvable does not mean land infinitely improved, as matter infinitely divisible does not mean matter infinitely divided. The position of Malthus is therefore as follows: given a people's skill, and given its standard of living at any time, its numbers are always tending to be the utmost that can be furnished by that skill with a living up to that standard,—that is to say, with what, according to that standard, are the necessaries of human life. Either a diminution of that skill or an increase in that standard would cause over population. The question is always a relative one.

[1] 2nd ed., p. 44; 7th ed., p. 32.

The human as distinguished from the animal character of the problem appears not only in that relativity (which affects mainly the preventive checks), but in the indirect way in which the positive checks, if we may say so, prefer to act. It is as if they were always desirous of resolving themselves as far as might be into preventive. The ultimate check, Malthus says, is starvation; but, he adds, it is seldom the immediate one. The higher up we go in the scale, the more it is hidden away out of sight. Starvation is interpreted, by all grades of society above the lowest, to mean the loss of what they conceive to be the necessaries not of a bare living but of endurable life; and even the lowest, instead of apprehending some pain, apprehend some bringer of it. They do not allow famine to kill them; they create manners and customs that do the work for it, keeping the famine itself afar off. "Both theory and experience uniformly instruct us that a less abundant supply of food operates with a gradually increasing pressure for a very long time before its progress is stopped. It is difficult indeed to conceive a more tremendous shock to society than the event of its coming at once to the limits of the means of subsistence, with all the habits of abundance and early marriages, which accompany a largely increasing population. But, happily for mankind, this never is nor ever can be the case. The event is provided for by the concurrent interests and feelings of individuals long before it arrives; and the gradual diminution of the real wages of the labouring classes of society slowly and almost insensibly generates the habits necessary for an order of things in which the funds for the maintenance of labour are stationary. . . . The causes [of the retardation of population] will be generally felt and [will] generate a change of habits long before the period arrives."[1] "An insufficient supply of food to any people does not show itself merely in the shape of famine, but in other more permanent forms of distress, and in generating certain customs which operate sometimes with greater force in the prevention of a rising population" than in the destruction of the risen.[2] Robertson the historian truly says, that whether civilization has improved the lot of men may be doubtful, but it has certainly improved the condition of women. Among the Indians and almost all savages, "servitude is a name too mild to describe their wretched state." The hard life of the men kills their instinctive fondness for the women; the latter are therefore less likely to become mothers, while, if they do, their own hardships and heavy tasks are a great hindrance to nursing. It is not surprising that the surviving children are of good physique; none but the exceptionally strong could weather the cruel discipline of childhood.[3] In South America the difficulty of upbringing actually led to an enforced monogamy, as well as to late marriages and their not unfrequent accompaniment, irregularities before marriage. Such customs diminish numbers. But even the adult savages do not find life easy. They are not the men to think of providing for a

[1] Malthus in *Edin. Rev.*, July 1808, p. 345.

[2] *Essay*, 2nd ed., p. 25; 7th ed., p. 18. [3] *Ibid.* p. 29; 7th ed., p. 21.

rainy day; in the short moments of plenty they do not think of the long days of want. Intemperate living as well as the rigour and the accidents of a hunting life cut off numbers in their prime. They are subject to diseases and invent no remedies. Their acquiescence in dirt leads to pestilences, but they invent no sanitary reforms; and their thinly peopled country loses its natural exemption from epidemics. Their wars are internecine, for they are largely prompted by sheer self-preservation, and the thought that if the one combatant lives the other cannot. Cannibalism itself was at first due to extreme want, though what occasional hunger had begun, hate perpetuated in a custom. This and the low cunning and mean strategy, due to a resolve to survive at all costs, are the prime inventions of the struggle for existence on these low levels.

Such are the causes by which the numbers of the North American Indians are kept down to a very low figure; but, low as it is, the figure is high enough for the food. Apart from a difference in the standard of living, the proportion of population to food is similar over the inhabited world; and in the same neighbourhood or among cognate races it will be almost identical. A diminution in one Indian tribe, not being voluntary, will not be the cause of plenty to the survivors; it has been the effect of want, and it will simply weaken the collective force of the tribe in the struggle against others.[1]

The supremacy of want as the ultimate check on

[1] 2nd ed., pp. 37, 45; 7th ed., pp. 27, 32.

population is illustrated by the instant expansion of population which is produced in these grades of humanity by an accession of plenty. When a tribe falls upon fertile land, its numbers swell, and its collective might, depending on numbers, becomes greater. The increase of food, however, seems in this case to lead to nothing else than increase of numbers. There is a melancholy equality of suffering between tribe and tribe, as well as between members of the same tribe. There is no distinction of rank, but only of sex and bodily strength, as regards endurance of hardships.

It is in this connection that Malthus throws some light on the question how progress could ever take place at all. His answer is not unlike Adam Smith's remark about the connection of high wages with good work. He says, that beyond a certain limit, hard fare and great want depress men below the very capacity of improvement; comfort must reach a certain height before the desires of civilized life can come into being at all. If the American tribes, he says, have remained hunters, it is not simply because they have not increased in numbers sufficiently to render the pastoral or agricultural state necessary to them. Reasons which Malthus does not pretend to particularize,[1] and which he allows to be unconnected with mere increase or decrease of numbers, have prevented these tribes from ever trying to raise cattle or grow corn at all. "If hunger alone could have prompted the savage tribes of America to such a

[1] Though, like Coleridge (MS. note below, 371), he mentions brandy.

change in their habits, I do not conceive that there would have been a single nation of hunters and fishers remaining; but it is evident that some fortunate train of circumstances, in addition to this stimulus, is necessary for this purpose; and it is undoubtedly probable that these arts of obtaining food will be first invented and improved in those spots which are best suited to them, and where the natural fertility of the situation, by allowing a greater number of people to subsist together, would give the fairest chance to the inventive powers of the human mind." "A certain degree of [political] security is perhaps still more necessary than richness of soil to encourage the change from the pastoral to the agricultural state."[1] These passages are remarkable because they seem to contradict the general tenor of the author's writings. We were told with great emphasis in the first edition of the essay that difficulties generate talents,[2] and even the second and later are full of approving commentaries on the proverb, "Necessity is the mother of invention."[3] The contradiction is soon solved. Malthus has no faith in the civilizing power of competition when it means a struggle among starved men for bare life, but much faith in it when it means the struggle for greater comfort among those who already have the animal necessaries.[4] The signifi-

[1] 2nd ed., pp. 43, 92; 7th ed., pp. 31, 64. Cf. I. vi., 2nd ed., p. 82 n.; 7th ed., p. 57 n.

[2] See above, pp. 35, 36.

[3] *E.g.* 2nd ed., II. ii. 199; 7th ed., p. 135.

[4] Compare the suggestive remarks of Rogers, *Six Centuries*, pp. 270, 271. He thinks that a movement like Lollardism could not have succeeded in times of utter depression.

cance of his admissions will be noticed later. Meanwhile it must be observed that the passage just quoted is not perfectly precise. The larger the society, the greater might be the division of labour and consequent stimulus to invention; but a tribe might be large and yet have little in it of a society, and still less of a division of labour. Without such favouring circumstances as Malthus mentions the progress cannot take place; but even with them it need not; they are therefore not the real motive power.

The account of the state of population among the South Sea Islanders,[1] which comes next in order to the chapter on the American Indians, is an illustration of these remarks. These savages live in a fertile country and yet they make no progress. As this is not the only point illustrated, it is worth while to look at the chapter in detail.

Malthus begins by observing that population must not be thought more subject to checks on an island than on a continent. The Abbé Raynal, in his book on the Indies, had tried to explain a number of modern customs that retarded population[2] by referring them to an insular origin. He thought that they were caused at first by the over-population of Britain and other islands, and were imported therefrom into the continents, to the perplexity of later ages. But as a matter of fact population on the mainlands is subject to the same laws as on the islands, though the limits are not so obvious to

[1] *Essay*, Book I. ch. v. [2] *E. g.* cannibalism and late marriages.

common observation, and the case is not put so neatly in a nutshell. A nation on the continent may be as completely surrounded by its enemies or its rivals, savage or civilized, as any islanders by the sea; and emigration may be as difficult in the one case as in the other. Both continent and island are peopled up to their actual produce. "There is probably no island yet known, the produce of which could not be further increased. This is all that can be said of the whole earth. Both are peopled up to their actual produce. And the whole earth is in this respect like an island."[1] The earth is indeed more isolated than any island of the sea, for no emigration from it is possible. The question, therefore, to be asked about the whole earth as about any part of it, is, "By what means the inhabitants are reduced to such numbers as it can support?"

This was the question which forced itself on Captain Cook when he visited the islands of the Pacific and Indian Oceans. Some of his experiences there, especially in New Zealand, show that the native population was kept down in nearly the same way as the American. Their chief peculiarity is the extreme violence of their local feuds. The people of every village he visited petitioned him to destroy the people of the next, and "if I had listened to them I should have extirpated the whole race." A sense of human kinship is impossible at so low a level of being; and the internecine wars of the New Zealanders were the chief check to their numbers,

[1] 2nd ed., p. 46; 7th ed., p. 33. Cf. pp. 290 and 339.

which, from the distressing effects of occasional scarcities, would seem always at the best to have been close to the limits of the food.

The first impression of common sense is that distress is natural where food is scanty, and unnatural where it is plentiful. But "if we turn our eyes from the thinly-scattered inhabitants of New Zealand to the crowded shores of Otaheite and the Society Islands" we find no such phenomenon. "All apprehension of death seems at first sight to be banished from a country that is described to be fruitful as the garden of the Hesperides." But reflection tells us that happiness and plenty are the most powerful causes of increase. We might, therefore, expect a large population in Otaheite; at its first start it might double itself not in twenty-five but in fifteen years. Captain Cook estimated it (on his second voyage in 1773) as 204,000. How could a country about one hundred and twenty miles in circuit support an increase that doubled these numbers in twenty-five years? Emigration is impossible, for the other islands are in the same situation. Further cultivation is inadequate, for scientific invention is quite wanting. The answer is that the increase does not take place, and yet there is no miracle. Licentiousness among the higher classes, and infanticide amongst all classes, are freely practised. The free permission of infanticide no doubt, as Hume remarks,[1] tends as a rule rather to increase than to diminish

[1] In *Essays*, vol. i., Essay XI., *Populousness of Ancient Nations*, p. 444 (ed. 1768).

population, for "by removing the terrors of too numerous a family it would engage many people in marriage," and such is the force of natural affection, that comparatively few parents would carry out their first intentions. But in Otaheite in its old state custom had made infanticide easy, and it was a real check. War against other islands was a third check, frequently destroying the food as well as the people, thus striking down two generations at once. All these checks notwithstanding, the population was up to the level of the food, and there was as much scarcity and keen distress as on any barren island.

Such at least was the state of things discovered by Captain Cook in his three voyages (the last in 1778) and Captain Vancouver (in 1791). On the other hand, the author of *A Missionary Voyage to the South Pacific Ocean in* 1796-8 (London, 1799) found a people very scanty as compared with the food. The accuracy of both accounts is borne out by the description of the habits of the people at these two periods. Captain Cook says they were careful to save up every scrap of food, and yet suffered often from famine. The missionaries observe the frequency of famine in the Friendly Islands and the Marquesas, but say of the Otaheitans that they are extremely wasteful, and yet never seem to be in want. Even in the intervals between one of Cook's voyages and another the state of the island had altered. Malthus sees here an illustration of two facts. The one is that, apart from changes in the standard of living, population fluctuates between great excess and great defect, great numbers with great mortality, and great comfort with rapid multiplication of numbers. The other, which explains the first, is that any cause affecting population, either towards increase or towards decrease, continues to act for some time after the disappearance of the circumstances that first occasioned it. For example, over-populousness would lead to wars,[1] and the enmities of these wars would long survive their first occasion. Again, over-populousness would lead to greater infanticide and vice, which would become habitual. New circumstances would, no doubt, after a time bring new habits, and, to use the author's words, would "restore the population, which could not long be kept below its natural level without the most extreme violence. How far European contact may operate in Otaheite with this extreme violence and prevent it from recovering its former population is a point which experience only can determine. But, should this be the case, I have no doubt that on tracing the causes of it, we should find them to be aggravated vice and misery."[2] As a matter of fact either European contact has caused a diminution, or exacter inquiry has made a lower estimate of the population of all Polynesia. The people of the whole Society Islands is reckoned at between 15,000 and 18,000,[3] which is a long way from Cook's estimate of 204,000 for Otaheite alone. We can hardly believe, however, that the vice and misery of Otaheite are more than ten times as great as they were in

[1] Cf. Plato, *Repub.*, ii. [2] 2nd ed., p. 57; 7th ed., p. 41.

[3] Behm and Wagner (Bevölk. d. Erde, 1882) give it at 16,300.

1773; and perhaps we may suppose Malthus to mean that, if the European influences were of the same character at the end as they were at the beginning, and were as pernicious to the Polynesian as to the Red Indian, the language of pessimism would be justified. The passage at least shows how unfair it is to suppose Malthus to desire at all costs a small population; he is careful to say that, while vice in Otaheite by reducing the numbers caused a transient plenty among the survivors, still "a cause which may prevent any particular evil may be beyond comparison worse than the evil itself."[1] Life itself may be bought too dear.

No good is done, however, by denying that excessive numbers are an evil, or by optimistic assertion that if men are only good they will be happy. There is at least one Polynesian island whose past history gives a picturesque proof of the contrary. Pitcairn, "the lonely isle of the Mutineers," was a moral contrast to Otaheite. The inhabitants owed nothing good to their parents, who were the mutineers of H.M.S. 'Bounty,' and the women of Otaheite that came with them in 1790, when they first took refuge in Pitcairn Island. They owed all to the religious teaching of John Adams, which made them so good, that there were few like them on the earth.[2] But in latitudes just touching the tropics, with a single square mile of poor soil, surrounded by wide ocean, they had no outlet for trade and

[1] 2nd ed., p. 57 n.; 7th ed., p. 40 n.
[2] Report of Admiral D'Horsey to the Admiralty, 1878.

modern arts. Like the inhabitants of Godwin's Utopia,[1] they soon peopled the little country to the full extent of the food that could be got by the old methods, and, unlike the Utopians, they had not skill to invent new. If they had not drawn the line for themselves, misery would have done it for them. Their little colony at its first founding consisted of fifteen men and twelve women. Fourteen men and many women died off in the course of the ten years which passed before the time of moral regeneration. But they left many children; and, when the patriarch John Adams was visited by a passing ship in 1814, he was surrounded by a happy circle of devout families. Rapidly outgrowing the resources of the place, these simple folk removed in 1831 to Tahiti, eighty-seven strong. Some remained there; others had no pleasure in their new abode, and came back to suffer affliction with the people of God, believing with Malthus that "a cause which may prevent any particular evil may be beyond all comparison worse than the evil itself." The evil was real, however, and, in default of celibacy or new ways of bread winning, their only cure seemed emigration. So in 1855, Tahiti seeming ineligible, they journeyed further west to Norfolk Island. Though there are more than four hundred and forty to the square mile in England and Wales, two hundred people of this primitive sort had been certainly too many for the single square mile of Pitcairn Island; and they did not leave a moment too soon. Home sickness

[1] See above, pp. 17, 18.

brought back two entire families (of seventeen persons) in 1859. One or two stray travellers joined them five years afterwards; but, with allowance for these, we find that the increase of population on Pitcairn Island reaches the highest estimate of Malthus. When the English Admiral D'Horsey visited the place in 1878, the quarter of a hundred had grown in nineteen years, at the moderate cost of twelve deaths, to a population of ninety[1] persons. The primeval virtues will avail little without the modern arts.

Returning to Malthus, we find him following an order of his own, in rough conformity with the orthodox progress from deer to sheep, and from sheep to corn. He takes us from Polynesian savages to the nomad pastoral nations of ancient Europe.[2] The vast migrations and their momentous historical effects he ascribes to the "constant tendency in the human race to increase" beyond its food, and thinks that when history has been rewritten it will contain more of this.[3] "The misfortune of history is, that while the particular motives of a few princes and leaders are sometimes detailed with accuracy, the general causes which crowd their standards with willing followers are totally overlooked."[4] At first sight the phenomenon of civilized agricultural nations unable to repel the invasion of shepherds seems incredible; a country in pasture cannot possibly support so many inhabitants as a country

[1] Behm and Wagner say ninety-three.

[2] *Essay*, Book I. ch. vi.

[3] See above, p. 83.

[4] 2nd ed., p. 68 n.; 3rd ed., p. 115 n. He afterwards altered "totally" to "often entirely," 7th ed., p. 47 n.

in tillage. A shepherd, it is true, is nearer to the skilled labourer than a hunter; he does not simply take what nature gives him, where nature puts it; he keeps the desired objects of consumption under his own control, and his life is stronger because more social. Early African colonization, as Adam Smith pointed out, was less successful than early American, because the natives, being shepherds and even farmers rather than fishermen, were stronger in their resources and more united than the American aborigines, so that the European intruders were not able to displace them.[1] We should have expected the Scythian, Cimbrian, and Gothic invaders of ancient times to have had a similar rebuff. "But what renders nations of shepherds so formidable is the power which they possess of moving altogether, and the necessity they frequently feel of exerting this power in search of fresh pasture for their herds."[2] They have always in their breeding stock a reserve of food for an emergency. The mere consciousness that their mode of life does not bind them to one place gives them less anxiety about providing for a family. Therefore, when they exhaust one region and begin to feel the pinch of want, they make an armed emigration on the scale of whole tribes at once, for the occupation of more fruitful regions, and, as a rule, the conquest of them by force. The law of their life is a series of periodical "struggles for existence"[3] between one nation and another, in which the fittest

[1] *Wealth of Nations*, Book IV. ch. vii. Part iii. p. 286 (ed. MacC.).
[2] 2nd ed., p. 66; 7th ed., p. 46.
[3] His own word: 2nd ed., p. 67; 7th ed., p. 47.

survive at the cost of a prodigious waste of human life.

The milder initial stage of this process is illustrated by the separation of Abram and Lot in the book of Genesis.[1] Abram "was very rich in cattle." "Lot also had flocks and herds and tents. And the land was not able to bear them that they might dwell together, for their substance was great, so that they could not dwell together. And there was a strife between the herdmen of Abram's cattle and the herdmen of Lot's cattle." They agreed, therefore, to separate, Lot choosing the fertile valley of the Jordan, Abram going to the left into the land of Canaan. Migrations of the same sort, more or less peaceable, are described by modern writers as extending the Russian people from time to time farther and farther to the south and east.[2] In the instances best known to history the migrations were far from peaceable, and the puzzle has been to account for their recurrence. The slaughter of the German barbarians by Marius, Cæsar, Drusus, Tiberius, Germanicus did not prevent the reappearance of similar hordes of invaders a generation later. Claudius destroyed a quarter of a million of Goths; Aurelian and Probus had the same work to do again. Under Diocletian the barbarians, finding the conquest of Rome too much for them, slaughtered one another in frontier wars. No losses seemed to exhaust the permanent possibilities of population in those quarters. At last in the fourth

[1] Gen. xiii. 1—9. *Essay*, 2nd ed., p. 65; 7th ed., p. 45.

[2] See *e. g.* Mackenzie Wallace: *Russia*, vol. ii. pp. 48, 90, &c.

century "clouds of barbarians seemed to collect from all parts of the northern hemisphere. Gathering fresh darkness and terror as they rolled on, the congregated bodies at length obscured the sun of Italy and sunk the Western world in night."[1]

Why were the resources of the North so inexhaustible? Simply because the power of increase is inexhaustible. The North was not, it is true, more densely peopled then than now. "The climate of ancient Germany has been mollified and the soil fertilized by the labour of ten centuries from the time of Charlemagne. The same extent of ground which at present maintains in ease and plenty a million of husbandmen and artificers, was unable to supply a hundred thousand lazy warriors with the simple necessaries of life. The Germans abandoned their immense forests to the exercise of hunting, employed in pasturage the most considerable part of their lands, bestowed on the small remainder a rude and careless cultivation, and then accused the scantiness and sterility of a country that refused to maintain the multitude of its inhabitants. When the return of famine severely admonished them of the importance of the arts, the national distress was sometimes alleviated by the emigration of a third, perhaps, or a fourth part of their youth."[2] In short, the countries were more than fully peopled up to their actual produce; and, though by agriculture the actual produce would have been made greater, yet agriculture was not extended. The

[1] *Essay*, 2nd ed., p. 72; 7th ed., pp. 50, 51. [2] *Gibbon*, ch. ix. p. 175.

passion of the Germans for wine did not lead them to plant vineyards by the Rhine and Danube, but to rob the vintage of Italy. "Pigrum quin immo et iners videtur sudore acquirere quod possis sanguine parare."[1] Malthus supposes that even the Mark system of land-holding, with its absence of cities and its periodical redistributions of land, may have sprung from a political motive, the fear of accustoming the people to a settled agricultural life, and the desire to make emigration less irksome to them.[2] So long as there were weaker peoples to be plundered, the northern nations might freely double their numbers every twenty-five years, or oftener, and descend again on Italy and the South. Only when the whole was occupied by their own people who were not likely to be less stout for defence than for conquest, were the hordes forced back. Not perhaps till gunpowder was invented was Europe finally safe against them. Long after their last inland invasions, the Norsemen found their way by sea to the shores of England and France.

Gibbon's account of the matter is, according to Malthus, substantially true. The only flaw is that he thinks it necessary, in denying the greater populousness of North Europe in ancient times, to deny the possibility of a rapid increase of population.[3] The German people were on the whole virtuous and healthy in their manners of living, and, the checks to increase being mainly the positive ones of war and famine, the increase itself was prodigious. But

[1] Tacitus, *Germ.* 14. [2] 2nd ed., pp. 74, 77; 7th ed., pp. 52, 53.
[3] Ch. ix. 176: "indeed the *impossibility* of the supposition."

Gibbon is greatly in advance of Montesquieu, who believes with Sir William Temple, Mariana, and Machiavelli, that the northern countries were, as a matter of fact, more densely peopled then than they are now, and that, further, when the Romans repelled them, a huge multitude was driven far north and remained there biding its time. The same (says Montesquieu) happened under Charlemagne, and would happen again if a modern prince were to make the same ravages in Europe; "the nations repulsed to the north, backed against the limits of the universe, would there make a firm stand, till the moment when they would inundate and conquer Europe a third time."[1] We are to suppose these immense multitudes living "at the limits of the universe" on ice and air for some hundreds of years. If this is to answer to the question-begging question, why the North is less fully peopled than it once was, it involves a miracle. But nothing more supernatural than ordinary laws is really needed to explain the movements of pastoral nations a thousand years ago. They are the same that govern the Tartars and Bedouins now.[2]

In the modern nomads,[3] it is true, the comparative simplicity of the circumstances and the comparative thoroughness of our knowledge about them, enable us to see plainly that the local distribution of the people is in strict accordance with the local distribution of the food, in other words, with

[1] *Grandeur et Décadence des Romains*, ch. xvi. p. 138, ed. 1876.
[2] *Essay*, 2nd ed., p. 76; 7th ed., p. 53. [3] *Ibid.* Bk. I. ch. vii.

"the quantity of food the people can obtain in the actual state of their industry and habits." We should see the same thing of the rest of the world's inhabitants, if the complicated commerce of civilized nations did not make it less gross and palpable. The power of the earth to support life may be compared with the power of a horse to carry burdens. He is strong in proportion to the strength of his weakest part, as a chain to the strength of its weakest link; and the earth's powers of nourishment are great in proportion to their greatness in the worst seasons of the year.[1] Again, owing to imperfect facilities for distribution, one part of a society may suffer want when another is in plenty.[2] Among the Tartars and the Arabs this is plainly seen; and it is clear, too, how the waste of life from war not only acts as a direct check on population, but checks it indirectly by repressing productive industry. Its fruits would have no chance of preservation. "Even the construction of a well requires some funds or labour in advance, and war may destroy in one day the work of many months and the resources of a whole year."[3] When once warlike habits have become fixed, the two evils, war and scarcity, reproduce and perpetuate one another. The encouragements held out to large families by the Mohammedan religion have a like effect. "The promise of Paradise to every man who had ten children would but little increase their numbers, though it might greatly increase their

[1] 2nd ed., p. 99; 7th ed., p. 68.
[2] 7th ed., p. 82.
[3] 2nd ed., p. 92; 7th ed., p. 63.

misery."[1] It could only increase their numbers if it increased their food, and it could not increase their food without changing their warlike habits into habits of industry. Failing this, it simply creates a constant uneasiness (through want and poverty) that multiplies occasions of war. Fortunately for himself, the Arab often proportions his religious obedience to the extent of his resources,[2] and in hard times, "when there is a pig at hand and no Koran," he thinks best to eat what God has given him.

Nothing but increase of food will permanently increase population, and where there is food the increase will reach up to it. In those parts of Africa that have furnished the Western slave supplies, there has been no discernible gap from the "hundred years' exportation of negroes which has blackened half America." Even in Egypt, where there is a striking contrast between natural fertility and human lethargy, the cause is not any deficiency in the principle of increase. It is that property is insecure, the government being despotic and its exactions indefinite. It is not the want of population that has checked industry, but the want of industry that has checked population; and it is bad government that has occasioned the want of industry. "Ignorance and despotism seem to have no tendency to destroy the passion which prompts to increase, but they effectually destroy the checks to it from reason and forethought. . . .

[1] 2nd ed., p. 94; 7th ed., p. 65.

[2] *Ibid.* p. 104; 7th ed., p. 72.

Coleridge (MS. notes) reminds our author that Mahomet allowed oblations of *sand* for water.

Industry cannot exist without foresight and security; the indolence of the savage is well known, and the poor Egyptian or Abyssinian farmer without capital, who rents land which is let out yearly to the highest bidder, and who is constantly subject to the demands of his tyrannical masters, to the casual plunder of an enemy, and not unfrequently to the violation of his miserable contract, can have no heart to be industrious, and, if he had, could not exercise that industry with success. Even poverty itself, which appears to be the great spur to industry, when it has once passed certain limits almost ceases to operate. The indigence which is hopeless destroys all vigorous exertion, and confines the efforts to what is sufficient for bare existence.[1] It is the hope of bettering our condition, and the fear of want rather than want itself, that is the best stimulus to industry; and its most constant and best directed efforts will almost invariably be found among a class of people above the class of the wretchedly poor."[2] This passage repeats an idea expressed in every book of the essay.[3] Government can retard the increase of population both directly and indirectly, but can only advance it indirectly, namely, by encouraging industry, more especially agriculture. For example, industrious agriculture has made China capable of bearing a great population, though other causes of a more equivocal character have made it exceed its great capacities, and its excessive numbers are cut down by famine and child

[1] Cf. above, p. 96, &c.
[2] 2nd ed., III. xi. 474-5; 7th ed., III. xiv. 381.
[3] Especially Book I. ch. x., the chapter on Turkey.

murder.[1] The Roman emperors found it impossible by legislation to promote the increase of the old Roman stock, because they found it impossible to restore the old Roman habits of industry, though believers in the superior populousness of ancient nations used to mistake their intentions for accomplished facts

In the eighteenth-century dispute about the populousness of ancient nations (one particular skirmish in the general battle of the books) we have seen that Malthus declares for the moderns. He gives his opinion in detached passages; but, putting together the different parts wherever we can find them, we discover his proof to depend on two principles, which are corollaries of the primary doctrine of the essay. The first is, that without the extension of agriculture or the better distribution of its fruits there can be no increase of population;[2] the second is, that whatever is unfavourable to industry is to that extent unfavourable to population.[3]

Now in the early days of Greece and Rome[4] the population ought on these principles to have been a large one, for not only was agriculture actively prosecuted, but property and wealth were more equally divided among the people than in later times. On the other hand, the numbers were always up to the level of the resources; and the smallness of the political divisions made law-givers like Solon, and

[1] *Essay*, Bk. I. ch. xii., 'China and Japan.'

[2] 2nd ed., p. 162; 7th ed., p. 112. [3] *Ibid.* p. 175; 7th ed., p. 120.

[4] See *Essay*, Bk. I. chs. xiii., xiv.

theorists like Plato and Aristotle, conscious of the risk of over-population and full of plans to provide against it. It is one of Aristotle's criticisms of Plato's Republic that Plato has not sufficiently met this difficulty, or realized that a community of goods or an equal distribution of property is impossible without a limitation of families. If every one may have as many children as he pleases, the result will soon be poverty and sedition. Of the preventive checks actually recommended by the highest wisdom of the Greek world, the mildest is late marriages; the rest include exposure and abortion. Colonization was rather adopted in practice than recommended in theory. Frequent wars and occasional plagues were the chief positive checks.

In Rome even more evidently than in Greece[1] the causes that produced inequality of property led also to thinness of population. In our own days the absorption of small proprietors by large would have this effect in a less degree, because the large would need to employ the labour of the small. In Rome the labour was done by slaves; and the wonder was not that the number of free citizens should decrease, but that any should exist at all, except the proprietors.[2]

Yet the legislation of Augustus in favour of marriage, and the universal lamentation of the later Roman writers over the extinction of the old Roman stock, are no more than a presumption that the population was decreasing, not a proof of its actual

[1] Sparta is the chief Greek instance.
[2] 2nd ed., p. 172; 7th ed., p. 118.

smallness, while the prevalence of war and infanticide, so often used to prove the same point, tend really to do the opposite. They are for the time positive encouragements to marriage, for people will not hesitate to bring children into the world, if they are either free to kill off the superfluous or certain to find sad vacancies ready for them.[1] In the former case, as we noticed, parental feeling will often interfere with the infanticide, and save rather too many than too few.[2] Wars, on the other hand, may injure the quality of the population by removing the most stalwart and even the most intelligent men; but there is as much food as before, there is more room, and there are therefore more marriages, till all the gaps are filled, even to overflowing.[3] Livy need not have wondered that in the Volscian wars the more were killed the more seemed to come on. The like is true of plague and famine; epidemics, like the small-pox, have never permanently lessened the population, though they have increased the mortality of the infected countries.[4] To take only one instance (from Süssmilch)—a third of the people in Prussia and Lithuania were destroyed by the plague in 1710, and in 1711 the number of marriages was very nearly double the average.[5] Emigration in like manner may drain off the best blood of a nation, but cannot reduce its numbers for any length of time, unless the nation

[1] 2nd ed., p. 150; cf. pp. 164, 172-3. 7th ed., p. 104; cf. pp. 113, 118.

[2] See above, p. 99.

[3] 1st ed., p. 119; 7th ed., Appendix, p. 515. [4] *Essay*, 7th ed., p. 122.

[5] 2nd ed., p. 254; 7th ed., p. 246. Cf. 2nd ed., pp. 172, 175, and 67; 7th ed., pp. 118, 120, and 47. Cf. Hume, *Pop. of Anc. N.*, pp. 487, and especially 504.

is learning a new standard of comfort. Greece and Rome were not less populous because they were great colonizers.[1] The known existence of a number of very active checks to population, instead of proving that the population was absolutely small, might more naturally, other things being equal, prove it to have been absolutely large. It might be argued that, if the population had not been great, fewer and less potent checks would have done the work.[2]

But other things were not equal. We know that the gratuitous distribution of foreign corn had ruined Roman husbandry.[3] We know that even the labour of the slaves who had supplanted the free labourers of Italy had not been sufficiently (or sufficiently well) directed to agriculture. Moreover, the increase by marriage in the number of slaves did not even balance the decrease in the number of the free men; else why should the Romans need to import fresh cargoes of slaves every year from all parts of the world?[4]

In short, the Roman habits had become "unfavourable to industry, and therefore to population." The very necessity for such a law as the Papia Poppæa would indicate a moral depravity inconsistent with habits of industry. This strong argument had escaped even Hume, who thought that the people would increase very fast under the Peace of Trajan and the Antonines, forgetting that the people could

[1] 7th ed., pp. 163, 387, 394; 2nd ed., pp. 113, 287, 292. Cf. 1st ed., pp. 118-19, 123 n.

[2] 2nd ed., p. 178; 7th ed., p. 122.

[3] 7th ed., p. 380, top.

[4] 2nd ed., p. 175; 7th ed., p. 120.

not unlearn their habits in so short a time; unlearning is harder than learning, especially for a whole people; and, "if wars do not depopulate much when industry is in vigour, peace does not increase population much when industry is languishing."[1] Contrariwise, it might be argued that the prevention of child-murder in India will not cause over-population, when it is part of a general policy accustoming the people to European habits.

Allow, then, that general viciousness is inconsistent with general industry, and it follows that those ancient nations in which the first prevailed were less populous than the modern. This seems to be the argument of Malthus brought to a focus. From the absence of censuses,[2] it is strictly deductive; there *could* not have been so many people as now, and therefore there *were* not.[3]

Expressed in more technical language, the meaning is, that where there is nothing present but the positive check and the lower kind of preventive, the habits of the people are necessarily such as to hinder an increase of food and thereby of population. When Europe was less civilized, it was not more, but less thickly peopled.[4]

[1] 2nd ed., p. 175; 7th ed., p. 120.

[2] 2nd ed., p. 180; 7th ed., p. 124. "It is therefore upon these causes alone,—independently of [2nd ed. says 'besides'] actual enumerations,—on which we can with certainty rely."

[3] Dr. Wallace, *Dissertation*, p. 55, had given Attica in its palmy days a population of 608 to the square mile; England in the nineteenth century has only 445, and crowded Belgium 487.

[4] *Essay*, 1st ed., p. 54; 7th ed., pp. 120, 122; cf. pp. 262, 434. Cf. *Wealth of Nations*, IV. vii. 254, 255.

This argument seems to be weakened by one consideration—that the poor in our day put more into their idea of necessaries; they have a higher standard of living than the poor 2000 years ago. It might therefore be said with justice that over-population (a peopling beyond the food) begins much sooner with us than with them, for it begins at a point much farther removed from starvation, and that therefore with the ancients a given amount of food would go farther and feed more. But, if we look only to the poor in each case, the difference between the ancient standard of comfort and the modern is unhappily much smaller than the difference between their meagre industrial resources and our ample ones, for our powers of production have grown far more rapidly than the comfort of our labouring population. Such difference as there is in the standards is only made possible by moral restraint, which has a closer affinity with modern civilization than with ancient or mediæval.[1] The history of modern civilization is largely the history of the gradual victory of the third check over the two others; and, as one of the chief allies of the third has been commercial ambition, the victory of moral restraint, by causing a larger industry, has caused in the end not a smaller, but a larger population.[2] The increase by being deferred has been made only the more certain and permanent.

[1] *Essay*, 2nd ed., p. 598; 7th ed., p. 476.
[2] *l. c.* cf. 2nd ed., pp. 175, 178; 7th ed., pp. 120, 122.

CHAPTER V.

NORTH AND MID EUROPE.

Different Effects of Commercial Ambition in different Countries—No single safe Criterion of National Prosperity—Süssmilch's "Divine Plan"—Malthus in the Region of Statistics—His Northern Tour—In Norway the truth brought home by the very nature of Place and Industries—In Sweden less obvious—In Russia quite ignored—Foundling Hospitals indefensible—Tendency of People to multiply beyond, up to, or simply with the Food—Author tripping—Facts the Interpreters and the Interpreted—Holland—The best *pater patriæ*—Emigration in various Aspects—Evidence of the Author before Emigration Committee—Switzerland, St. Cergues and Leysin—The *pons asinorum* of the subject.

THE broad difference between a savage and a civilized population is, that the positive checks prevail in the one, the preventive in the other,—and between ancient and modern civilizations, that vice and misery prevail in the one, moral restraint in the other.[1] Yet every civilized nation in modern times has not only passed through these three stages in the course of its past history, but contains them all within it now as a matter of observation. Its early history was an endeavour after independence or bare life, its later history an endeavour after full development; but there are strata in it to which civilization has not descended, and in which the struggle for bare existence prevails, alongside of strata in which

[1] *Essay on Population*, 2nd ed., p. 180; 7th ed., p. 124.

the struggle is towards ideals of commercial ambition and social perfection.

The view which Malthus takes of commercial ambition is substantially that of Adam Smith. As soon as commerce is separated from slavery, as soon as wealth is a man's own acquisition, got by the sweat of his own brow, then the desire of wealth has a new social aspect. It becomes what Adam Smith calls "the natural desire of every man to better his own condition;" and as such it creates modern commercial society, as opposed both to the ancient society built upon slavery, and to the feudal built upon war.

This *vis medicatrix reipublicæ,* the desire of rising in the world, so glorified in the *Wealth of Nations*[1] and in the *Essay on Population,*[2] is really not easy to define. It is a very composite motive; and the same differences of race (whatever their origin), which lead to differences of intellect and language also affect a nation's standard of comfort, as soon as it can be said to have one. By the influence of good climate and much intercourse with foreigners, along with advantages of upbringing, and perhaps of race, a nation of Southern Europe comes to put into its notion of happiness a great many more elements than a northern nation, which has to hew its model out of much poorer materials. The Norwegian standard will be simpler than the Parisian. But there is more behind. The question is not simply one of like and

[1] *E. g.* II. iii. 152, 1; IV. ix. 304, 2 (ed. MacC.).
[2] *E. g.* 7th ed., pp. 307, 434, 473 4.

unlike elements, or of many and few elements, but of the treatment of them by the human subject. The English notion of comfort differs from the French in its elements, which are probably more in number as well as other in quality, and have a third peculiarity quite distinct from the other two, their effect on the habits of the persons concerned.

French writers have noticed that the English farmer works hard for such an income as will give him the innumerable little luxuries of toilet, dinner-table, and drawing-room, that make up the English idea of comfort, while the French farmer works hard that he may be able to buy another farm.[1] The one lives up to his income; and in his efforts to preserve it he is enterprising and persevering; he is always striving to rise to the class above him. The other, on the contrary, is more content with his position in society; and simply wishes to make it stronger, by gaining more property. His willing privations in time of plenty are rewarded by his secure provision in time of want; he has always his land to sell.

Both are moved by the civilizing "desire to better one's own condition"; but it leads in the one case to simple saving, the old stocking, the piece of land, or the *rentes*, in the other to active using, the steam-plough first, that the piano and pony-carriage may follow afterwards. There is some truth in M. Taine's paradox, "The Englishman provides for the future not by his savings but by his expenses."[2] If capitalizing means using as well as saving, there is a sense

[1] Taine, *Angleterre*, pp. 176, 232-3. [2] *Ibid.* p. 233.

in which the French and English divide the two functions between them.

This is what prevents the economist from making any exact predictions about the effect of the *vis medicatrix reipublicæ*. He may, like Adam Smith, find it doing good work in the undermining of feudalism,[1] and he may point out that at any rate it would make a better guide to the world than military glory, which means unhappiness to one half the world, and a very mingled happiness to the other half. But he cannot predict its effect on men whose characters are unknown to him. He cannot even tell whether a man is wealthy or not, till he knows what his wants are, for wealth exists to satisfy wants, wants change with human progress, the notion of wealth expands with civilization, and the luxuries of one age and one man are the necessaries of another. It is impossible to treat this relative question as if its conditions were absolute, and to deal with men as we would with figures on a slate. Two and two do not always make four in such a case, but sometimes five, and frequently only three. A new vista of comfort spread before different men may stimulate one, spoil another, and leave a third unmoved.

It is not surprising then that the question, "By what various modes is population kept to the level of the food in the states of modern Europe?" is not a simple one. On some grounds it would seem comparatively easy to get the answer. There are figures to be had, and in many cases a census; there is a

[1] *Wealth of Nations*, III. iv. 183, 2, &c.

general similarity of circumstances which produces a general similarity of habits, and, therewith, of the movements of population. But there is no invariable order of mortality and generation. The rates of births and deaths are not the same for all nations; they depend on the conduct of human beings, and may differ not only in different countries, but in different parts of the same country. In the same way, we have no single statistical criterion of the healthy state of a population, just as it might be said we have no single criterion of the commercial prosperity of a country, still less of its happiness. The two former stand to the last as the parts to the whole. A healthy population and a prosperous trade are parts of the happiness of a nation, though they do not constitute the whole of it. To ascertain whether a nation is happy or not, we have to take into account these two parts of happiness along with many others. The parts in their turn consist of many parts. We measure the state of trade not only by imports and exports, railway, banking and Clearing House returns, and the gains of the public revenue, but by subscriptions to churches, charities, and schools, by savings banks and benefit societies, sales of books, pictures, and luxuries of all kinds, by the state of workmen's wages, by the poor-law returns, by the number of marriages, emigrants, and recruits for the army; and we could make little use of most of these figures without the census returns and the reports of the Registrar General. In the same way, to measure the healthiness of a population and ascertain whether it is safely under the level of its food, tending to pass beyond it, or simply rising up to it, and to ascertain by what ways and means the process is going on, we need instead of one single general criterion a whole array of particular tests. It is in the infancy of statistical science that men yield to appearances and "suppose a greater uniformity in things than is actually found there."[1]

This was, for example, the failing of Johann Peter Süssmilch, one of the earliest inquirers into the movements of population. A book like Süssmilch's had the same relation to the *Essay on Population* as astrology to astronomy, or alchemy to chemistry; it prepared the way for the more accurate study. Süssmilch first published his researches in 1761, while the Seven Years' War was still in progress. He dedicated it to Frederick the Great, as became a patriot and Church dignitary; and entitled it, *The Divine Plan in the Changes through which the Human Race passes in Birth, Death, and Marriage.* The Divine plan is the one set forth in the exhortation to Noah in Genesis—the peopling of the earth;[2] and the book tries to show the particular arrangements by which the plan is carried out. One condition is, he says, that fertility be greater than mortality; the births must exceed the deaths. On an average at present each marriage produces four children; and "the present law of death" is on an average, taking town and country together, 1 in 36; out of 36 men now living, 1 must die every year. In the country it is from 1 in 40 to 1 in 45; in the town, from 1 in 38

[1] Bacon, *Nov. Org.*, I. xlv. [2] See below, Bk. IV.

to 1 in 32. There is a yearly excess of births represented by 1 in 10 and 5 in 10. The increase must have been faster at first than it is now; and the means God took to effect His end in each case was the lengthening and shortening of human life. In the times of Methuselah there must have been a very different law of mortality, perhaps one death in a hundred; the length of life was greater; and probably the power of parentage lasted longer. The average number of children might be about twenty in a family instead of four; and the doubling of population would take place in ten or twenty years, instead of as now in seventy or eighty. Antediluvians were long lived because their long lives were needed for the replenishment of the earth; and the extreme length was shortened so soon as the time came when the same end could be reached in other ways. When we observe the remarkable adaptiveness of man which enables him alone among the creatures[1] to live in any latitude, and when we observe how he has been preserved while many animals have become extinct, we need have no doubt that the replenishment of the earth was really the Divine purpose. It is remarkable too that, though more sons are born than daughters, death equalizes their numbers before mature life. The "system" which prevails in the increase of man is like the march of a military regiment, in which all the men have their places, actions, and accoutrements determined for them. The proportion of sons to

[1] Except the hog, adds Gibbon, *Decl. and F.*, ch. ix. p. 171 n.

daughters, and deaths to births, Süssmilch regards as a tolerably fixed one; the discovery of unexpected uniformities overjoys him greatly, and he regards the man who first used the London bill of mortality to detect these uniformities as a sort of statistical Columbus. In short, his book is an economical Théodicée, a long piece of pious deductive reasoning; and it is curious to find Germany producing two such optimistic books at a time when it was even further from the millennium than its neighbours.

The facts of Süssmilch, ill-sifted as they were, gave Malthus a much firmer ground of reasoning than the scanty patches of evidence about the population of ancient and barbarous nations. He is at last in the region of statistics as opposed to conjecture, and in the region of the personal observation and travel of men who were at least asking his own questions. But the fate of the bills of mortality and other records, in the hands of Price and Wallace, to say nothing of Petty and Süssmilch, shows how important was Malthus' work as an interpreter of statistics. Statistics were a novelty in his day. As Adam Smith wrote on the *Wealth of Nations* without any full statistics of the wealth, and none at all of the population, of his own country, Malthus wrote his first essay when there was no census; and, for some time afterwards, so comparatively isolated were the nations of Europe, that to be at all certain of his facts, an author needed to verify and collect them by journeying in person, and seeing the scenes with his own eyes. This essential work of an investigator Malthus did not leave undone; and his chapters on the state of population in modern European nations are to a large extent a record of his own observations. He went for a summer trip in 1799 with three college friends, Dr. Edward Clarke, Mr. Cripps, and Mr. Otter, afterwards Bishop of Chichester. They went by Hamburg to Sweden, and there the party broke up into two, Clarke and his pupil Cripps going farther north, Otter and Malthus going on through Norway to visit Finland and St. Petersburg.[1] These were the only European countries where English travellers could easily make their way in those years.[2] In 1802 he saw France and Switzerland,[3] but seems not to have left the kingdom again till 1825, when the journey was taken for the sake of his wife's health, on the death of one of his children, and he was little in the mood for investigations. The tours of 1799 and 1802 are the only ones that have left substantial traces on his economical work.[4]

In all his travels he found the foreigner as ignorant as the Englishman on the subject of population. Only twice did he hear the truth expounded to him; in Norway during his first tour, and in Switzerland during his second. In the latter case

[1] See above, p. 48.

[2] The phrase on p. 216 of 2nd ed. (p. 148 of 7th), "in the preceding summer of 1788," is probably a slip. We do not hear elsewhere of any visit so early. See below, Bk. V.

[3] See above, p. 49. Cf. 2nd ed., p. 281; 7th ed., p. 173, &c.

[4] For his other movements and other details of his life, see Bk. V. (Biography).

the enlightenment was confined to one individual; but in the former the whole nation was wise. While the Swedish Government was continually crying for more people, and trying to "encourage population," the Norwegian Government and people seemed to have understood that the first question must be, "Are there means to feed more people?" If not, then we multiply the nation without increasing the joy. Of course there are cases where we might thin down the nation and still less increase the joy. Mere scantiness of numbers is no advantage to a nation, any more than fewness of wants to an individual; it may mean a low state of civilization, in both cases. It is not by any means so good for a country to be wasted by a pestilence as to be opened up by a new trade. The denser the population, the better;—so says Malthus himself;—but, he adds, let it be a population of strong, comfortable citizens, or let us stand by the small numbers and the slow increase.

Look now at Norway.[1] If we were dealing with uncivilized times under the reign of positive checks, we should expect an overflowing population, a large body of poor, and in times of scarcity a great deal of distress. There had been no wars for half a century, the cold climate kept away epidemics, and what else was left but famine to keep down the population to the limits of the food? Vice was not taken into the service, and emigration was seldom practised then in these regions. But Malthus visited

[1] 2nd and 7th edd., Bk. II. ch. i.

the country in one of the hardest years ever known in Europe, 1799, and found the Norwegians "wearing a face of plenty and content, while their neighbours the Swedes appeared to be starving."[1] He found the death-rate lower in Norway than in any country in Europe.[2] The population, however, was hardly increasing at all; and the proportion of marriages to the whole numbers of the people was smaller than in any country except Switzerland.[3] The positive check was largely superseded by the preventive. The virtue of foresight, he says, is elsewhere forced upon the upper classes by the smallness of their circle and the fewness of openings in business or professions; in Norway it is forced upon all classes alike by the evident smallness of the country's resources, and by the peculiarities of the national industry. There is almost no variety of occupation or division of labour. The humbler classes are almost all "housemen" (*husmänd*), labourers, who receive from a farmer in quasi-feudal fashion a small house and a little piece of land in return for occasional labour on his fields. In other countries men may easily fall into the fallacy of crediting the whole of the land with a greater power of supporting people than the power possessed by the sum of its parts. In the great towns of Central Europe a man has perhaps some excuse for trusting to the chapter of accidents; in the great variety of occupations he may have some excuse for thinking

[1] *Essay*, 2nd ed., p. 189; 7th ed., p. 129.
[2] The Russian figures being incredible. See later, p. 133.
[3] 2nd ed., p. 184; 7th ed., p. 126.

there will surely be a vacancy for him, and he may "e'en take Peggie." Norway, however, is to manufacturing countries what the country districts elsewhere are to the towns elsewhere. In the country districts an excess of population cannot be hidden, and the superfluities must go to the towns. Those who marry, therefore, when there is no vacancy for them, do so with the alternatives of poverty or migration clearly before their eyes. In Norway every peasant, not to say every farmer, knows quite certainly whether there is an opening for him or not, and, if there is not, he cannot marry.[1]

The conditions of the problem were in this way simplified, and the problem itself was satisfactorily answered. The only districts where Malthus saw signs of poverty were on the coast, where the people live by fishing; the openings for a fisherman are not so distinctly limited in their numbers as the openings for a farmer.

Time united Norway and Sweden under one king (1814), and Sweden now presents no unfavourable contrast with Norway. Even in 1825 Malthus wrote[2] that the progress of agriculture and industry, and the practice of vaccination, had caused a steady and healthful increase of population since 1805. He would be pleased to find too by the census that the population of Norway had increased very greatly in proportion to its poor. The improvement continues. The paupers were about one per cent. of

[1] 2nd ed., pp. 188, 189; 7th ed., pp. 128, 129. Cf. Thornton's chapter (II.) on the "Social Effects of Peasant Proprietorships," *Peas. Prop.* (ed. 1874), p. 55.

[2] In 6th ed., 1826. See 7th ed., p. 144.

the population in 1869 (when they were nearly five per cent. in England), which seems to have meant a decrease from previous years;[1] but between 1865 and 1875 the population had increased fourteen per cent. in spite of considerable emigration.[2] Malthus would have recognized with satisfaction that the nation had been "either increasing the quantity or facilitating the distribution" of its food,[3] that is to say, improving either its agriculture or its manufactures. It has really done both. Though the growth of the population has been greater in the centres of manufacture, there has been progress also in the country districts. Many of the old customs and laws that hampered agriculture have ceased to exist.[4] Malthus himself says that, if Government would remove hindrances to agriculture, and spread sound knowledge about it, it would do more for the population of the country than by establishing five hundred foundling hospitals.[5] He need not have confined his recommendation to agriculture; and elsewhere he states the truth in broader terms: "The true encouragement to marriage is the high price of labour, and an increase of employments which require to be supplied with proper hands."[6] Remove hindrances to trade and spread sound knowledge of it—that (in his view) is the way to increase the quantity and facilitate the distribution of the products of agriculture; and, to judge by results, the Norwegian Government has followed it.

[1] *English Blue Book on Foreign Poor Laws*, 1875, p. 109.
[2] *Statesman's Year Book*, 1880, p. 439.
[3] *Essay*, 7th ed., p 112.
[4] *E. g.* that of *Essay*, 7th ed., p. 130.
[5] *Essay*, 7th ed., p. 139; cf. pp. 151, 152.
[6] *Ibid.* p. 152.

Sweden,[1] as it then was, furnished a striking contrast to Norway. Malthus had the advantage there of the earliest and most regular of European censuses, beginning with the year 1748, and continued at intervals first of three and then of five years. He found that there was a large mortality, though the conditions of life were superficially the same as in Norway. The only explanation he could see was that the size and shape of the country, as well as its mode of government, did not so forcibly bring home to the people the need of restraint as in Norway, while at the same time the hindrances to good farming were even more serious than in the smaller country. From the very contiguity and general similarity of the two countries, they proved Malthus' point, by the Method of Difference, almost as well as a deliberate experiment could have done. It was not that Norway had an absolutely small and Sweden an absolutely large population; considerations of absolute greatness or smallness never enter into this, if into any, economical question. But Norway had a moderately large population in proportion to her food, while Sweden had in the same regard an excessive population, a population which was sparely fed even in average years, and decimated by famine and disease in years below the average.

Russia,[2] which was the third scene of Malthus' travels, had this in common with Norway and Sweden, that the movement of its population was unlike that of Central Europe, and that the eccentricity was due

[1] *Essay*, Bk. II. ch. ii. [2] *Ibid.* Bk. II. ch. iii.

to a clearly definable cause. In Norway the shape and climate of the country and the fewness of the available occupations forced the Government and the people to restrain rather than to encourage the increase of numbers; in Sweden, under conditions less simple, the habits of the people conspired with a false policy of the Government to produce an excessive increase. In both cases we have something different from the typical modern society of Central Europe, with its full division of labour, its system of large factories, and its extensive substitution of machinery for hand labour. Russia was as old-fashioned as Norway and Sweden in this respect; and her physical vastness made her a difficult country to know, in these days of slow communication. It is not surprising that the statistics available in the days of Malthus were open to grave suspicion. The death-rate was given as 1 in 60, while in Norway itself it had not been lower than 1 in 48 **[and it is about 1 in 73 in England now]**, yet the number of marriages and of births and the size of families were no smaller than elsewhere.[1] These facts by themselves would simply suggest a great rate of increase going on in the country concerned; and Malthus allows that there is great scope for such in Russia. But there was one other fact that strengthened his doubts about the vital statistics of that country; contrary to the experience of all other countries, it was said that in Russia more women were born than men. In others, more men are born

[1] 2nd ed., pp. 213-14; 7th ed., pp. 146, 147.

than women, and the numbers are only equalized gradually, by the greater risks of masculine life, as the years go on. In Sweden, with a climate not milder than Russia, this had long been observed.[1] It turned out on inquiry that the Russian method of registration allowed loopholes for more omissions in the deaths than in the births. Public institutions, including hospitals and prisons, had been left out of account; and the deaths in the foundling hospitals were alone quite sufficient to alter the average very significantly for the worse. Malthus' hatred of Foundling hospitals is only equalled by his dislike of Poor laws. The idea of such institutions was, like that of Pitt's Poor Bill, purely philanthropic. They were "to enrich the country from year to year with an increasing number of healthy, active, and industrious burghers,"[2] that would otherwise be doomed to death soon after birth. It used to be said of the bounty, granted by the Government of India, on slaughtered snakes, that it really kept up the supply, for the natives bred them to catch the bounty. The foundling hospitals had an opposite effect. They were meant to multiply and they tended to destroy. They encouraged a mother to desert her child at the precise time it needed the minute and careful attention that only a mother can give. "It is not to be doubted that, if the children received into these hospitals had been left to the management of their parents, taking the chance of all the difficulties in which they might be involved, a

[1] 2nd ed., pp. 214-15; 7th ed., p. 147, foot.

[2] *Ibid.* p. 218; 7th ed., p. 150. Cf. above, p. 30.

much greater proportion of them would have reached the age of manhood and have become useful members of the state."[1] But, besides increasing the mortality of children, they injure the very "mainspring of population"[2] by discouraging marriage and encouraging irregularities. In his talks with his father, Malthus had no doubt discussed the propriety of Rousseau's conduct in sending his children to the Paris Foundling Hospital. He would certainly have declared against Rousseau. To those who argue that the foundling basket may prevent child-murder, he answers that an occasional murder from "false shame" is saved at a very dear price by the violation of "the best and most useful feelings of the human heart," which the existence of such an institution teaches to the poor. To relieve parents of the care of their children is bad for the parents,[3] because it takes away from them a responsibility essential to full citizenship and civilizing in its effects on human character;—and it is unjust to their fellow-citizens, because, like the Poor Laws, it relieves one portion of society (in this case rather the worst than the poorest) at the expense of all the rest, and finds a career for pauper apprentices to the prejudice of independent workmen and their children.[4] In the third place, like the Poor Laws, it promises an impossibility—to relieve all that come. If children are to be received without limit, the resources for maintaining them should be without

[1] 2nd ed., p. 219; 7th ed., p. 151. Compare Price, *Observations*, p. 280 note; and especially Hume, *Pop. of Anc. N.*, p. 445 (ed. 1768).

[2] *Essay*, ibid.

[3] *Essay*, 2nd ed., p. 220; 7th ed., p. 151.

[4] *Ibid.* p. 221; 7th ed., p. 152.

limit; otherwise an excessive mortality is quite unavoidable.[1] The second reason is no doubt an economical commonplace; it is the first and third that are most characteristic of Malthus. He never forgets that human wants and human wills are an element in every economical phenomenon, and therefore considers that the effects of character on actions and of actions on character are of great economical importance. He will not allow that it can be right, even for a Government, to make promises that cannot be performed. These two plain principles give the tone to the later chapters, where he interprets for us the comparatively full statistics of Central Europe and our own England.[2]

The law of population may be described (though not in the exact words of Malthus) as among savage peoples the tendency to increase beyond the food, and among civilized to increase up to it. So Professor Rogers founds his estimate of the numbers of the English people in the thirteenth and fourteenth centuries on the principle that "there were generally as many people existing in this country as there have been, on an average, quarters of wheat to feed them with."[3]

In the case of highly progressive modern nations such statements would be beyond the truth; and we must either say that they tend to increase not beyond but along with the food, or else we must

[1] *Essay*, 2nd ed., pp. 216-17; 7th ed., p. 149.
[2] *Ibid.* 7th ed., Bk. II. chs. iv. to x., as rearranged in the 3rd ed.
[3] *Six Centuries of Work and Wages*, pp. 118, 119.

define food itself very widely. In the first case "tendency" will mean the abstract possibility depending on the one physiological condition; in the others it is the concrete nett possibility depending on all the various conditions together. In a general preface to his chapters on Central Europe, Malthus quite recognizes these distinctions and warns us against exact statements. "It seldom happens," he says, "that the increase of food and of population is uniform; and when the circumstances of a country are varying either from this cause or from any change in the national habits with respect to prudence and cleanliness, it is evident that a proportion which is true at one period will not be at another. Nothing is more difficult than to lay down rules on this subject that do not admit of exceptions."[1]

After this it is hard to believe what he tells us elsewhere, that "the only criterion of a real and permanent increase in the population of any country is the increase of the means of subsistence."[2] It would be at best a negative criterion and *sine quâ non*,—there can be no increase of numbers without increase of food,—though even then it is not true of a "forced population," living down to a lower food.[3] But there clearly may be an increase of food without an increase of numbers, unless the character of the people is such that they do nothing with the food except increase by it. Therefore, though, within certain wide limits fixed for us by invariable qualities

[1] *Essay*, 2nd ed., II. v. p. 245; 7th ed., II. iv. p. 159. Cf. 2nd ed., p. 320; 7th ed., p. 206. [2] *Ibid.* 2nd ed., p. 347; 7th ed., p. 260.
[3] *Ibid.* 2nd ed., p. 348; 7th ed., p. 260.

of human nature, predictions are justifiable on the ground of the law of population[1] or any other economical laws, none that specify a particular course of action as a result of a particular event are trustworthy, till we know the character of the people concerned.[2] Malthus always tries to bear this in mind; and, when he tells us that the lists of births, marriages, and deaths in Mid Europe give more information about its internal economy than the observations of the wisest travellers,[3] he is at once interpreting those figures in the light of a principle, and interpreting the principle by means of the figures. This appears when we look at the four chief conclusions of the general chapter in question. The first is the proposition that in the present state of our industrial civilization the marriages depend very closely on the deaths, and the births on the marriages.[4] Montesquieu says that wherever there is room for two persons to live comfortably a marriage will certainly take place.[5] In old countries experience is usually against any sure expectation of the means of supporting a family; the place for a new marriage is only made by the dissolution of an old. As a rule therefore the number of annual marriages is regulated by the

[1] See above, p. 18.

[2] So in substance Cairnes in his rehabilitation of the Wages Fund. *Leading Principles*, pp. 196 *seq.* Cliffe Leslie *passim.*

[3] *Essay*, 2nd ed., p. 240; 7th ed., p. 155.

[4] *Ibid.* p. 247; 7th ed., p. 160.

[5] "Partout où il se trouve une place où deux personnes peuvent vivre commodément, il se fait un mariage."—*Esprit des Lois*, Bk. XXIII. ch. x. (not XXII., as in 7th ed.).

number of annual deaths. "Death is the most powerful of all the encouragements to marriage,"[1] while on the other hand the marriages are a frequent cause of the deaths. In almost every country there is too great a frequency of marriages, which causes as it were a forced mortality. Which of these two mutual influences is the more powerful depends on circumstances. In last century the proportion of annual marriages to inhabitants was in Holland generally as 1 in 107 or 108. But in twenty-two Dutch villages it was as 1 in 64. Süssmilch explained this anomaly by the number of new trades in Holland and the new openings for workmen. Malthus would not have denied this possibility, his startling paradox about death being only a particular case of the general principle that "the high price of labour is the real encouragement to marriage."[2] But in this case the explanation ought to have applied to all Holland if to any part of it. The real reason came out when Malthus observed that the mortality, which was as 1 in 36 in Holland generally, was as 1 in 22 in those villages. The additional marriages did not really increase the population. They were caused by the high number of deaths which provided openings for the living; and the high number of deaths was caused by the unhealthiness of the region and of its prevailing industries, which were manufacturing rather than agricultural. The choice in every large population is between having

[1] *Essay*, 2nd ed., p. 247; 7th ed., p. 160.
[2] *Ibid.* 2nd ed., p. 221; 7th ed., p. 152.

many lives which end soon, and few which last long. Greater healthiness in the conditions of life will result in the latter. We find as a matter of fact that, where there has been the sanitary improvement as well as simply the "replenishment" of an old country, the marriage-rate goes down at the expense of the death-rate, and there is an economy of human life and suffering.

Putting the parts of his exposition together, we get something like a deductive scheme of the growth of population in old countries under an industrial revolution like that of the eighteenth century. The first effect of the discovery of new minerals, and even (with some qualifications) of the invention of new machines, is to provide new employment for working men, and many new opportunities for marriage; the proportion of marriages therefore becomes at once greater without any alteration (from this cause at least) in the death-rate. But, when the first burst of progress has passed, and the succeeding improvement is not by leaps and bounds, but at a uniform rate, then the proportion of marriages will decrease, as the new situations are filled up and there is no more room for an increasing population. Once the country is really "old" in the sense of fully peopled and unprovided with new sources of employment, then the marriages will be regulated principally by the deaths, and (the habits of the people remaining the same) will bear much the same proportion to each other at one time as at another. It is not, however, exactly the same proportion for all old countries, simply because the habits and standards of living are different, to say nothing of healthiness or unhealthiness of climate and occupation. For similar reasons it is not the same for towns as for country districts.[1] "A general measure of mortality for all countries taken together" would be useless if procurable; but it cannot be procured.[2]

Habits, however, are sufficiently fixed to make us certain that "any *direct* encouragements to marriage must be accompanied by an increased mortality."[3] They spur a willing horse. Montesquieu and Süssmilch, although they both enlarge on the evils of over-population, still think it a statesman's duty to be, like Augustus and Trajan, the father of his people by encouraging their marriages. But, if many marriages mean many deaths, the princes or statesmen who should really succeed in this patriotic policy might more justly be called the destroyers than the fathers of their people.[4]

If Malthus had been asked how a prince could best become a real *pater patriæ*, he would have named two or three ways. The prince might direct his mind to the improvement of industry, especially of agriculture.[5] He might circulate news and knowledge on these subjects;[6] or, as we should say now, he might institute agricultural exhibitions, and regular agricultural statistics of home and foreign production.

[1] *Essay*, 2nd ed., pp. 248-9; 7th ed., pp. 161-2. [2] *Ibid.*
[3] 2nd ed., p. 246; 7th ed., p. 159. The Italics are the author's.
[4] *Ibid.* p. 247; 7th ed., p. 160. [5] *Ibid.*
[6] 2nd ed., p. 205; 7th ed., p. 139.

He would in this way increase the population by helping to increase the food.

In the second place, he might benefit trade everywhere by giving it the security of good government and impartial justice, a peaceful foreign policy and light taxation.

In the third place, he might, together with all these, encourage Emigration. Malthus devotes a special chapter of the essay to this subject; and, though the chapter is in a later part of his work (Bk. III. ch. iv.[1]), this seems the best place to touch on the subject. Emigration, he says, is, apart from political distinctions, the same thing as migration; and, if it is economically good for a man to go from a poor land at his door to a rich in the next county, it cannot be economically bad for him to go from a poor district of his own country to a rich across the sea. The mere length of the journey or the difference of latitude does not affect the economical nature of the change.

Economical motives, however, have come very late in all the great European emigrations. It was not the desire of finding room for the over-crowded families at home, but desire of the metal gold, or else it was the simple love of adventure, or ambition of conquest, that first sent the Spanish, Portuguese, English, and Dutch to the far East and far West.[2] "These passions enabled the first adventurers to triumph" over obstacles that would have deterred

[1] *Essay*, 2nd ed., pp. 387 *seq.*; 7th ed., pp. 287 *seq.*

[2] *Ibid.*

quiet industrial emigrants, "but in many instances in a way to make humanity shudder, and to defeat the very end of emigration. Whatever may be the character of the Spanish inhabitants of Mexico and Peru at the present moment, we cannot read the accounts of the first conquests of these countries without feeling strongly that the race destroyed was, in moral worth as well as numbers, superior to the race of their destroyers." The settlers that followed on the heels of these pioneers, though they were more like real emigrants, went unskilfully to work. They seemed to expect that "the moral and mechanical habits" which suited the old country would suit the new,[1] and everything would go on as it did at home. At first therefore there would be a redundant population[2] in the new country rather than in the old, for, however great the possible produce of the colony, the actual produce would be less than the wants of the new-comers on their first arrival. To all this must be added the fact that, though economically a far and a near place are alike, they are very different to the sentiments of men. Patriotism is no fault, and the breaking of home ties is a real evil to the individuals, however beneficial the emigration may be to the nation. Men are slow to move, not only from the uncertain prospects of success, but from that *vis inertiæ* in man which is always counteracting the *vis medicatrix* of commercial ambition. In addition, therefore, to the mere uneasiness of poverty and the desire of getting a living, there is need of some spirit

[1] *Essay*, 2nd ed., p. 391 ; 7th ed., pp. 289-90. [2] *Ibid.*

of enterprise, to make men willing and successful emigrants.[1] Those who felt distress most would often have been the most helpless in a new country; they needed leaders who were "urged by the spirit of avarice or enterprise, or of religious or political discontent, or were furnished with means and support by Government;" otherwise, "whatever degree of misery they might suffer in their own country from the scarcity of subsistence, they would be absolutely unable to take possession of any of those uncultivated regions of which there is such an extent on the earth." Emigration then (according to Malthus) is not likely to happen unless political discontent and extreme poverty have brought the emigrants to such a plight that it is better for their country as well as for themselves that they should go. "There are no fears so totally ill-grounded as the fears of depopulation from emigration."[2] Emigration is not even a cure for an over-population; and is much recommended only because little adopted. Gaps made in the population of old countries are soon filled up; room found in the new is soon occupied. If emigration is proposed as a means of securing an absolutely unrestricted increase of population by placing old countries in the position of new colonies, the hope will be soon and for ever cut off.[3]

Towards the end of his life, Malthus had an opportunity of explaining his views on this subject to an audience of statesmen. He appeared as a witness

[1] *Essay*, 2nd ed., p. 393; 7th ed., p. 291.
[2] 2nd ed., p. 395; 7th ed., p. 292. [3] *Ibid.*

before the Select Committee[1] of the House of Commons "to inquire into the expediency of encouraging emigration from the United Kingdom," and his influence is traceable in their Reports. They reported[2] that there had been in the United Kingdom a "redundant population," in Ireland agricultural, in Scotland and England manufacturing; that one cause of it had been the unavoidable displacement of hand labour by machinery;[3] that meanwhile the British colonies in America, Africa, and Australia had few men and plenty of land, and that it would benefit the whole empire if parishes could convert their probable or actual paupers into emigrants, always provided that the remaining population could be induced not to grow so fast as to fill the whole gap thus created.[4] "The testimony" (said the Committee in their third Report[5]) "which was uniformly given by the practical witnesses has been confirmed in the most absolute manner by that of Mr. Malthus, and your Committee cannot but express their satisfaction at finding that the experience of facts is thus strengthened throughout by general reasoning and scientific principles." They were more disposed than their witness himself to *a priori* reasoning, and in many of their leading

[1] Appointed in March 1826, in the last thirteen months of Lord Liverpool's Government. Malthus came before them on 5th May, 1827. See *Third Report of Emigration Committee*, pp. 9, 10, and for his evidence pp. 311 *seq.*

[2] 1st Report, 1826 (May); 2nd, 1827 (April). The free use of technical terms is not surprising, for political economy was then a popular study. For examples see 1st Report, pp. 46, 57; 2nd Report, pp. 63, 102; 3rd Report, pp. 261, 308.

[3] 2nd Report. [4] 3rd Report, 1827 (June). [5] p. 9.

questions he declined to follow them.[1] But he agreed with their main conclusions, allowing that under certain conditions it would be even a financial advantage to remove unemployed workmen to the colonies rather than suffer them to become paupers at home, and adding, that, if he was against the admission of any legal claim to relief in ordinary cases of pauperism, still more would he be against it when the pauper had before him the alternative of assisted emigration.[2] His own view of emigration had not changed since he wrote in 1803. It was to him a partial remedy; and it is more useful when spontaneously adopted by the people[3] than when pressed on them by their Government. Under the torture of the question he conceded no more.[4]

As a temporary expedient, the essay tells us,[5] "with a view to the more general cultivation of the earth and the wider extension of civilization, it seems to be both useful and proper," and is to be encouraged, or at least not prevented, by Governments. All depends on the rate of wages. If wages were high enough to enable people to live with what they counted reasonable comfort at home, we may be sure their domestic and patriotic ties would be strong enough to keep them there. The complaint that emigration raises wages is most unreasonable. At the utmost it prevents wages from falling too low,

[1] Cf. below, ch. vii. (on Ireland), especially pp. 197 and 199.

[2] 3rd Report, p. 315, qu. 3257.

[3] The Emigration Committee recommended that the help of the state should only be given on condition of a local initiative and local contribution.

[4] See *e. g.* qu. 3370.

[5] 7th ed., p. 292.

and helps to heal the mischief caused by fluctuations in trade.

We shall find at a later stage that Malthus is keenly aware of the unhappiness caused in modern industrial societies by changes in the demand for goods, occurring even in the natural (or uninterrupted) course of trade. A movement in favour of emigration in 1806 and 1807 led him to insert a paragraph in the fourth edition of his essay which explains the relation of emigration to these changes. He accepts the statement of Adam Smith, that "the demand for men, like that for any other commodity, necessarily regulates the production of men;"[1] but he adds (as Cairnes added later) that it takes some little time to bring more labour into the market when there is demand for it, and some little time to check the supply when once it has begun to flow.[2] A family may be reared to catch high wages, and the high wages may have gone before the family has arrived at maturity. Malthus distinguishes between a normal or slight "oscillation" of this kind, and an excessive redundancy caused by an unusual stimulus to production—the stimulus, for example, of the foreign wars and the foreign trade of the years before Waterloo. In the normal case we must submit to the inevitable; in the exceptional we may find an outlet in emigration. No doubt, even if there be no emigration, in the long run the labour market will

[1] *W. of N.*, I. viii. 36 (MacC.'s ed.). "Other" is not a slip; the writer is conscious of his cynicism.

[2] *Essay*, III. iv. 293, of which the concluding paragraph was added in 1817.

right itself; but the process will be a very painful one to the workmen concerned. Emigration is the humane and politic remedy.

In some cases, such as Norway and the uplands of Switzerland,[1] there would seem to be no need for Government to teach the people to emigrate. Circumstances should do it for them; but human beings are influenced by habit and "chance" as much as by any deliberate motive, commercial or otherwise. In the Swiss uplands, as Malthus knew them, "a habit of emigration depended not only on situation but often on accident." Three or four successful emigrations "have frequently given a spirit of enterprise to a whole village, and three or four unsuccessful ones a contrary spirit."[2] This is illustrated by the contrast of two parishes, both in the Canton de Vaud, St. Cergues in the Jura, and Leysin[3] in the Bernese Alps near Aigle. The movements of population in Leysin puzzled M. Muret, the Swiss economist, who drew up a paper on the depopulation of Switzerland for the Economical Society of Berne in the year 1766. He found that in this parish of four hundred people there were born every year on an average only eight children, whereas, elsewhere in Canton de Vaud, to the same number of people eleven (in Lyonnais sixteen) children were a common proportion. The difference, he observed, disappeared by the age of twenty, when, if we may say so, the difference died off, the eight in Leysin being healthier than the

[1] *Essay*, 7th ed., Bk. II. ch. v. [2] 2nd ed., pp. 275-6; 7th ed., p. 169.
[3] Or "Leyzin," as Malthus spells it.

eleven (or sixteen) elsewhere. Muret infers from this, that "in order to maintain in all places the proper equilibrium of population, God has wisely ordered things in such a manner as that the force of life in each country should be in the inverse ratio of its fecundity."[1] There is, however, no need to suppose a miracle. The fact was simply that the place and the employments were healthy, that the people had not formed habits of emigration, that their resources were stationary, that, therefore, they married late, had few children, and were long-lived.[2] The subsisting marriages were to the annual births as 12 to 1; the births were to the living population as 1 to 49; and the number of persons above sixteen were to those below as 3 to 1.[3] This would show that mere number of births is no criterion of the size of a population, for it took only about half of the ordinary number of births to keep up a population of four hundred in the parish of Leysin. In St. Cergues the subsisting marriages were to the annual births as 4 to 1 (instead of 12 to 1 as at Leysin), the births were to the living population as 1 to 26, and the number of persons above and below sixteen just equal. That is to say, St. Cergues had nearly twice as many births a year in proportion to the population, and more than twice as many marriages; but, instead of three-fourths of its living population being above sixteen (as at Leysin), those above and those below were equal in number, and St. Cergues had a smaller proportion of adults

[1] *Essay*, 2nd ed., p. 271; 7th ed., p. 166.
[2] Average sixty-one years. [3] 2nd ed., p. 274; 7th ed., p. 168.

than Leysin. On the other hand, the death-rate was nearly the same; the healthiness was nearly as great. How came it then that the population of St. Cergues was only one hundred and seventy-one, as against the four hundred and five of Leysin? What became of the children born? Seeing that they did not die, and did not appear on the registers of the living, we infer that they left their native village; that is all. The situation of the parish of St. Cergues, on the high road from Paris to Geneva, suggested emigration; and, as a matter of fact, the place had become, like most highland hamlets, a breeding-place for the lowlands and the manufacturing towns. The annual drain of adults made room for the favoured remnant to marry and have large families. Even Leysin, though it lay on no high road, might conceivably (says Malthus) have exchanged its stay-at-home character for a habit of emigration, and might then have doubled its birth-rate without raising the death-rate. It is one of the fallacies of old statisticians to infer a large population from a high birth-rate; in an old country, if the rate of births is high in comparison with the number of living inhabitants, it means either many deaths or much emigration.

The people of an old country, if they cannot or will not emigrate, must, according to Malthus, either look for a high death-rate or accustom themselves to late marriages. M. Muret's figures showed that many cantons of Switzerland had adopted this last course in the eighteenth century. In the Canton de Vaud, for example, the proportion of marriages to living inhabitants (1 to 140) was lower than in Norway itself. In a pastoral country the limits of human resources are so obvious that the people cannot fail to be impressed with the need of limiting their numbers. Pastoral industry, again, feeds more than it employs,[1] and the unemployed must look for employment elsewhere. This was one reason why there were so many Swiss in foreign service. "When a father has more than one son, those who are not wanted on the farm are powerfully tempted to enrol themselves as soldiers, or emigrate in some other way, as the only chance to enable them to marry."[2] Malthus was a little disappointed with the condition of the Swiss peasantry when he saw them in 1803. Perhaps, he says, they were still suffering from the wars in which the "Helvetic Republic" had been involved by its French allies; but more probably they were suffering from the unwise attempts of their Government in the previous century to "encourage" what they then thought was a declining population.[3] The peasant who guided Malthus to the sources of the Orbe[4] talked freely to him on the poverty of the district, which he ascribed to early and imprudent marriages, "le vice du pays"; he would have a law passed to prevent a man marrying till he was forty, and a woman till she was elderly. He said that at one time the introduction of stone polishing had given the people high wages and led them to expect constant

[1] 2nd ed., p. 280; 7th ed., p. 173, top. The remark savours of paradox.
[2] *Ibid.* p. 280, foot; 7th ed., p. 173.
[3] *Ibid.* p. 281; 7th ed., p. 173.
[4] See above, p. 127.

employment; changes of fashion[1] had helped to drive the industry away, but the habits taught by it had remained so fast rooted in the people that emigration itself brought no relief to their overflowing numbers. But this self-taught Malthusian had not learned his lesson perfectly. He fancied that the fertile lands of the low countries, with their abundance of corn and employments, could never experience the evil of over population. This was true only in the unhappy sense that they had greater unhealthiness and a greater mortality, providing room for early marriages and many births.

It is easy to see that Malthus over-valued his prize. The *pons asinorum* of the subject is the doctrine that over-population is not a question of absolute numbers or absolute quantity of food and fertility of soil, but of the numbers in relation to the food, in whatever place or time; and the young peasant had not crossed it.

[1] Compare above on "oscillations," p. 147, and below, Bk. II. chs. ii. and iii.

Note.

The warning of the Preface (p. viii) is much needed in this and the following chapter.

In regard to Norway and Sweden (again separate, 1905), a short section in Mr. John M. Robertson's *Evolution of States* (Watts, 1912, pp. 282–5) gives the desired supplement to the above sketch of population in those countries, with sympathetic but frank criticism of Malthus. Malthus was quite aware of the defects of his illustrations. See page next following (153 foot.).

CHAPTER VI.

FRANCE.

French Numbers a Problem to Europe in 1802, because Law of Increase not understood—Effects of War—Lament for the unborn millions eighty years ago—More fitting now—Good Distribution and Production sometimes inseparable—The Stationary State—Malthus and the French Revolution.

In the order of his writing Malthus follows the order of his travels, and takes France[1] after Switzerland. France presents us with facts of an almost unique kind. But before the Revolution it had no trustworthy parish registers to show to the English inquirer; and Malthus would not have lingered over it, if in 1802 the public mind had not been perplexed by a riddle, about French population and its increase during war, of which he had the key.[2]

The essay is not meant for a mere history, and its author is not careful to be full in his historical details if he has a body of facts sufficient for his purpose. He even says, about some conjectures of his own based on French figures, that he had only adopted the figures for the sake of illustration, and had not supposed them to be strictly true. "It will be but

[1] *Essay*, 7th ed., Bk. II. chs. vi., vii.

[2] 2nd ed., p. 285; 7th ed., p. 175.

of little consequence if any of the facts or calculations which have been assumed in the course of this chapter should turn out to be false. The reader will see that the reasonings are of a general nature, and may be true though the facts taken to illustrate them may be inapplicable."[1] This is not a wary admission. Nevertheless, the chapter on France is one of the most telling in the essay. The substance of it may be stated very shortly.

"It has been seen," he says, "in many of the preceding chapters, that the proportions of births, deaths, and marriages are extremely different in different countries, and there is the strongest reason for believing that they are very different in the same country at different periods and under different circumstances."[2] The truth of this remark is borne out not only by the contrast between the France and the Switzerland of that time, but, as we shall find, by the contrast between the France of 1803 and the France of to-day. It is not singular that Malthus should (wrongly) expect the Swiss to become his pupils more easily than the French, for in his day both the mortality and the number of marriages were greater in France than in Switzerland.[3]

He spends most pains in illustrating the contrast between the France before the Revolution and the

[1] 2nd ed., p. 296; cf. 7th ed., p. 182 n. "Indeed in adopting Sir F. d'Ivernois's calculations respecting the actual loss of men during the Revolution, I never thought myself borne out by facts, but the reader will be aware that I adopted them rather for the sake of illustration than from supposing them strictly true."

[2] 7th ed., p. 188.

[3] 7th ed., p. 176; cf. p. 175.

France at the Peace of Amiens. In many ways it was fortunate that he confined himself to the Republican period. It was the time when the moral position of France was highest, and she was warring not for conquest but for defence. Switzerland had exemplified the fact that Emigration does not permanently check population, but, on the whole, encourages it. France, at the time chosen, exemplified the fact that even the most destructive Wars have a similar effect on the growth of numbers. What Malthus had proved more or less deductively in regard to ancient nations he was able to show more inductively by statistics in regard to modern. Great surprise was expressed in the early days of this century that, in spite of her enormous losses, France had not diminished in population. Malthus says she had rather increased than diminished. According to the estimate of the Constituent Assembly, which was confirmed by the calculations of Necker, the population in 1792, before the war, was 26,000,000. In 1801 it seems, from the returns of the Prefects, to have been about 28,000,000.[1] In ten years the increase had been 2,000,000, or 200,000 a year. Yet at a medium calculation France, in addition to the ordinary deaths, had lost by the war about 1,000,000 of men up to that time,[2] or 100,000 a year. How, on the principles of Malthus, were the two facts to be reconciled?

To reconcile them he shows, first, how, according to the figures given by Frenchmen themselves, the numbers of the unmarried survivors at home were

[1] 7th ed., pp. 177, 181 n. [2] *Ibid.*, p. 178 and n.

more than enough to have kept up in case of necessity the old number of marriages and the old rate of increase; second, how from general principles there was a presumption in favour of a rapid increase at such a time; and third, how the social and industrial conditions of the French people since the Revolution were favourable to an increase of population. First, then, he shows that the entire body of unmarried persons was large enough in spite of the war to fill the vacancies and keep up the old rate of increase. The body of the unmarried is formed by the "accumulation" year by year of the numbers of persons, rising to marriageable age, who are not married (or say briefly of the marriageable unmarried, including widows and widowers). This accumulation will only stop when the yearly accessions thereto are no more than equal to the yearly mortality therein. The size of this body will therefore vary with the character of the particular nation considered. In the Canton de Vaud it was equal to the whole number of the married; but in France both the mortality and the marriage rate were higher than in Switzerland, and the unmarried were therefore a smaller fraction of the total numbers. Assuming from the French authorities[1] a certain birth and death rate, and assuming from the same authorities that the unmarried men for the period before the Revolution were one and a half millions out of five millions that were marriageable, it would appear that every year there were 600,000 persons arriving at the marriageable

[1] Not above suspicion. See 7th ed., p. 176 n.

age, of whom (since about 220,000 is the annual number of marriages) 440,000 marry. The surplus of unmarried is therefore 160,000 persons, or about 80,000 men. It follows that for war purposes (if mere numbers be considered) the reserve fund of men would be nearly one and a half millions, and every new annual surplus of 80,000 youths above eighteen might be taken for military service without any diminution in the number of marriages.[1] As a matter of fact, it is putting the case somewhat strongly to suppose as many as 600,000 to be taken for service in the first instance, and 150,000 additional troops to keep up the supply every year. But this would still leave in the first instance nearly 900,000 for the reserve fund, which with the annual 80,000 could bear a drain on it of 150,000 for ten years, and leave a balance of 200,000 altogether, or 20,000 a year. In other words, there would be room for an increase in the number of marriages of nearly 20,000. It would not be miraculous then if the French population should continue to increase in the face of great losses in war, for the increase before the war had been very much less than the greatest possible.

In the second place, the circumstances of the civilian population made an increase very likely. Many out of the reserve fund of unmarried men will in the course of ten years be past the military age, but not past the age of marriage. The 150,000 recruits would probably be taken from the 300,000

[1] The military advantage of an increasing population is pointed out also in the article on Newenham's 'Ireland,' *Edin. Rev.*, July 1808, p. 350.

who every year rose to marriageable age, and the marriages would be kept up from the older unmarried men, in the scarcity of younger husbands. It may be remembered, too, that in the early years of the war so many youths married prematurely to avoid service,[1] that the Directory were obliged (in 1798) to extend the conscription to the married men. But even when the husbands were removed to the war the marriages were not necessarily childless, and would thus, at the least, be a means of adding to the people's numbers that did not exist before the Revolution. The facility of divorce, too, though bad both in morals and in politics, would at least, in the existing scarcity of men, act somewhat like polygamy, and make the number of children greater in proportion to the number of husbands. It is said, too, that there were more natural children born in France after the Revolution than before it; and, since the peasants were better off after it than before it, there was a better chance that more of the children than formerly should survive.

In the third place, there is no doubt, says Malthus, that the division of the domain lands and the creation (or at least the multiplication) of peasant properties have had a great influence both on wealth and on population. They add to population more than to wealth, for they increase the gross produce of food at the expense of the nett surplus. "If all the land of England were divided into farms of £20 a year, we should probably be more populous than

[1] Cf. Josiah Tucker, *On Trade*, p. 17 (3rd ed., 1753).

we are at present, but as a nation we should be extremely poor. We should be almost without disposable revenue, and should be under a total inability of maintaining the same number of manufactures or collecting the same taxes as at present."[1] But the division of lands was at least in favour of the gross produce, and even the passing traveller was inclined to think, from the appearance of the fields and the style of the field labour, that, however severely the manufacturing industry of France might have suffered during the war, her agriculture had rather gained than lost.[2] The absence of so many strong men with the armies would not only raise wages at home and make the labourers better off, but by *pro tanto* lessening the demand for food and taking from those at home the burden of supporting so many men, would not raise the price of food with the wages, but would allow real wages to rise. This would co-operate with political causes in making the people desert the towns for the country, and thereby it would reduce the death-rate, which is always higher in towns than in the country. It is attested by Arthur Young (no friend to the *Essay on Population*) that the high mortality of France before the Revolution (according to Necker 1 in 30) was caused by an over-population which the changes at the Revolution tended to remove. The probability is, therefore, that

[1] *Essay*, 2nd ed., p. 297 n; 7th ed., p. 185, which omits one clause. Cf. 2nd ed., pp. 290-1; 7th ed., pp. 179, 180.

[2] 2nd ed., p. 291; 7th ed., pp. 179, 180. Cf. the often-quoted passages about the bleak rock and the garden, written (be it remarked) before and not after the Revolution, in Arthur Young's *Travels in France* (Bury St. Edmunds, 1792), pp. 36, 37, 42; cf. p. 341.

the births increased and the deaths decreased during the ten years after the Revolution; and there could be no difficulty in understanding the increase of population in spite of the war. In the later editions of the essay[1] Malthus confesses that his French figures need revision; the returns of the Prefects for 1801-2 and other Government papers had given a smaller proportion of births than he had thought probable, for the period before the Revolution. But (he remarks) the Prefects' returns do not embrace the earlier years of the Revolution, precisely the time when the encouragement to marriage would be greatest and the proportion of births highest. In any case they show that the population of France is not less but greater since the Revolution. If in the latter part of this period the increase was affected by the decrease of deaths rather than by increase of births, they not only leave his position untouched, but give him a result that would highly please him. Certainly in England and in Switzerland, and probably in every European country, the rate of mortality has decreased in the last two hundred years, through the greater healthiness of the conditions of life; and it is not at all surprising that a population should be kept up or even made to increase with a smaller proportion of births, deaths, and marriages than before.[2]

The French labouring classes at the beginning of the Revolution were seventy-six per cent. worse fed, clothed, and supported than their fellows in England.[3]

[1] *E. g.* 5th, 1817; 7th ed., ch. vii.
[2] 7th ed., p. 188.
[3] Arthur Young, *Travels in France*, pp. 410, 437.

Their wages were 10*d.* a day (as compared with 1*s.* 5*d.*), while the price of corn was about the same; but their condition and their remuneration had been decidedly improved by the Revolution and the division of the national domains. Wages in money (since Young wrote) had risen to 1*s.* 3*d.* a day; and, according to some authorities, the real wages had become even higher than in England.[1] The new distribution of wealth had been followed by an immense increase in the production of it, shared by the producers themselves, and making France immensely stronger as a nation either for offence or defence.[2] Such an improvement in the condition of the people would naturally be followed by diminution in the deaths; and a diminution in the deaths must lead either to an increase of population or to a decrease in the marriages and births. The latter (which is presumably an increase of moral restraint) has followed. In the ten years after the Peace of Amiens the population seems to have increased only at a very slow rate. "There is perhaps no proposition more incontrovertible than this, that in two countries, in which the rate of increase, the natural healthiness of climate, and the state of towns and manufactures are supposed to be nearly the same, the one in which the pressure of poverty is the greatest will have the greatest proportion of births, deaths, and marriages," and *vice versâ.*[3]

Malthus' survey of population in France applies

[1] *Essay*, 7th ed., p. 189. [2] Cf. Fyffe, *Mod. Europe*, i. 124.
[3] *Essay*, 7th ed., p. 189.

only to his own lifetime, and indeed only to the earlier part of that. To do him full justice we must place his picture of the real losses of war alongside of his description of the compensations.

The constant tendency of population to increase up to the limits of the food may be interpreted (in the case of war) as the tendency of the births in a country to supply the vacancies made by death. The breaches are not permanent; they are among the reparable as distinguished from the irreparable mischiefs of war. But this does not, from a moral or political aspect, afford the slightest excuse for the misery caused thereby to the existing inhabitants.

"Can you by filling cradles empty graves?"

There is an exchange of mature beings in the "full vigour of their enjoyments"[1] for an equal number of helpless infants. Not only is this a waste of the men who died, but it is a deterioration, for the time being, of the quality of the whole people; they will consist of more than the normal proportion of women and children; and the married will be men and women who in ordinary times would have remained single. When the drain of men for military service begins to exhaust the reserve of unmarried persons, and the annual demands are in excess of the number annually rising to marriageable age, then of course war will actually diminish population.[2] Till that point is reached, war may alter the units and spoil the quality of the population, but will not lessen its

[1] A characteristic utilitarian touch. 2nd ed., p. 295, top; 7th ed., p. 183. [2] *Ibid.*

total volume. Sir Francis Ivernois, from whom Malthus took some of his figures, went too far in the other direction when he told us we must not look so much at the deaths in battle or in hospital, when we are counting up the destructive effects of war or revolution, as at the remoter results; "the number of men war has killed is of much less importance than the number of children whom it has prevented and will still prevent from coming into the world." He supposes one million of men to have been lost in the Revolution itself, and one and a half millions in its wars; and he says that, if only two millions of these had been married, they would have needed to have had six children each in order that a number of children equal to the number of their parents (*i. e.* four millions) should be alive thirty-nine years afterwards. We ought, he thinks, to mourn not only for the two and a half millions of men killed, but for the twelve millions whom their death prevented from being born. To which Malthus wisely answers that the slain, being full-grown men, reared at no little cost to themselves and their country, may be fitly mourned, but not the unborn twelve millions, whose appearance in the world would only have sent or kept a corresponding number out of it,—and "if in the best-governed country in Europe we were to mourn the posterity which is prevented from coming into being, we should always wear the habit of grief."[1]

If Sir Francis Ivernois could have foreseen the history of French population for seventy years after

[1] 2nd ed., p. 294; 7th ed., p. 183.

the time when he wrote, he would have had more reason to utter his curious lament.

"The effect of the Revolution," wrote Malthus in 1817, "has been to make every person depend more upon himself and less upon others. The labouring classes have therefore become more industrious, more saving, and more prudent in marriage than formerly; and it is quite certain that without these effects the Revolution would have done nothing for them."[1] The country districts which took the least active part in the Revolution have been the most resolute in conserving the results of it. Over-population in France is known only in the towns. At the beginning of the eighteenth century—say one hundred and fifty years ago (1732)—under Louis XV. the population of France was estimated at twenty millions of people.[2] There is good reason to believe that the habits of the people were entirely different from what they are now; they were even said to be famous for their large families.[3] In 1776 their numbers were about twenty-four mil-

[1] *Essay*, 7th ed., p. 320 (III. vii.).

[2] Levasseur, *France avec ses Colonies* (1875), p. 842. According to Anderson, *Chron. Ded.*, Vol. III. p. xliii, some said twenty, others seventeen. But Kitchin cites Vauban to show that there had been a decline in population from fifteen to thirteen millions between the beginning of the war of Succession and the end of it (1702, 1713).—*History of France*, vol. iii. p. 342. Cf. Fox Bourne's *Life of Locke*, i. p. 350; Vauban's *Dime Royale*, pp. 162-3.

[3] Josiah Tucker, *Essay on Trade* (3rd ed., 1753), p. 14. There may be rhetorical exaggeration in his statements. "The subordination of the common people is an unspeakable advantage to the French in respect to trade. By this means the manufacturers [workmen] are always kept industrious. They dare not run into debauchery; to drunkenness they are not inclined. They are [practically by the law of military service] obliged to enter into the married state, whereby they raise up large families to labour, and keep down the price of it; and consequently, by working cheaper, enable the merchant to sell the cheaper."

lions,[1] at the Revolution of 1789 about twenty-six millions,[2] in 1831 thirty-two and a half, and in 1866 thirty-eight. At the present time, from loss of territory and from decrease of numbers in certain parts of the country, they are little more than thirty-seven and a half millions—not much more than the population of Great Britain, a country neither so large nor so fertile. Even in 1815 Malthus spoke of France as having a more stationary and less crowded population than Britain, though it was richer in corn.[3] The population of 1881 showed an increase of 766,260 over that of 1876, and was in all 37,672,048.[4] It increases not by augmentation in the number of births, for that has been actually lessening, but by diminution in the deaths. The population of Britain has trebled itself within the present century ; that of France has not even doubled itself in a century and a half, with every allowance for a varying frontier. The fears which Malthus expressed,[5] that the law of inheritance and compulsory division of property would lead to an excessive and impoverished country population, have not been realized. The industrial progress of the country has been very great. Fifty years ago the production of wheat was only the half of what it is

[1] *Wealth of Nations*, IV. iii. pp. 220-1.

[2] See above, p. 155. Levasseur makes it twenty-five ; Arthur Young, who considers France over-populated by five or six millions, makes it twenty-six (*Travels in France*, pp. 468-9 ; cf. p. 474). Price had made it thirty.

[3] *Grounds of an Opinion*, &c., p. 12. See below, Bk. II. ch. i.

[4] Census as given in *Annuaire de l'Économie Politique* (1882), p. 899.

[5] *Political Economy* (1820), pp. 433 *seq.* Cliffe Leslie (*Mor. and Pol. Essays*, 1879, p. 424) attributes the few births to the very Law of Succession of which Malthus was afraid.

to-day, of meat less than the half. In almost every crop and every kind of food France is richer now than then in the proportion of more than 2 to 1. In all the conveniences of life (if food be the necessaries) the increased supply is as 4 to 1, while foreign trade has become as 6 to 1. Since property is more widely distributed in France than elsewhere, an increase of production is much more certain to mean a benefit to the whole people. But there are certain classes of goods, chiefly necessaries, of which (even in a land like England, where the great wealth is in a few hands) it is impossible profitably to extend the production without *pari passu* extending the distribution. When articles of food are imported in vast quantities, they cannot, from the nature of things, go entirely to the rich; the rich can easily eat and drink beyond the normal value, but not much (without Gargantua's mouth) beyond the normal quantity; and, at least in the case of our own country, very little is exported again. Generally speaking, it is a true saying that, the more the food, the more are fed. But what is true of necessaries in England is true even of other goods in France.[1] The "average wealth of each person" is not there, as often elsewhere, a mere arithmetical entity, but a very near approach to the ordinary state of the great majority of the people; and this average wealth is thought by good authorities[2] to have more than doubled since the beginning of the

[1] In the country districts at least. On the relation of luxury to trade, &c., see below, Bk. II. ch. iii. p. 268.

[2] *E. g.* by M. Levasseur in *La France avec ses Colonies* (1875), p. 853.

century. The population, on the other hand, has only increased by one-half; and the average duration of life has lengthened from twenty-eight to thirty-seven years. In a paper of Chateauneuf's (1826) quoted by MacCulloch,[1] it was said that the French people were improving their condition by diminishing their marriages. The statistician Levasseur, on the contrary, with the facts of another half-century before him, tells us that married people in France are the *majority* of the population,[2] the average age of marriage being twenty-six for the women, and rather more than thirty for the men. The birth-rate, however, is the lowest in Europe,[3] being 1 in 37, as opposed to 1 in 27 for England. It is by refusing to fill the cradles that they leave the graves empty. Yet France is less healthy than England. Its death-rate in 1882 was 22·2 per thousand, while in England it was 19·6.[4]

There are other features which make the case unique. There are few foreigners in France except in the largest towns; the numbers of the French people are little swelled by immigration and not reduced by emigration. Since the expulsion of the Huguenots and the colonization of Canada, few nations have been so rooted in their own country; even Algerian and Tunisian conquests are due to no popular passion for colonizing. The peasant properties have made the people averse to movement.

At present most Frenchmen remain during life in

[1] Appendix to *Wealth of Nations*, note iv. p. 465.
[2] Levasseur, *l. c.* pp. 845, 846 ft. [3] *Times*, Jan. 1883.
[4] *English Registrar-General's 45th Report*, for 1882, pp. cii, cvii.

the same Department in which they were born;[1] and recent observers tell us[2] that a military career is becoming distasteful to all classes. Taking the absence of immigration as balanced by the absence of emigration, we are brought to the conclusion that the population of France is stationary by its own deliberate act.

How far this is in accordance with the views of Malthus it is impossible to say in one word. It is at least the result of the prudence which he was always preaching. But his prudence lay in the deferring of marriage; and this is not the form which prevails in France. Moreover, he thought with Adam Smith that the progressive state and not the stationary was the normal one for humanity; if the whole world became contented with what it had got, there would, in his opinion, be no progress, and the resources and capacities of human beings and of the world would not be developed. In fact, he retained the aspirations of the Revolution, which the country-folk in France seem in danger of losing; he wished men to have hopes for the future as well as a comfortable life in the present; he saw no virtue in mere smallness any more than in mere bigness of numbers; he desired as great as possible a population of stalwart, well-instructed, wise, and enterprising men; he thought that, without competition, ambition, and emulation, and without the element of difficulty and hardship, human beings would never fully exert their best powers, though he also thought that a time might

[1] Levasseur, *La France*, l. c. [2] E. g. *Times*, l. c.

come when the lower classes would be as the middle classes, or, in his own words, when the lower would be diminished and the middle increased, and when, mainly through the action of the labourers themselves, inventions would become a real benefit, because accompanied by lighter labour and shorter hours for the labourers.[1] As for that love of humanity, that was so much present in the words and thoughts if not in the deeds of the men of the Revolution, he had a full share of it. He desired a longer life for the living, and fewer births for the sake of fewer deaths. His work was like that of the lighthouse, to give light and to save life.

[1] *Essay*, 7th ed., IV. xiii. p. 474; 2nd ed., IV. xi. p. 594.

Note.

Much has changed in France since 1885. The lost provinces have been regained. But the population with this allowance has remained stationary. In this respect New France (Quebec) deserves rather to be called Old France (see p. 164).

CHAPTER VII.

ENGLAND, SCOTLAND, AND IRELAND.

Prevailing Checks — Proposed Census of 1753 — Brown's Estimate — Depopulation of England in Eighteenth Century—Opposing Arguments — Census of 1801 — Interpretation of Returns — Relative Nature of the Question of Populousness—Scotland to England as Country to Town—Industrial changes since the Union—Ireland under English rule in Eighteenth Century and after—The Wall of Brass—Virtue without Wisdom—The Potato Standard—The Emigration Committee—The New Departure.

In dealing with the question of population in his own country,[1] Malthus tries to answer at least three distinct questions:—What were the checks actually at work in those days? Had the numbers of the people increased, or not, in the eighteenth century? What conclusions on either point may be drawn from the English census?

The first question was answered with comparative fulness in the essay of 1798. It is remarked there that in England the middle and upper classes increase at a slow rate, because they are always anxious to keep their station, and afraid of the expense of marriage.[2] No man, as a rule, would like his wife's

[1] 2nd ed., II. ix.; 7th ed., II. viii., ix.

[2] 1st ed., pp. 63, 64.

social condition to be out of keeping with her habits and inclinations. Two or three steps of descent will be considered by most people as a real evil. "If society be held desirable, it surely must be free, equal, and reciprocal society, where benefits are conferred as well as received, and not such as the dependant finds with his patron or the poor with the rich." So it happens that many men, of liberal education and limited income, do not give effect to an early attachment by an early marriage. When their passion is too strong or their judgment too weak for this restraint, no doubt they have blessings that counterbalance the obvious evils; "but I fear it must be owned that the more general consequences of such marriages are rather calculated to justify than to repress the forebodings of the prudent."[1] What Malthus desires, as we infer from the general tenor of his book, is that all classes without exception should show reluctance to impair their standard of living; and his hatred of the Poor Laws is due to his conviction that they hinder this end. The subject will be more fully discussed by-and-by.[2] In the chapters on England it is little more than mentioned, the author devoting himself chiefly to the statistical data of the census and registers.

In this connection it was impossible for him to avoid the question that had long agitated the minds of politicians. Had the numbers of the English people been decreasing or increasing since the

[1] 1st ed., pp. 65-6; cf. 2nd ed., p. 300, and 7th ed., p. 193.
[2] See below, Bk. II. ch. iv., &c.

Revolution of 1688, and especially in the course of the eighteenth century? Economists of the present day are overloaded with statistics; but, when Adam Smith wrote the *Wealth of Nations*, he was unaware of the numbers of his own nation. To estimate population without a census is to study language without a dictionary; there had been no census since the coming of the Armada,[1] and it was not till one hundred years after that event that statistical studies came much into favour. An annual enumeration of the people was proposed in the House of Commons in 1753, as a means of knowing the numbers of our poor.[2] But the proposal was resisted as anti-Scriptural and un-English, exposing our weakness to the foreigner and spending public money to settle the wagers of the learned. There was probably a fear[3] that the tax-gatherer would follow on the heels of the enumerator, as he had done in France. The House of Lords beat off the bill, and left England in darkness about the numbers of its people for another half-century, though something like a census of Scotland was made for Government in 1755.[4] As without the Irish Famine we might not have had the total Repeal of the Corn Laws, so without the worst of all possible harvests in 1799 we might have had no census in 1801, for Parliament, when

[1] The numbers given then were five millions.—Froude, *Hist. of England*, i. 3.

[2] See Hansard, *Parl. Hist.*, xiv. 1317.

[3] Not unfelt in 1801. So Arthur Young speaks as if the agricultural interest had not unfrequently regarded the Board of Agriculture as a new instrument of taxation. (*Report on Suffolk*, p. 16.)

[4] In charge of Rev. Alexander Webster.

they passed Mr. Abbot's Enumeration Bill in 1800, looked to an enumeration of the people to guide them in opening and closing the ports to foreign grain. The practical question about the increase or decline of English numbers was connected, in logic as well as in time, with the controversy about the comparative populousness of ancient and modern nations. The same year (1753) which saw the attempt to settle by census the question of England's depopulation, saw also the publication of Dr. Robert Wallace's reply to Hume's *Essay on the Populousness of Ancient Nations*, in his *Dissertations on the Numbers of Mankind in Ancient and Modern Times*. One of Henry Fox's objections to Hardwicke's Marriage Act (of 1753) was that it would check population.[1] We are told[2] that the academical discussion roused attention on the Continent, and a French savant, Deslandes, published an estimate of the numbers of modern nations, in which England was made much inferior to France, having only eight millions against twenty. This was too much for English patriotism. Even in our own day a great war and a few reverses usually fill England for a year or two with forebodings of decay. Written in 1757 (at the beginning of the Seven Years' War), Dr. John Brown's *Estimate of the Manners and Principles of the Times* was only the most popular of a host of gloomy pamphlets too

[1] *Parl. Hist.*, vol. xv. p. 69, quoted by Mahon, *Hist. of England*, sub dato, ch. xxxi. p. 39. Cf. Trevelyan, *Early Life of Fox*, ch. i. p. 14.

[2] Dr. Adam Anderson, *Chronological Deduc. of Commerce*, Introd., p. xliii; first printed in 1762.

prejudiced to be of much use for statistics.[1] Dr. Adam Anderson[2] sides with the moderns and the optimists. The contributions of Dr. Brackenridge and Richard Forster to the discussion survive by the mention of them in Price's *Observations* (pp. 182-3) and in George Chalmers' *Estimate* (ch. xi. 193), this last giving on the whole perhaps the most lucid history of the whole depopulation controversy. We know from Goldsmith's *Traveller* (1764) and *Deserted Village* (1770), with its charming illogical preface, that even in peace the subject was not out of men's thoughts. A similar panic in Switzerland, which owed its beginning to England,[3] seems afterwards to have reacted on England itself. The American War of Independence revived the languishing interest in the controversy. This time it was the English and not the antiquarian topic that fell into powerful hands. Dr. Richard Price, the Radical dissenter, the friend of Dr. Franklin, and the inventor of Pitt's Sinking Fund, did battle, in his *Observations on Reversionary Payments* (1769), on behalf of the pessimistic view; Arthur Young, the agriculturist, the traveller and the talker, led the opposition to him,[4] and was supported by Sir Frederick Eden, William Wales, John Howlett, and last but not least by George Chalmers.[5]

[1] See especially *Estimate* (7th ed., 1758), Vol. I. Pt. II. sect. viii. pp. 186 *seq.*

[2] *Chron. Ded.*, ibid.

[3] *I. e.* to the discussion described by Dr. Anderson. Cf. Malthus, *Essay*, 7th ed., p. 164. Muret's pessimistic paper was printed in 1766.

[4] In his *Political Arithmetic*, 1774.

[5] *Estimate of the Comparative Strength of Britain during the present and four preceding Reigns*, by George Chalmers, F.R.S., S.A., 1st ed., 1782.

Gregory King[1] and Justice Hale[2] in the seventeenth century, Dr. Campbell[3] in the eighteenth, had agreed that the numbers of Norman England must needs have been small, for the government was bad; Dr. Price, on the contrary, had maintained the paradox that, though the Revolution of 1688 brought a "happier government," the numbers of the people had ever since declined.[4] He reasoned from the decreased number of dwelling-houses assessed to window tax and house duty, as compared with those assessed to hearth (or chimney) money before the Revolution.[5] Opponents denied the accuracy of his data, and thought his estimate of four and a half or five inhabitants to a house too low. He pointed to the evil influence of a "devouring metropolis," a head too large for the body, and of great cities that were the "graves of mankind."[6] Here, too, both the data and the inference were doubtful. He argued from the decreasing produce of the Excise duties. Opponents answered that, even if the figures were right, a changed public taste had lessened the consumption of many taxable articles, and many taxed ones were supplied free by smuggling.[7] He laid stress on the

1 *Natural and Political Observations*, 1696. *Apud* Davenant and Chalmers.

2 *Primitive Origination of Mankind.*

3 *Political Survey of Great Britain*, 1677.

4 Cf. Chalmers, *Estimate*, p. 4, Pref. p. cxxxviii, and John Howlett's *Examination of Dr. Price's Essay* (Maidstone), 1781.

5 Cf. Macaulay, *History*, ch. iii. 137.

6 *Observations*, supplement, p. 366. Cf. Malthus, *Essay*, App. p. 519. Arthur Young, *France*, p. 409. The whole subject will be considered later in connection with Scotland.

7 See *Observations on Smuggling*, 1779.

difficulty the Government found in raising troops in the middle of the eighteenth century as compared with the end of the seventeenth, though he took this as a symptom, not a cause, and complained at the same time quite consistently that the increase of the army and navy and of military expenditure in three great wars had been a potent cause of diminished population. Opponents answered that the first was really a symptom not of decline but of prosperity; the abundance of other employments kept men from the need of enlisting in the army; and they answered too often, that the second (the war expenditure) was good for trade. They were safer in urging that for the first part of the century the long peace (1727-40) and the good harvests (1731-50) made the presumption of increase very strong.[1] Price made much of the emigrations to America and to the East and West Indies. It was answered that the known possibility of emigration would give men at home the greater courage to have a family. Even the engrossing and consolidation of farms and the enclosure of commons, which he considered to be against population, would, said his opponents, increase the food, and therefore the people, though perhaps not the people on the spot;[2] and the increase of paupers was thought to be a sign of overflowing numbers. He saw a cause of

[1] But see the *caveat* in the *Registrar-General's 44th Report* (for 1881), p. vi: The price of wheat and the marriage rate do not always vary inversely.

[2] In the same way the returns to the Board of Agriculture at the end of the century are full of (not quite disinterested) praises of enclosures as an encouragement of population.

depopulation in the increased luxury and extravagance of the people of England. At the beginning of the century gin-drinking was credited with an evil effect on population.[1] When the opponents of Price did not meet this with Mandeville's sophism, luxury benefits trade, they answered that what had become greater was not the national vices but the national standard of comfort, the expansion of which implied an increase of general wealth and presumably of population.[2] Beyond doubt too (it was argued) the general health was better, and medical science had won some triumphs.[3] Malthus, however, warns us against this argument; great unhealthiness is no proof of a small population nor healthiness of a large.[4] In the ten years after the American War of Independence (1783-93) the prosperity of the country seems to have advanced by leaps and bounds, only to make the subsequent depression the more observable. Dr. Price, who did not live to see the relapse, seems to have confessed his error. "In allusion to a diminishing population, on which subject it appears that he has so widely erred, he says very candidly that perhaps he may have been insensibly influenced to maintain an opinion once advaneed."[5] Yet public

[1] Lecky, *Eighteenth Cent.*, i. 261, 479 *seq.* Restrictions on the sale were successfully adopted by Pelham in 1751, at the time when the question of depopulation was coming to the front.

[2] An unsafe presumption. See below, Bk. II. ch. ii., &c.

[3] *E. g.* inoculation.

[4] *Essay*, 2nd ed., p. 317; 7th ed., p. 198, compared with 7th ed., p. 189, &c., above, pp. 115-16.

[5] *Essay*, 7th ed., p. 198 note; first printed in 3rd ed. (1806), p. 461 n.

opinion was not fully convinced till 1801, when "the answers to the Population Act at length happily rescued the question of the population of this country from the obscurity in which it had been so long involved."[1]

There is no good reason to believe that at the end of the century the fear of depopulation had given place to a fear of over-population.[2] Malthus and Arthur Young stood almost alone in their opinion.[3] Alarm was felt by the agricultural interest, not lest there should be an excessive population, but lest the population should get its food from abroad. The population it was feared had grown beyond the English supplies of food; but of over-population, in the wider sense of an excess beyond any existing food, the general public and the squires had learned little or nothing in these years; and we have no reason to attribute to Malthus any share in the merit of passing the Enumeration Bill. It was brought forward in an autumn session of Parliament (Nov. 1800) specially convened because of the scarcity. It was moved by Mr. Abbot,[4] who had made his name more as a financier than as an economist, and was chiefly remarkable afterwards as a vigorous opponent of

[1] 2nd ed., p. 302 n.; 7th ed., p. 194 n.

[2] This is asserted in the *Preliminary Report* to the English census (1881). Against the idea, see the *Annual Register's* reviews of Eden's work on the *Poor* (1797), and of his *Estimate* of English numbers (1800). The *Register* had numbered Burke and Godwin among its writers, and was not likely to be behind public opinion.

[3] See the review of Arthur Young's *Question of Scarcity plainly stated*, 1800, in *Ann. Register*, sub dato.

[4] Chairman of the Committee on the Public Finances 1797, Speaker of the Commons 1802, Lord Colchester 1817.

Catholic Emancipation. The motion was seconded by Mr. Wilberforce; and the combination of finance and philanthropy was irresistible. Malthus, though he is the true interpreter of the census, neither caused it in the first instance nor found it of immediate service in spreading his doctrines.

The first census would hardly have justified him in treating as obsolete the old quarrel about depopulation; it had decided only the absolute numbers in the first year of the nineteenth century, not the progress or relapse during the eighteenth. Besides giving the actual numbers of the people in 1801, the census no doubt gave "a table of the population of England and Wales throughout the last century calculated from the births." But the births, though a favourite, were an unsafe criterion; and, for the population at the Revolution of 1688, Malthus would depend more on "the old calculations from the number of houses."[1] He finds no difficulty of principle in admitting with Mr. Rickman, the editor of the census returns and observations thereon, that the rapid increase of the English people since 1780 was due to the decrease of deaths rather than to the increase of births.[2] Such a phenomenon was not only possible but common, for the rate of births out of relation to the rate of deaths could give no sure means of judging the numbers. After a famine[3] or pestilence,

[1] 2nd ed., p. 318; 7th ed., p. 204. Cf. 2nd ed., p. 317; 7th ed., pp. 192, 203, 206, 219, &c.

[2] 2nd ed., p. 311; 7th ed., pp. 201, 202, foot. Compare *44th Rept. of Reg.-Gen.* (England), p. v.

[3] As *e. g.* in 1800-1 compared with 1802-3; 7th ed., p. 214.

for example, the rate of births might be twice as high as usual, and by the standard of births the numbers of the people would be at their maximum, when a comparison with the rate of deaths or an actual enumeration would show them to be at the minimum,[1] whereas a low rate of births, if lives were prolonged by great healthiness, might certainly mean an increase, perhaps a high increase, of numbers. But at the particular time in question the factory system was coming into being, and manufacturing towns were growing great at the expense of the country districts. The conditions of life in towns are at the best inferior to those in the country; new openings for trade would add not only to the marriages but to the deaths and the births.[2] The presumption was not all in favour of healthiness; and the registers at that particular time could not tell the whole truth;—the drain of recruits for foreign service would keep down the lists of burials at home, while allowing an increase of births and marriages.[3] For these and other reasons, Malthus, while he agrees with Rickman that the general health has improved, trusts little to his calculations from registers; and concludes that even the census gives us no clear light on the movement of population in the eighteenth century. We can be certain that population increased during the last twenty years of it, and

[1] 2nd ed., p. 319; 7th ed., p. 205. Cf. passages cited on last page.

[2] Cf. *Essay*, 2nd ed., pp. 308-9; 7th ed., pp. 198-9.

[3] 2nd ed., pp. 312-13; 7th ed., p. 201. The 2nd ed. has a reference to "the late scarcities" wanting in the later edds. Registration, be it remembered, was then of baptisms and burials, not births and deaths.

almost certain that the movement was not downwards but upwards since the Peace of Paris; and we have good ground for believing that it was rather upwards than downwards even in the earliest years of the century, during the good harvests and the long peace of Walpole,[1] and that over the whole country the movement of population was less fluctuating in England than on the Continent.[2] The author's admission, that the proportions of the births, deaths, and marriages were very different in our country in his time from what they used to be,[3] seems to put the census of 1801 out of court altogether in the question of depopulation, especially as there were no previous enumerations with which to compare it. The figures from the parish registers for the whole of the century, that were included in the "returns pursuant to the Population Act," in addition to the enumeration, turned out on examination to be unsatisfactory.[4]

Malthus, however, was able to prove some solid conclusions from the census of 1801. It had shown, for example, as regards marriages, that the proportion of them to the whole numbers of the people was, in 1801, as 1 to $123\frac{1}{5}$, a smaller proportion than anywhere except in Norway and Switzerland,[5] and the more likely to be true, because Hardwicke's Marriage Act had made registration of marriages more careful

[1] See above, p. 176. Cf. on the other hand the concession, 2nd ed., p. 317; 7th ed., p. 203, middle.

[2] *Essay*, 2nd ed., p. 319; 7th ed., pp. 205-6.

[3] 7th ed., p. 188.

[4] Rickman himself allowed their defectiveness. See *Essay*, 2nd ed., p. 304; 7th ed., p. 196. Cf. above, p. 179.

[5] 2nd ed., p. 302; 7th ed., p. 194. By the *Registrar-General's Report* for 1882 it was as 1 in $64\frac{1}{2}$ in that year. Now 1922, 1 in 73.

than of burials and baptisms. In the early part of the eighteenth century, the pessimist, Dr. Short, had estimated the proportion (with much probability) as 1 to 115; and it would appear, therefore, that at neither end of the century were the marriages in a high proportion to the numbers, or had population increased at its highest rate. Again, Malthus thinks it proved by the census that, since population has as a matter of fact increased in England in spite of a diminished rate of marriages, the increase has been at cost of the mortality, the fewer marriages being partly a cause, partly a consequence, of the fewer deaths of the later years.[1] Those that married late might have consoled themselves with the reflection that they were lessening not the numbers but the mortality of the nation. It was no doubt difficult to estimate the extent to which such causes operated, or the degree in which the national health had been improved. In any case the census guides us better than the registers,[2] for it carries us beyond the inferred numbers to numbers actually counted out at a given time. Neither the census nor the registers can be rightly interpreted without a knowledge of the social condition, government, and history of the people concerned. In undeveloped countries, like America and Russia, or in any old countries after special mortality, a large proportion of births may be a good sign; "but in the average state of a well-peopled territory there cannot well be a worse sign than a large proportion of births, nor can there well

[1] 2nd ed., p. 303; 7th ed., p. 195. [2] 7th ed., p. 205.

be a better sign than a small proportion." Sir Francis d'Ivernois had very justly observed that, if the various states of Europe published annually an exact account of their population, noting carefully in a second column the exact age at which the children die, this second column would show the comparative goodness of the governments, and the comparative happiness of their subjects;—a simple arithmetical statement might then be more conclusive than the cleverest argument. Malthus assents, but adds that "we should need to attend less to the column giving the number of children born, than to the one giving the number which reached manhood, and this number will almost invariably be the greatest where the proportion of the births to the whole population is the least."[1] Tried by this standard, which is much more truly the central doctrine of Malthus than the ratios, our own country was even then better than all, save two, European countries. Tried by it to-day, we have still a good place. Though no great European countries, except Austro-Hungary and Germany, have had more *marriages*, in the twenty years from 1861 to 1880, not only these, but Holland, Spain, and Italy, have had more *births*, and all of them except Denmark, Norway, and Sweden have had more *deaths*, in proportion to their numbers.[2]

One great advantage of the census is, that it enables the registrars to calculate from their own data, with certain sure limits of told-out numbers behind and

[1] 2nd ed., pp. 213-14; 7th ed., p. 202.
[2] *45th Report of Registrar-General* (England), (1882), p. ci.

before them. "When the registers contain all the births and deaths, and there are the means [given by the census] of setting out from a known population, it is obviously the same as an actual enumeration."[1] Malthus suggested in 1803 that the experiment of 1801 should be repeated every ten years, and that registrars' reports should be made every year.[2] This has been done; and, if both have been accurate, then the registers of the intervening years, on the basis of the decennial enumeration, ought to make us able to calculate the numbers for any intervening year. Accordingly, the population of England in 1881, as calculated from the births and deaths, was little more than one-sixth of a million different from the numbers as actually counted over on the night of the 4th of April in that year.[3] The growth in the last decade, 1871 to 1881, was higher than in any since 1831-41;[4] the births were more and the deaths fewer than usual. Another London has been added to our numbers in ten years.[5]

This gives no sure ground, however, for prediction. To suppose a country's rate of increase permanent is hardly less fallacious than to suppose an invariable order of births and deaths over the world generally. Even if we are beyond the time when we need to make any allowance for increasing accuracy and fulness, and if we may assume that no given census has any

[1] 7th ed., p. 210. [2] 2nd ed., p. 302; 7th ed., p. 194 n.

[3] Numbers calculated by "natural increment," *i. e.* births and deaths —26,138,248; numbers actually enumerated—25,968,286.—*Preliminary Report*, p. iii.

[4] '31-'41, incr. 14·52; '71-'81, incr. 14·34.

[5] Or three and a quarter millions of people to England and Wales alone.

units to sweep into its net that through their fear or an official's carelessness escaped its predecessor, still we cannot take the rate of increase from one census to another as a sure indication of the future. With some qualifications the words of Malthus apply to us in 1881 quite as accurately as to our fathers in 1811: "This is a rate of increase which in the nature of things cannot be permanent. It has been occasioned by the stimulus of a greatly increased demand for labour, combined with a greatly increased power of production, both in agriculture and manufactures. These are the two elements which form the most effective encouragement to a rapid increase of population. What has taken place is a striking illustration of the principle of population, and a proof that, in spite of great towns, manufacturing occupations, and the gradually acquired habits of an opulent and luxuriant people, if the resources of a country will admit of a rapid increase, and if these resources are so advantageously distributed as to occasion a constantly increasing demand for labour, the population will not fail to keep pace with them."[1] It was a rate of increase which he saw would double the population in less than fifty-five years; and this doubling has really happened. The numbers for England in 1801 were 8,892,536; and in 1851 they were 17,927,609. Malthus had not anticipated any greater changes in manufacture and trade than those of his own day; and he clearly expected that the rate of increase would not continue and the numbers

[1] 7th ed., II. ix. p. 215 (written first in 5th ed., 1817).

would not be doubled. The one thing certain was the impossibility of safe prediction on the strength of any existing rate. A writer at the beginning of this century prophesied the extinction of the Turkish people in one hundred years; Sir William Petty at the end of the seventeenth century predicted that in 1800 London would have 5,359,000 inhabitants. But the Turks are not yet extinct; London in 1800 had less than a million of people, and has taken eighty years more to raise them to the number in the prophecy.[1]

If prediction was difficult in the case of England, it was not less so in the case of the other parts of the United Kingdom. The conditions of society and industry were quite different in the three countries; and to judge of the actual or probable growth of population in Scotland or Ireland, we must first, as with England, clearly understand these conditions. In the early part of this century even more than now, Scotland[2] stood to England as the country districts of England now stand to its great towns. Continual migration from country to town may be said to have been its normal state; and the largest towns were in England. The change from a militant and feudal to an industrial society was nowhere so marked as in Scotland after the Union, and especially after the rebellion of 1745. The hereditary judgeships of highland chiefs were swept away; the relation

[1] *Essay*, 7th ed., p. 258; cf. *Prel. Rept. Census*, 1881, p. ix.

[2] The account of Scotland in the *Essay*, Bk. II. ch. x., is taken from the *Statistical Account* of Sir John Sinclair, 1791-99. Sinclair was acting, on the south side of the Tweed, as President of the Board of Agriculture. See below, Bk. II. ch. i. p. 218.

between chief and clansmen became the unromantic relation of landlord and tenant. The displacement of household work by the factory system, and of hand labour by machinery, crowded the great towns of Scotland at the expense of the country districts; and crowded the great towns and manufacturing districts of England at the expense of Scotland. The flood of North Britons into England was not of Bute's making; and it was greatest after and not before the Peace of Paris, although under that peace and a stable government the farming, the manufacturing, the banking, and the foreign trading of Scotland itself had grown great enough (it might have seemed) to employ the whole population at home. Cotton manufacture, which on the whole is the typical industry of these latter days, was peculiarly English.[1] Sheep-farming at home and cotton-spinning in England combined to depopulate the Scotch highlands and much of the lowlands. The highlands, with their strongly-marked physical features and strictly limited industrial possibilities, were somewhat in the position of Norway. In the highlands proper there were no mineral riches; there were moorlands, mountains, streams, lochs, heather, bracken, peat, and bog; the patches of cultivable soil would bear a scanty crop of oats, and perhaps clover, barley, or potatoes.[2] This description applied to a large half

[1] There was very little in Scotland. It is seldom mentioned by Adam Smith. MacCulloch says "never," but he had overlooked *Wealth of Nations*, IV. vii. 251-297.

[2] The last of late introduction. See *Reports to Board of Agriculture: Central Highlands* (1794), p. 21.

of entire Scotland; and we must bear it in mind to understand the saying of Malthus in 1803: "Scotland is certainly over-peopled, but not so much as it was a century or half a century ago, when it contained fewer inhabitants."[1] The highlands are over their whole extent what the lowlands are as regards their hills, fit only for sheep. Sutherland has about thirteen inhabitants to the square mile now, and Midlothian seven hundred and forty-six; but Sutherland and not Midlothian may be over-peopled. Sutherland as compared with her former self, when she had thirty or forty to the square mile, may be more or she may be less over-peopled than she once was; we cannot tell till we know what her wealth was and how it was distributed.

Under the patriarchal government[2] of early times the wealth of the country consisted literally in its men. If a chief were asked the rent of his estate, he would answer that it raised five hundred men; the tenant paid him in military service. Adam Smith remembers that in the Jacobite Rebellion, which disturbed his country at the time he was studying at Oxford, "Mr. Cameron of Lochiel, a gentleman of Lochaber in [the west highlands of] Scotland, whose rent never exceeded £500 [English] a year, carried, in 1745, eight hundred of his own people into the rebellion with him."[3] Subdivision of land meant more retainers and greater honour; and so the highlands were peopled not to the full extent of the work to be done, but actually to

[1] 2nd ed., p. 334; 7th ed., p. 229.

[2] Not feudal but pre-feudal, or allodial. See *Wealth of Nations*, III. iv. 183, 1.

[3] *Wealth of Nations*, ibid.

the full extent of the bare food got from the soil.[1] On the establishment of a strong government and the abolition of their hereditary judicial privileges, the chiefs soon became willing to convert the value in men into a value in money, exchanging dignity[2] for profit. They no longer encouraged their tenants to have large families; and yet they made no efforts to remove the habits, which the tenants had formed, of having them.[3] It was this change that gave Sir Walter Scott the materials for his most powerful pictures in *Waverley* and other novels. But it is the distress of the chiefs that is tragic to him, rather than the misery of the clansmen. The clansmen for their part had under feudalism been brought up to be farmers or cattle-dealers and nothing else; there was as little variety of occupation in the highlands then as in Ireland now. Undoubtedly too they had that customary right of long possession, which law so often construed into a legal title in the case of more influential men. It was true also that, if the native highlanders would not cultivate that poor soil, no strangers would, and, if it was politically desirable that the country should remain peopled, the only way to secure this was to prevent the native exodus.[4] No such attempt was made; but, on the contrary, the highland landlords followed the way that led to the highest rents; they consolidated their

[1] Selkirk, *Highlands*, 1805, p. 25. [2] See the *Legend of Montrose*, &c.

[3] Adam Smith, *l. c.*; cf. I. viii. 36, 1 (the often-quoted description of "half-starved highland women" with their twenty children in contrast to the "pampered fine lady" with few or none.

[4] *Reports to Board of Agriculture: Central Highlands*, 1794, p. 52.

farms; they exchanged agriculture for pasture; they substituted deer for sheep. Almost every highland district has sooner or later passed through all these three stages, and with the same result, the employment of fewer and fewer men.[1] The discarded men had two courses before them, migration to the lowlands[2] or emigration to the colonies. The farm labourer would migrate, the farmer emigrate. The landlords incurred and often deserved odium for the manner of their evictions; but they treated the evicted better than the average British capitalist treats his dismissed hands. They usually provided passages and often procured settlements abroad for them. Lord Selkirk, one of the few writers on this subject that preserves a judicial calmness, advised his countrymen to acquiesce in the "depopulation" of the highlands, but to draw the stream of emigration to our own colonies. He himself drew it, so far as he could, to the Red River settlement and Prince Edward Island.

From the middle of last century to the beginning of this, emigration went on except when war made it impossible. The dangerous qualities of the highlanders made them very valuable in the three great wars that prevented them from leaving the country

[1] *Wealth of Nations*, III. iv. 184, 1 (written 1774), a passage which shows that the clearances and the consequent cry of Depopulation are to be looked for as early as the middle of the century. We are sometimes told that from the '45 to the end of the century was the golden age of highland farmers. But the willingness of the clansmen to enter Chatham's highland regiments would hardly imply great contentment.

[2] Cf. *Essay on Pop.*, pp. 332 (2nd ed.), 227 (7th ed.), and Selkirk, *l. c.*, pp. 43 *seq.* *Contra*, see *Report of Crofters Commission*, 1884, p. 51.

with their families. It may be that this very military consideration induced the English Government to connive at the clearances at first; and interference at any later stage was very difficult. As it is, in the end even the Sutherland evictions[1] seem simply to have shifted the population and not removed it. In spite of emigration Sutherland had as many inhabitants at the last census of 1881, as at the first in 1801, namely, above 23,000. Fishing, an industry new to a great part of the highlands, made this phenomenon possible. Fishing villages have grown at the expense of inland farms. But this is not the whole truth. Till the time when free trade began to distend Glasgow and other great towns of Scotland, the highland counties taken altogether had actually increased in population, as compared with what they were in 1801. The subsequent fall is due not to any great clearances or emigrations, but to another cause that had been acting though not conspicuously for some time before. This was migration to the industrial centres of the lowlands. In the days of the Tudors there were complaints in England of the decay of towns, because a strong government had at last made the protection of walled towns superfluous, and industry had spread itself in peace, where it was wanted. But two centuries later there was decay not of the towns but of the country districts, because industry was taking forms that made concentration necessary. At first, both in

[1] Made under the Marquis of Stafford between 1807 and 1820, in which year the popular odium was at its height, and the landlord made his defence in a well-known pamphlet by his factor, James Loch.

England and Scotland, there was a real diminution in the rural population; there had been for the time a real diminution of the work to be done in the country, and a transference of it to the towns. The hand-loom weaver had been supplanted by the power-loom. The little villages, where the workman lived idyllically, half in his farm and half in his workshop, now either sent their whole families to the towns, thus stopping their contributions to the parish registers in the country and swelling those of the town, or, still keeping the parents, sent three-fourths of the children there, thus making the country registers a very untrustworthy reflection of the real state of the population in the country districts. That country villages in every part of Scotland, but especially near the large cities, are "breeding grounds" of this latter description[1] is perfectly well known; and the same is true, in a less degree, of England. This is one reason why even the purely rural districts of Scotland have greatly increased in apparent population since 1801, and most of them are increasing still; the readiness of the Scotch to emigrate has caused the large families quite as much as the large families the emigration. Another reason is, that even in the country districts there is now more work to be done and it is done better. Orthodox economists may count this an example of the self-healing effects of an economical change that causes much suffering at first. It is fair to say that this eventual cure is

[1] Cf. Malthus, *Essay*, 7th ed., p. 229, top; cf. pp. 221 ft., 223 ft.; 2nd ed., pp. 326-7.

neither more nor less complete than the cure of the analogous hardships of the newly-introduced factory-system, and the temporary inconveniences of sudden free trade. What keen commercial ambition can do it has done, and its success is at least sufficiently complete to justify us in saying of Scotland to-day what Malthus said of it many years ago: it was most over-populated when it had fewest inhabitants. Modern improvements, however short of perfection, have at least both in England and in Scotland absolutely put an end to periodical famines. Even the scarcities of 1799 and 1800, though they caused great distress in both countries, were not famines in either of them; and, since the repeal of the Corn Laws in 1846, even such general distress as was caused in Scotland by the potato blight cannot occur again. That distress itself was as nothing compared with the terrible dearths from which Scotland used to suffer five or six times a century, and which England experienced as late as the seventeenth.[1] The dismal picture[2] which Malthus draws of the condition of the Scottish peasantry reminds us that it is not much more than a century since Scotland took her first steps in civilization and turned her energies from war to commerce. Her population at the '45 was about one and a quarter millions, in 1801 about one and a half; but in 1861 more than three, and in 1881 three and three-quarters. Population therefore

[1] See Malthus, *Essay*, 7th ed., p. 227. Cf. Farr in *Statist. Journ.*, 16th Feb. 1846.

[2] Drawn chiefly from the *Statistical Account of Scotland*, 1791-99.

has more than doubled within the century. But even now there are only a hundred and twenty-one inhabitants to the square mile, as compared with four hundred and forty-five in England. The wealth of the country has increased immensely faster than the population; it has multiplied fivefold since the middle of the century, and tenfold since the beginning of it.[1]

The history of population in Ireland would have furnished Malthus with still more striking illustrations of his principles, if his life had lasted a few years longer. He contents himself (till the 6th edition of the *Essay*[2]) with a single paragraph: "The details of the population of Ireland are but little known. I shall only observe, therefore, that the extended use of potatoes has allowed of a very rapid increase of it during the last century. But the cheapness of this nourishing root, and the small piece of ground which, under this kind of cultivation, will in average years produce the food for a family, joined to the ignorance and depressed state[3] of the people, which have prompted them to follow their inclinations with no other prospect than an immediate bare subsistence, have encouraged marriage to such a degree, that the population is pushed much beyond the industry and present resources of the country; and the consequence naturally is, that the lower classes of people are in the most impoverished[4] and miserable state. The checks to the population are of course chiefly of the

[1] Lavergne, *Econ. Rur. de l'Angleterre*, ch. xx. p. 310.

[2] The 6th simply adds the numbers of the people from the census of 1821, with hardly any comment.

[3] 2nd ed. says "barbarism."

[4] 2nd ed., "depressed."

positive kind, and arise from the diseases occasioned by squalid poverty, by damp and wretched cabins, by bad and insufficient clothing,[1] and occasional want. To these positive checks have of late years been added the vice and misery of intestine commotion, of civil war, and of martial law." [2]

In his review of Newenham's *Statistical and Historical Enquiry into the Population of Ireland* in 1808,[3] and in his evidence before the Emigration Committee in 1827, Malthus uses even stronger language. We may quote from the latter document as the less known of the two. In 1817 he had spent a college vacation in visiting Westmeath and the lakes of Killarney,[4] and was able to speak from personal knowledge of the country. He was asked :—

Qu. 3306. "With reference to Ireland, what is your opinion as to the habits of the people, as tending to promote a rapid increase of population?"—"Their habits are very unfavourable in regard to their own condition, because they are inclined to be satisfied with the very lowest degree of comfort, and to marry with little other prospect than that of being able to get potatoes for themselves and their children." [5]

[1] 2nd ed. adds, "by the filth of their persons."

[2] 2nd ed., pp. 334-5 ; 7th ed., p. 229. He refers to the rebellion of 1795-98, that was prelude to the Union of 1800, and was fresh in his memory.

[3] *Edin. Review*, July 1808, one review in that journal assigned to him by express testimony.

[4] *3rd Report of Emigration Committee* (1827), Evid., qu. 3225.

[5] In the article on Newenham he incidentally utters the paradox that in view of the low standard of food the people's indolence is almost an advantage, for it prevents wages falling quite down to that level.—Art. p. 341. Cf. *Essay*, IV. xi. 456-7. For his view of potatoes in Ireland, *ibid.*, 453.

3307. "What are the circumstances which contribute to introduce such habits in a country?"—"The degraded condition of the people, oppression, and ignorance."

3311. "You have mentioned that oppression contributes to produce those habits to which you have alluded; in what way do you imagine in Ireland there is oppression?"—"I think that the government of Ireland has, upon the whole, been very unfavourable to habits of that kind; it has tended to degrade the general mass of the people, and consequently to prevent them from looking forward and acquiring habits of prudence."

3312. "Is it your opinion that the minds of the people may be so influenced by the circumstances under which they live, in regard to civil society, that it may contribute very much to counteract that particular habit which leads to the rapid increase of population?"—"I think so."

3313. "What circumstances in your opinion contribute to produce a taste for comfort and cleanliness among a people?"—"Civil and political liberty and education."[1]

Then the subject of one acre holdings is introduced, and Malthus is asked:—

3317. "What effect would any change of the moral or religious state of the government of that country produce upon persons occupying such possessions?"—"It could not produce any immediate effect if that system were continued; with that system of

[1] Cf. *Review of Newenham*, p. 352.

occupancy there must always be an excessive redundancy of people, because, from the nature of tolerably good land, it will always produce more than can be employed upon it, and the consequence must be that there will be a great number of people not employed."

3318. "Is, therefore, not the first step towards improvement in Ireland necessarily to be accomplished by an alteration of the present state of the occupancy of the land?" This was a leading question, but Malthus would not be led. He replied, "I think that such an alteration is of the greatest possible importance, but that the other (the change in the government) should accompany it; it would not have the same force without." In his answers to later questions he gave his view at greater length on the causes of the difference between English and Irish character.

Answ. to qu. 3411. "At the time of the introduction of the potato into Ireland the Irish people were in a very low and degraded state, and the increased quantity of food was only applied to increase the population. But, when our [English] wages of labour in wheat were high in the early part of the last century, it did not appear that they were employed merely in the maintenance of more families, but in improving the condition of the people in their general mode of living." [1]

3413. "You attribute the difference of the character of the people to the difference of food?"—"In a great measure."

[1] Cf. Rogers, *Six Centuries of Work and Wages* (1884), p. 484.

3414. "What circumstance determines the difference of food in the two countries?"—"The circumstances are partly physical and partly moral.[1] It will depend in a certain degree upon the soil and climate whether the people live on maize, wheat, oats, potatoes, or meat."[2]

3415. "Is not the selection in some degree dependent on the general state of society?"—"Very much on moral causes, on their being in so respectable a situation that they are in the habit of looking forward, and exercising a certain degree of prudence; and there is no doubt that in different countries this kind of prudence is exercised in very different degrees."

3416. "Does it depend at all on the government under which they live?"—"Very much on the government, on the strict and equal administration of justice, on the perfect security of property, on civil, religious, and political liberty; for people respect themselves more under favourable circumstances of this kind, and are less inclined to marry, with[out] the prospect of more physical sustenance for their children."

3417. "On the degree of respect with which they are treated by their superiors?"—"Yes; one of the greatest faults in Ireland is that the labouring classes there are not treated with proper respect by their

[1] In a sense already frequently noticed. So in answer 3401, where he seems to accept the phrase "moral degradation" as applied to Ireland.

[2] Cf. above, pp. 95 and 195 n. Professor Rogers must have forgotten such passages as these when he wrote the 62nd and 63rd pages of his *Six Centuries of Work and Wages* (1884), though he furnishes his own correction on a following page (484).

superiors; they are treated as if they were a degraded people."

Thereupon he is again asked a leading question of a somewhat cynical character, but he is again cautious in his answer.

3418. "Does not that treatment mainly arise from their existing in such redundancy as to be no object to their superiors?"—"In part it does perhaps; but it appeared to take place before that [redundancy] was the case, to the same degree."

The questioner, however, begs the question and asks:

3419. "The number being the cause of their treatment, will not their treatment tend to the increase of that number? and the answer is: "Yes, they act and react on each other."

Accordingly his opinion in 1827 is, as it was in 1803, that emigration conjoined with other agencies will be good for Ireland, but by itself will leave matters no better than they were.

Alongside of his weighty words in the essay and in the evidence it is worth while to place the words written by Adam Smith half a century earlier:—

"By the union with England, the middling and inferior ranks of people in Scotland gained a complete deliverance from the power of an aristocracy which had always before oppressed them. By a union with Great Britain, the greater part of the people of all ranks in Ireland would gain an equally complete deliverance from a much more oppressive aristocracy, an aristocracy not founded, like that of Scotland, in the natural and respectable distinctions of birth and fortune, but in the most odious of all distinctions, those of religious and political prejudices; distinctions which, more than any other, animate both the insolence of the oppressors and the hatred and indignation of the oppressed, and which commonly render the inhabitants of the same country more hostile to one another than those of different countries ever are."[1]

With such passages before us, we cannot consider the two economists to have been behind their age in their Irish policy. In regard to accurate figures, the later economist was little better off than the earlier. Ireland was not included in the first two censuses of 1801 and 1811. In 1695 its population was estimated by Captain South as little more than one million;[2] in 1731, by inquiry of Irish House of Lords, at two millions; in 1792 by Dr. Beaufort at a little above four millions;[3] in 1805 by Newenham at five and a half millions; in 1812 an imperfect census gave it as nearly six millions; in the census of 1821 it was 6,800,000. It was clear that the population of Ireland was increasing even then faster than that of England.[4] But between these dates and our own

[1] *Wealth of Nations*, V. iii. 430, 1, 2.

[2] Sir Wm. Petty made it 1,100,000 in 1672. See MacCulloch, Append. to *Wealth of Nations*, (IV.) 462.

[3] See Sir H. Parnell's evidence in *3rd Report to Emigration Committee*, 1827, p. 200. He thinks that between 1792 and 1821 the population of Ireland had doubled itself.

[4] Malthus, Evidence before Emigration Committee, 1827; *3rd Report*, qu. 3430, p. 327.

times comes an episode striking enough to provide all economical histories with a *purpureus pannus*.

For about two generations England had perpetrated in Ireland her crowning feats of commercial jealousy, a jealousy not more foolish or wicked against Ireland than it was against the American colonies, or, till 1707, against Scotland, but more easily victorious. Ireland had not begun to be in any sense an industrial country till the reigns of Elizabeth and James I.; and the wars of the succeeding reigns hampered her early efforts. She had fair corn and meadow lands, and perhaps the best pastures in the world for sheep and cattle. The English farming interest became impatient of Irish competition, and a law was passed to forbid the importation of Irish sheep and cattle and dairy produce into England (1665, 1680). By reason of the later Navigation Acts, Ireland could not make amends for this by trading with America, for all such trading must be by way of England and in English ships, nor by trading with France for the same reason. England in her jealousy would have surrounded her with a cordon quite as close as Berkeley's wall of brass.[1] As soon as a considerable woollen manufacture grew up, England stopped it by legislation, which (in 1699) forbade the exportation of Irish woollens not only to England but to any other country whatever. English interference,

[1] Querist (1735) 134: "Whether if there was a wall of brass a thousand cubits high round this kingdom, our natives might not nevertheless live cleanly and comfortably, till the land, and reap the fruits of it?" The "caged rats" of the Corn Law pamphlets give us the other side of the question.

if it had done no more, added immensely to the uncertainties[1] and fluctuations of Irish trade. The growth of industries like the woollen manufacture had set on foot a growth of population which did not stop with the arrest of the industries. As often happens,[2] the effects of an impulse to marriage lasted far beyond the industrial progress that gave the impulse. But this means hunger and suffering, if not death. In the case of Ireland, the ruin of all industries but farming over more than three-fourths of the land led to an absolute dependence of the people on the harvest of their own country; and, where it failed them, they were brought face to face with dearth or famine. It led also to the peopling of the country districts at the expense of the towns,[3] instead of (as usual) the towns at the expense of the country. If Goldsmith's *Deserted Village* is not English, it is not Irish. By the year 1780, when Lord North from fear of rebellion granted free trade to Ireland with Great Britain, the mischief had been made almost incurable. The great increase in the Irish population, like the great increase in the English, may be said to begin in a free trade movement. In the worst days of legal persecution it might have been said of the Irish Catholic population, the more they were afflicted the more they multiplied and grew. Lavergne[4] thinks their greater increase was

[1] "Of such consequence in the encouragement of any industry is a steady unvarying policy."—Arthur Young, *France*, p. 388.

[2] See above, p. 151, &c.

[3] See above, pp. 191-2.

[4] *l. c.* p. 399. Cf. Lecky, *Eighteenth Cent.*, vol. ii. pp. 222 *seq.*; *Review of Newenham*, pp. 349, 350.

due first to the physiological law, that in the case of all animals the means of reproduction are multiplied in proportion to the chances of destruction [?], and second to the instinctively sound tactics of a people otherwise defenceless. The probability is, too, that they remained quiet under their multitudinous industrial, political, and religious disqualifications so long, because they were reduced to that depth of misery that kills the very power of resistance; and poverty at its extreme point is a positive but not a preventive check on population. Where things are so bad, marriage, it is thought, cannot make them worse, and marriage would go on at the expense of a high mortality, general pauperism, or continuous emigration. The pureness of marriage relations in Ireland, though in itself a much greater good than its consequences were evil, acted as it would have done in Godwin's Utopia;[1] apart from wisdom, virtue itself had its evils. Potatoes by-and-by came into general use; and the bad harvests, which taught even the Scotch and English poor[2] to make frequent use of this substitute for corn, converted it in Ireland from a substitute into a staple. Economists viewed this change with almost unanimous disapproval. In the view of Malthus it was the cheapness of this food that made it dangerous for the labourers; his theory of wages led him to object to cheap corn on the same grounds.[3] On the principle that it needs difficulties

[1] See above, p. 18.

[2] 7th ed., p. 378 ft. Cf. *Polit. Econ.*, 1st ed., pp. 252, 290, and 394 *seq.*

[3] *Essay*, III. viii. 323 (first in 5th ed.). See later, p. 268, &c.

to generate energy, the Irish are made indolent by their cheap food, and make no use of it except to increase by it. Living on the cheapest food procurable, they could not in scarcity fall back on anything else. Every man who wished to marry might obtain a cabin and potatoes.[1] At the lowest calculation, an acre of land planted with potatoes will support twice as much as one of the same quality sown with wheat.[2] There are other objections to a potato diet. It is a simple (as opposed to a composite) diet, and it involves a low standard of comfort. The second is not the same as the first, for a people that had no variety in their food might conceivably have a great variety in their other comforts. As a matter of fact, however, it was none of these three supposed disadvantages of the potato that proved the bane of the Irish population, but a fourth one, its liability to blight.[3]

The figures of the census tell their own tale. In 1821 the Irish people numbered 6,801,827; in 1831, 7,767,401; in 1841, 8,199,853; but in 1851, 6,514,473. In each previous decade the increase approached a million; in the last there was not only no increase, but a decrease of more than a million and a half. There had been a disastrous famine followed by great emigrations. What happened on Lord Lansdowne's estate in Kerry is an example of what took place over Ireland generally.[4] That estate comprehended

[1] *Essay*, 7th ed., pp. 452-3; 2nd ed., pp. 575-6.

[2] *Ibid.*, p. 323 ft. (7th); MacCulloch, Appendix to *W. of N.*, p. 467, 2.

[3] *Essay on Pop.*, 2nd ed., p. 576; 7th ed., p. 453 ft.

[4] *Lavergne*, pp. 423-4.

about 100,000 acres, on which before the famine there was a population of 16,000 souls. When the famine came a fourth part of them perished and another fourth emigrated. In course of time, thanks to money sent by relatives from America and advances made by Lord Lansdowne, the emigration continued with such rapidity that only 2000 souls were left on the estate. The famine taught the people how to emigrate, and gave them some idea of the meaning of over-population. The rural districts of Ireland are probably over-peopled now; but there seems reason to believe that a body of tenants, who are little short of peasant proprietors in security of tenure, and who have been forced into a knowledge of the world outside Ireland, will not retain the habits of the old occupiers.[1] Without a change of habits, peasant proprietorships would have done little for France, and will do little for Ireland.

This would certainly have been the judgment of Malthus on things as they are now in Ireland, after Catholic Emancipation, Disestablishment, and the Land Act. In his own time he was wise enough to see that the first could not be delayed without injustice and danger. The rapid increase of the Catholic population would soon, he foresaw in 1808,[2] bring the question of Emancipation within the range of "practical politics," and if the measure had been

[1] Even in 1875 the Registrar-General's Report showed that there were then fewer marriages in Ireland than in England, in proportion to the population, and that they came later. Cf. the 18*th Report*, for Ireland (1882), pp. 18, 19.

[2] *Review of Newenham*, pp. 351-4.

passed, as he urged, in 1808, instead of twenty years later, the labour of conciliating Ireland might have proved easier, and the political change might have helped to produce that change in the habits of the people which Malthus deemed essential to its permanent prosperity.

BOOK II. ECONOMICS.

CHAPTER I.

THE LANDLORDS.

Need of an Economical Digression—The Hegemony of Adam Smith's School—Cardinal Doctrines of the Malthusian Economy—Scope, Method, Details—Malthus doing Injustice to his Economics—Human Character of his Doctrines—Agricultural Situation in 1794—History of Corn Laws—Malthus on Rent in 1803 and afterwards—*Observations on the Corn Laws*—*Grounds of an Opinion*—*Nature and Progress of Rent*—Ricardo's Criticisms—Agricultural Improvements—Malthusian Ideal of Commercial Policy—The Wall of Brass—Limits to Commercial Progress.

THE *Essay on Population* deals with the past, the present, and the future. We have tried to follow its account of past and present, and must now consider the author's view of future prospects and of the various schemes (including his own) for making the future better than the present.

To do justice to this half of the essay, we must take further liberties with its arrangement. For the sake of explaining the historical genesis of the essay, we have already taken first[1] that criticism of Godwin and Condorcet which in the later essay comes in the centre of the work,[2] on the heels of the

[1] See above, Bk. I. ch. i.

[2] 2nd ed., Bk. III. chs. i. to iii.; 7th ed., Bk. III. chs. i. and ii.

account of population in the United Kingdom, the point where we have now arrived; and the chapter on emigration has been used before its time. There remain, out of the fourteen chapters of the third book of the essay, eleven still untouched; and in all but one[1] a knowledge of the general economical doctrine of Malthus is indispensable to a clear and just understanding of him. No apology is needed then for a somewhat long digression, in which the chief economical writings of our author are briefly analysed. It is not wholly a digression, as the substance of seven[2] out of ten chapters will be found incorporated with it, and their logical connection with the author's economical theories (so far as it exists) will be shown.

As a thoroughly practical man, Malthus knew that philanthropy can do little without sound doctrine; and his economical theories belong to the substance of his work. They were developed, unlike the *Essay on Population*, in quiet controversy among friends; Ricardo, James Mill, and Jean Baptiste Say, who were critics of the *Political Economy*, had been converts of the *Essay*. These were, however, the very men who came nearest to identify orthodox economics with rigorous abstraction. Malthus himself, labouring to build up the neglected pathology of economic science, was not chargeable with this fault. His first work had happily fixed into an intellectual principle his natural inclination to look at speculative questions

[1] 7th ed., ch. iii. (on Owen, &c.), which replaces a reply (2nd and 3rd edd.) to Godwin's first reply.

[2] All except those on pauperism. When pauperism is reached, the thread of the essay is again taken up.

in their relations to practice, and to look at "things as they are"[1] rather than as they might be. Ricardo's first work, bearing wholly on finance,[2] had unhappily fixed for him his inclination to treat every social question as a problem in arithmetic. In both cases the excitement of controversy would make the impression deeper.

The two economists both start from Adam Smith,[3] as theologians from the Bible. It was becoming clear that these Scriptures were of doubtful interpretation. Men were to choose between the Calvinism of Ricardo and the Arminianism of Malthus; and, when the two writers turned from their debates with the public to debates with each other, no less a prize was in question than the hegemony of the school.

This was won by Ricardo, whose *Principles of Political Economy and Taxation* (1817) were accepted by James Mill, MacCulloch, Nassau Senior, to say nothing of others, as the Institutes of their creed. MacCulloch thought it not worth his while to print what Ricardo had thought it worth his while to write, in vindication of his positions against Malthus.[4] The strongest ally of Malthus was Sismondi. It was not till Ricardo had reigned for thirty years that there was serious sign of defection, when the son of James Mill broke with his father's traditions;[5] and, though

[1] *Pol. Econ.*, 1820, Introd. p. 11. Cf. *Tract on Value*, p. 60 ft., and above, p. 37.

[2] *High Price of Bullion*, 1809. See below, p. 285.

[3] Malthus, *Pol. Econ.*, Introd. pp. 2, 5, 22, &c.; *Essay on Pop.*, Pref. &c.; Ricardo, *Principles of Pol. Econ. and Taxn.* (1817), Pref.

[4] Life of Ricardo in preface to *Works*, p. xxxi.

[5] J. S. Mill, *Political Economy*, 1848 and 1849. It was not a complete

in the hands of Thornton, Cliffe Leslie, Walker, and others, the reaction has been carried to the utmost, the eclipse of Ricardo has done nothing to rescue Malthus from obscurity. The very success of the *Essay on Population* may have deepened the oblivion of the other writings in virtue of the popular fallacy that a man cannot be equally great in general theory and in the advocacy of one particular reform.

The *Political Economy* of Malthus has its faults; but it contains in outline the main truths which writers of our own time think they have established against Ricardo. First and foremost, he maintains with them that the proper study of the science is not Wealth, but Man, or more definitely, Wealth in relation to Man. The qualities of man and the earth he cultivates are according to Malthus so many and variable in relation to each other that a study of their relations cannot be an exact science like mathematics; it may contain "great general principles" to which there are few exceptions, and "prominent landmarks" that will be safe guides to us in legislation or in life; but "even these when examined will be found to resemble the most general rules in morals and politics founded upon the known passions and propensities of human nature."[1] Human conduct is characterized by such variation and aberration that we must always be prepared for

breach. The new faith and the old perplex each other and the reader, in the pages of Mill.

[1] *Pol. Econ.*, Introd. Cf. the Discussions on the Measure of Value, *Pol. Econ.*, ch. ii., and pamphlet on the subject. So Roscher, *Nationalökonomie*, § 1 and n.

exceptions to our principles, and for qualifications which spoil the charm of uniformity, but are faithful to facts,[1] like George Eliot's "analyses in small and subtle characters," which stimulate no enthusiasm but alone tell the whole truth. In the second place, we are told that the nature of the subject makes a peculiarly cautious Method nécessary. Our first business being to account for things as they are,[2] till we are sure that our theories do so we cannot act on them.[3] A good economical definition must conform to the ordinary usage of words. We must take if possible a meaning which would agree with the ordinary use of words "in the conversation of educated persons."[4] If this does not give sufficient distinctness, we must fall back on the authority of the most celebrated writers on the science, particularly of the founder or founders of it; "in this case, whether the term be a new one born with the science, or an old one used in a new sense, it will not be strange to the generality of readers, or liable to be misunderstood."[5] If any word must have a different meaning from that adopted by either of these authorities, the new sense must not only be free from the faults of the old, but must have a clear and recognizable positive usefulness. The new definitions should be consistent with the old; and the same terms should be used in the same sense, except where

[1] Arist., *Ethics*, i. (3).

[2] "*Definitions in Political Economy*, preceded by an inquiry into the rules which ought to guide political economists in the definition and use of their terms, with remarks on the deviations from these rules in their writings" (1827), p. 5.

[3] *Pol. Econ.*, Introd. p. 11. [4] *Definitions*, p. 4. [5] *Ibid.*, p. 5.

inveterate custom insists on an exception. When all is done, it is still impossible in a social science like political economy to find a definition entirely beyond cavil.[1]

"Wealth" must include all the "material objects that are necessary, useful, or agreeable to mankind;"[2] "productive labour" must be the labour which realizes itself either in such material objects or the increased value of them; or else we wander from common language, and our discussions travel off into indefiniteness. Economical reasoning must be a deduction from observed facts of nature and of human nature verified by general experience. Malthus professes to have used this cautious method throughout, and the theory of population was only the particular instance where circumstances enabled him to make his verification most complete. "I should never have had that steady and unshaken confidence in the theory of population which I have invariably felt, if it had not appeared to me to be confirmed, in the most remarkable manner, by the state of society as it actually exists in every country with which we are acquainted."[3] On the other hand, Ricardo, legislating for Saturn, gives us little or no verification by experience. It is true that he admits qualifications and exceptions to his own statements; and he would have winced a little at his own

[1] *Definitions*, pp. 6, 7.

[2] *Pol. Econ.* (1820), p. 28. "And have an exchangeable value," was the Ricardian addition; and in the *Quarterly Rev.*, Jan. 1824, p. 298, Malthus weakly allows the addition to pass.

[3] *Pol. Econ.*, Introd. p. 11.

biographer's assertion that "Mr. Ricardo paid comparatively little attention to the practical application of general principles; his is not a practical work."[1] But he makes no use of the admissions; his illustrations as a rule are not historical, but imaginary cases and the verification is wanting. In a letter to Malthus (written on the 4th May, 1820) he says: "Our differences may in some respects, I think, be ascribed to your considering my book as more practical than I intended it to be. My object was to elucidate principles, and to do this I imagined strong cases, that I might show the operation of these principles."[2] In Malthus and Adam Smith, imaginary cases are rare exceptions, actual examples from life or history are the rule. Malthus goes so far in this direction that (to use his own phraseology) he is tempted to subordinate science to "utility." Even Adam Smith, though he had abundance of good-will to his kind, did not write to do good but to expound truth. To Malthus the discovery of truth was less important than the improvement of society. When an economical truth could not be made the means of improvement, he seems to have lost interest in it. His pointed warning to others against this error[3] may be regarded as a confession of his own liability to it; and, if he obeyed his own warning at all, his position was at the best like that of the latter-day utilitarians, who try to reach

[1] MacCulloch, *Life of Ricardo*, prefixed to *Princ. of Econ. and Taxation* (ed. 1876), p. xxv.

[2] Letter quoted by Empson in *Edin. Review*, Jan. 1837, misdated.

[3] *Pol. Econ.*, Pref. pp. 12, 13 (2nd ed.). Cf. above, p. 57.

happiness by making believe not to think of it. If his science had been less biassed by utility, it might have been more thorough; and we might not have had in our own time a Ricardian socialism, appearing like the ghost of the deceased Ricardian orthodoxy sitting crowned upon the grave thereof. He has the virtue of refusing to join the economical Pharisees,[1] who would not admit the elasticity of economical laws, lest they should discredit their science; but he is to blame for not pushing his quarrel against Ricardo with the same energy as against Godwin. His forces, in this campaign, were worse drilled and worse handled. It is justly said by Garnier (*Dict. de l'Écon. Pol.*, art. 'Malthus'), that in spite of its title, the *Political Economy* of Malthus is not the exposition of a system, but simply a collection of economical papers on various subjects that had been brought specially under his notice in discussion with his friends, or (we might add) in his college class. This itself would lead him to present a much less solid front to the enemy than he did in the *Essay*.

To come, in the third place, to Details, we find the human character of the *Political Economy* of Malthus appearing not only in his view of population, where all is at last made to depend on the personal responsibility of the individual man, and legislation is good or bad according as it strengthens or weakens that responsibility,—but in his view of the Value of goods, as measured by human labour,—in his view of demand

[1] Arist., *Ethics*, x. 1. Some thought pleasure was the goal, but, for the sake of others, "one must not say so."

and supply, as sharing the inconstancy of the human desires that enter into both of them,—in his view of the Rent of land, as determined by the effects of human industry and skill as well as by the natural qualities of the soil,—in his view of the Wages of labour, as regulated not by an unchangeable but by a progressive minimum,—in his view of luxury, as being equally with parsimony necessary to production, and preventive of over-production,—and in his view of free trade, as a rule to which we must make exceptions if we would not cause sufferings.

These doctrines had a distinct relation to current events. Political and social changes were reacting on political economy. As Godwin and Pitt provoked the essay of 1798, the scarcity of 1799 and 1800 called forth the pamphlet on High Prices (1800). As the latter bears directly on the Poor Law, it will best be considered when the thread of the *Essay on Population* is taken up again;[1] and the same applies to the letter of Malthus to Whitbread (1807). The distresses of a time when wheat went so high as £6 the quarter instead of its normal 40*s*. or 50*s*., would naturally make the relief of the poor a question of the day. The high prices of corn increased the number of enclosures and Enclosure Bills. More than three millions of acres, or about a twelfth part of the entire area of England and Wales, are said to have been taken from waste into cultivation between 1800 and 1820. The average price of wheat, always the staple food of the people when they could get it, had

[1] See below, ch. iv.

been 55*s.* 11*d.* for the years preceding, viz. from 1790 to 1799 inclusive; it was 82*s.* 2*d.* from 1800 to 1809 inclusive, and 88*s.* 8*d.* from 1810 to 1819 inclusive, after which it fell (for the next decade) to 58*s.* 5*d.*[1] In 1883-4 it was 35*s.* 8*d.* a quarter, which means a four-pound loaf (of medium quality) at 4½*d.* or 5*d.*; but at its lowest during the war (in 1803) it was at 57*s.* 1*d.*, and the loaf was at 6¾*d.* or 7*d.*

Yet agriculture had not been standing still. Arthur Young, whose eccentric energy benefited every one but himself, and fell little short of genius, betted his nineteen volumes of *Annals of Agriculture* against Sir John Sinclair's twenty-one volumes of the *Statistical Account of Scotland*, that the Government of Pitt would not establish a Board of Agriculture. But Farmer George did establish one, in 1793;[2] Young paid his bet and became Secretary; Sinclair gained his nineteen volumes and became President of the new Board; and together they did much to make farmers and landlords aware of the rotations of crops, disuse of fallows, new manures, road-makings, that the Secretary had been preaching in vain for thirty years.[3]

When the great scarcities of 1799-1800 took place, the Board was equal to the occasion. It urged the Government to get supplies of rice from India; it preached earnestly the cultivation of waste lands and the temporary conversion of grass lands into corn-

[1] Porter's *Progress of the Nation*, p. 148 (ed. 1851). Cf. MacCulloch, *Wealth of Nations*, Notes, p. 525.

[2] Dissolved in 1817.

[3] Between 1767 and his death in 1820, he wrote no less than a hundred volumes on agriculture. His bet is given in Sir J. Sinclair's *Life* by Archdeacon Sinclair, i. 253.

fields. The last was done widely enough when the prices of corn were high. The second, except when it meant enclosure of commons, was hardly done at all; and there was a strange impression that the efforts of the Board were at bottom a political movement against ecclesiastical titles and the Established Church. The importation of rice would have been of immense immediate service; but by the time the order had reached India and the rice ships had come back to England,[1] the famine was over, the people preferred wheat, and £350,000 of bounty were thrown away.[2] Nothing shows the insularity of English commercial policy better than the remedies generally proposed in those days for curing the evils of a bad harvest. The House of Commons passed self-denying ordinances[3] and brown-bread bills, and offered a bounty on potatoes.[4]

There was some talk inside the House of enforcing a minimum rate of wages, and outside of enforcing a maximum price of bread. The people were told to eat red herrings instead of bread; philanthropic soup shops were opened; distilleries and starch manufactories were threatened with prohibition. Relief from the poor rates was, however, the favourite way of cutting the knot. Better that our people should depend on each other than on the foreigner. This fear of dependence was the more pardonable then, as

[1] At the end of 1801.

[2] *Communications to Board of Agriculture*, iv. 232-5 (1805). Cf. *Ann. Reg.*, 1801, p. 131.

[3] *E. g.* that the members should always use mixed instead of pure wheaten flour.

[4] *Ann. Reg.*, 1801, p. 129.

there were times, in the war with Napoleon, when England was more completely alone against the world than she is ever likely to be again. It was a much more culpable folly to pretend[1] that the scarcity was due to "forestalling and regrating,"[2] and that England could have provided for herself well enough, even in 1799 and 1800, but for the corn-dealers and the large farms and the enclosures and the new-fashioned husbandry. The new learning, however, went on its way.[3] The benefits of it may have gone to farmer[4] or to landlord,—the question was much debated,—but they did not go to the labourers. The same is true of the improvements in cattle-breeding introduced by Bakewell of Leicester and Chaplin of Lincoln, and encouraged by the Smithfield Club (1798), which has long outlived the Board of Agriculture. The life of the country labourers was little changed. They and their wages could not remain entirely unaffected by the growth of manufacturing towns. But custom still had the chief power over wages, and had no little influence on rents. From the reports sent from the Scotch, English, and Welsh counties to the Board of Agriculture in 1794, it does not appear that wages were at all, or rent very closely, in correspondence with the amount of the produce.[5] Rents were far from being

[1] As was done, *e. g.*, by Chief Justice Kenyon, King's Bench, Rex *v.* John Rusby, Nov. 1799.

[2] See J. S. Girdler, *Forestalling*, &c. (1800), S. J. Pratt's poem on *Bread for the Poor* (1800).

[3] Girdler, *l. c.* pp. 46, 48, &c.

[4] Philps, *Progress of Great Britain*, p. 132.

[5] Cf. the figures given in Malthus' *Tract on Value*, pp. 69-79, and in

rack rents, and wages were far from varying with the necessary expenses of the labourer. In truth each country district in the days before railways and steamboats was nearly in the same isolation with regard to the rest as all England was with regard to foreign nations. The price of farm produce was indeed tending to be equal over England, as now over the world. Wages were displaying no such tendency. Of all goods a man is the most difficult to move,[1] for you must first persuade him; and human inertia by making men stationary will keep wages low. So it was in 1794. The exertions of landlord and tenant were directed therefore rather to keep up corn than to keep down wages. They were beginning to fear for their monopoly of the corn market. The English Government had done its best to keep their market for them. A law of Charles II. passed in 1670 virtually prohibited importation of foreign wheat till the price of home wheat was over 53*s.* 4*d.* a quarter, and made it free only when the home price was 80*s.* The Revolution of 1688 brought a new phase of commercial policy. The new rulers, to conciliate the agricultural classes and atone for the burdens which had been transferred to them from the industrial classes, granted a bounty of 5*s.* a quarter on the exportation of wheat so long as the home price was not over 48*s.* In this way, after exportation in the days of the Romans,

Professor Rogers' *Six Centuries of Work and Wages*, pp. 487 *seq.*,—both of them taken chiefly from Eden on the Poor.

[1] *Wealth of Nations*, I. viii. 44, 1.

and alternate exportation and importation according to the seasons in after times, there was, after the Revolution, exportation encouraged by a bounty, while importation was still hindered by duties. The intention was at once to attract capitalists to agriculture and to reward those already engaged in it. By this means not only would the farmers be attached to the new dynasty, but England would provide all her own food.[1]

But the very increase of tillage kept down prices and gave the landowners little benefit. Whenever a scarcity occurred the laws were suspended, and the bounty and duties were taken off together.[2] Exportation, however, was the rule till a little after the middle of the century, say at the beginning of George III.'s reign, when the tide had fairly turned. Especially after the Peace of Paris (Nov. 1762), commerce was extended and population with it. Canals were made, roads improved, and home trade prospered.[3] We could no longer raise enough corn for our own wants.[4] In 1766, the year of our author's birth, there were scarcities, Corn Riots, and suspensions of the Corn Laws;[5] but the bounty was kept up in name to the end of the century. In 1795 and 1796 the price of wheat rose to 80*s.* a quarter, in 1797 and 1798 it sank to 54*s.*; but, at the end of harvest, 1799, it rose to 92*s.*, in 1800 to 128*s.*, and before the harvest of 1801 to 177*s.* The quartern loaf (under 6*d.* in 1885)

[1] On the whole subject see Craik, *Hist. of Commerce*, ii. 142-5.

[2] Macpherson, ditto, iii. 148 (year 1728), 307 (year 1757).

[3] *Ibid.*, iii. 329, 331; MacC., *Comm. Dict.* (ed. 1871), p. 430.

[4] Cf. *Essay on Population*, p. 352 (7th ed.). Cf. above, p. 25.

[5] Macpherson, iii. 438, 452.

was once within ½*d.* of 2*s.*! Then came a time of comparative plenty. Wheat between 1802 and 1807 was at 75*s.* on an average, and a new Corn Law in 1804 prohibited importation till the home price should rise to 63*s.* Between 1808 and 1813 it was 108*s.* on an average; and it was as high as 140*s.* 9*d.* in the severe winter (1812-13) of Napoleon's retreat from Moscow. But in the spring of 1815 wheat was at 60*s.* If it should rise to 63*s.* the ports would be opened, and there was not even the Protection of war. The farmers and landowners were terror-stricken, the political economists divided, and the bill for raising the importation price to 80*s.* was hurried through the House. The bounty, relaxed in 1773, had been finally repealed, in 1814.[1] As the sliding scale of duties was not introduced till 1827, we are to regard Malthus and Ricardo as writing on rent (in 1815 and 1820) under the severe Corn Law of 1815, as well as when the wisdom of passing that measure was still under debate. All their discussions on rent bear consciously or unconsciously upon the Corn Laws of their own time.

Malthus is rightly considered the first clear expounder in England of the economical doctrine of rent. Dr. James Anderson, a contemporary of Adam Smith, was no doubt before his age in his view of the subject;[2] but, perhaps because he was better known

[1] Cf. Malthus, *Essay on Pop.*, p. 453 (2nd ed.); *Grounds of an Opinion*, &c., p. 43.

[2] E. g. *National Industry of Scotland*, vol. ii. pp. 208-9 (1779). MacCulloch has quoted other passages (*Wealth of Nations*, xlviii. n., and *Note on Rent*, p. 453, 1, and n.). Sir Edward West agrees with Malthus

as an agriculturist than as an economist, he does not seem to have made converts. The "simultaneous rediscovery" of the true doctrine by West and Malthus in 1815 may be compared with the simultaneous discovery of the Darwinian theory by Wallace and Darwin in 1859. The times were ripe for it. Malthus gives no certain sound on the subject in the early editions of the *Essay on Population*. In the second he even says that "one of the principal ingredients in the price of British corn is the high rent of land" (p. 460; cf. p. 444). However, needing to lecture on Rent to his pupils at Haileybury in 1805, he saw the unsoundness of this position, and in 1806, in the third edition of the essay, the passage is dropped, and we are told, "universally it is price that determines rent, not rent that determines price" (vol. ii. p. 266). The passage is repeated in the fourth edition (1807).[1] But when the time came for a fifth edition, in 1817, the whole of the chapters on Corn Laws and bounties, which are the only chapters of the essay that deal much with rent, were recast, to express the clearer views which the author had already expounded elsewhere. In the spring of 1814, in the excitement of debates on the abolition of the bounty and on new laws to keep out foreign grain, Malthus was led for the fourth or fifth time in his life to take the field as a pamphleteer.[2] This time, however, he came forward, he said, not to take a side but to act as arbitrator. His "*Observations on the effects of*

in his qualified approval of the Corn Laws. See *Price of Corn*, &c., p. 139.

[1] A reprint of the 3rd

[2] If we include the *Crisis*, it would be the fifth time.

the Corn Laws, and of a rise or fall in the price of corn on the agriculture and general wealth of the country" (1814),[1] professed to balance the arguments for and against the Corn Laws, and did it, he said, so judiciously, that his own friends were in doubt to which opinion he leaned.[2] To later readers the bias is not doubtful. It appears even in such a passage as the following, which, incidentally, shows us his view of rent, nearly matured :—"It is a great mistake to suppose that the effects of a fall in the price of corn on cultivation may be fully compensated by a diminution of rents. Rich land, which yields a large nett rent, may be kept up in its actual state, notwithstanding a fall in the price of its produce, as a diminution of rent may be made entirely to compensate this fall, and all the additional expenses that belong to a rich and highly-taxed country. But in poor land the fund of rent will often be found quite insufficient for this purpose. There is a good deal of land in this country of such a quality, that the expenses of its cultivation, together with the outgoings of poor's rates, tithes, and taxes, will not allow the farmer to pay more than a fifth or sixth of the value of the whole produce in the shape of rent. If we were to suppose the prices of grain to fall from 75*s.* to 50*s.* the quarter, the whole of such a rent would be absorbed, even if the price of the whole produce of the farm did not fall in proportion to the price of grain, and making some allowance for a fall in the price of

[1] It was popular enough to reach a 3rd edition in 1815.

[2] See *Grounds of an Opinion*, &c., p. 2.

labour. The regular cultivation of such land for grain would of course be given up, and any sort of pasture, however scanty, would be more beneficial both to the landlord and farmer."[1] The drift of the pamphlet may be shortly stated. The writer refused to go with Adam Smith in identifying corn with food, and attributing to it in that capacity an unchangeable value, which made any rise of price futile for the encouragement of tillage. He thought that it was perfectly possible to encourage tillage by Corn Laws; but was it good policy? Before he could answer this question, he felt bound to consider several others.[2] Under free trade would Great Britain grow her own corn?—if not, ought Government to interfere to secure this?—if so, would laws to hinder importation be the best kind of interference? The answer to the first is, that other countries have soils more fertile than Britain; Poland can ship corn at Dantzig for England at 32*s*. a quarter;[3] and, if there were free trade over Europe, the rich lands which are not English would send their plenty to relieve the wants of their neighbours. If Corn Laws have not made us grow our own corn, free trade would not. In answer to the second question, no doubt it is sound economy to buy in the cheapest market and sell in the dearest; and, if we had regard to nothing but the greatest "wealth, population, and power," the rule would be invariable; foreign imports of food are in every case a good thing for the country, and, if there

[1] *Observations*, pp. 20-1. [2] *Ibid.*, p. 17.
[3] The English price in Nov. 1884.

is evil in the matter, it is not in them but in the bad season which makes them necessary; moreover, a free trade in corn secures a steadier as well as cheaper supply of grain.[1] But, on the other hand, dependence on other nations for the first necessary of life is a source of political insecurity to the nation so depending; and, though the dependence is mutual, identity of commercial interests seldom prevents nations from going to war with each other; "we have latterly seen the most striking instances, in all quarters, of Governments acting from passion rather than interest."[2] And it might be argued that, if we give up agriculture for manufacture, we change the character of our people; manufacturing industry conduces to mental activity, to an expansion of comforts, to the growth of the middle classes, and to the growth with them of political moderation; but it is more subject than agriculture to the fluctuations of fashion, which lead to chronic destitution and discontent, and the conditions of artizan life are "even in their best state unfavourable to health and virtue."[3] Virtue and happiness after all are the end; wealth, population, and power are but the means. Malthus himself believes in something like a golden mean, a balance of the two industries, which legislation might possibly preserve.[4] There is another and less plausible

[1] *Observations*, pp. 19, 22, 23, 27.
[2] *Ibid.*, p. 28. If the Ricardian hypothesis is not true of individuals, it is still less true of Governments, as Cobden experienced.
[3] *Ibid.*, pp. 30, 31.
[4] *Ibid.*, p. 32: "Many of the questions both in morals and politics seem to be of the nature of the problems *de maximis et minimis* in

argument on the same side. Assuming that wages vary with the price of corn, high money wages, and therefore high prices of corn, are an advantage to working men, who would have more money to buy the goods of the foreign countries where prices of corn were low and goods were cheap. This argument, though our author is inclined to yield to it, is inconsistent with his own views of wages and the facts he cites in support of them.[1] More cogent is the plea that it would be unfair suddenly to withdraw a long-established protection, though (it might be replied) we are no more bound to be gradual in abolishing protection than in concluding peace during war. But the real question is, whether once protected is to mean always protected, and protected in an always increasing degree, for it was this increased protection that was proposed in 1814 and 1815. It may be true that if we protect manufacture we ought to protect agriculture; but, instead of protecting both, why not set both free? Statesmen had no courage, however, to be free-traders, in days when the separate articles protected were as many as the millions in the National Debt, and each article represented a vested interest. Malthus does not seem to expect Parliament to give free trade a moment's consideration. But the friends of the new Corn Laws, besides using the commonplaces of protectionism, argued from the change in the value of the English currency. When paper were paper prices,[2] the importation price of the

fluxions; in which there is always a point where a certain effect is the greatest, while on either side of this point it gradually diminishes."

[1] Cf. even *Observations*, pp. 5, 12, 13. [2] See below, chs. ii. and iii.

law of 1804 could be soon reached, and foreign corn came in much faster than the real or the bullion prices of it would have allowed. There was also the long array of standing arguments for Corn Laws that lay stress on the heavy taxation of the country, and are meant to show that the agricultural classes bear most of it, and are thus handicapped against the foreigner. From Malthus himself the old leaven of protectionism was never wholly purged away. Like Pitt, though in a less degree, he suffered his politics to corrupt his political economy, and drag him back from the "simple system of natural liberty" into "the mazes of the old system."[1] English people since the Repeal of the Corn Laws will hardly care to thrash the old straw out again. Perronet Thompson's *Catechism of the Corn Laws* is the best storehouse of the old arguments and their refutations, set forth with a liveliness to which no other English economical writing has the slightest claim.[2]

The real opinion of Malthus came out in the second Corn Law pamphlet on the *Grounds of an Opinion on the Policy of restricting the Importation of Foreign Corn* (1815). Between the two came the tract on Rent, which is rather an economical book than a political pamphlet, and will be noticed immediately. He now declares himself in favour of a temporary

[1] The expression of Grenville in a letter to Pitt, 1800. See Stanhope, *Life of Pitt*, ii. 371.

[2] Unless perhaps Mr. Bagehot's. Col. Thompson understood the theory of population only in its cruder form. In answer 337 of the *Catechism* (1839) he meets the objection that free trade would only increase population by saying: "No man has a right to prevent us running a constant race with hunger if we can."

duty on imported corn to countervail the artificially low value of the currency,—"to get rid of that part of our prices which belongs to great wealth, combined with a system of restrictions."[1]

He warns the Government that they should not take such a step to benefit a particular trade, but only to benefit the public. The motives are those constantly professed by defenders of the Navigation Act—not private interests but public policy. Since he wrote his *Observations* circumstances had changed. The sudden peace had brought the then unprecedented combination of a bad harvest and low prices; the value of the currency had fallen fast; and last, and not least, France, the best corn country in Europe, had begun to prohibit the exportation of grain[2] in dear years. We must therefore, he says, keep up the high farming which the war taught us, by keeping up the high prices of the war. Eighty shillings might not be too high a price, for the limit of prohibited importation.

It seems extraordinary that, after so clearly recognizing that "wealth does not consist in the dearness or cheapness of the usual measures of value, but in the quantity of produce," and that exports are not so good a criterion of wealth as the "quantity of produce consumed at home,"[3] Malthus should recommend the increase of abundance by means of artificial dearness. It is a poor consolation to us that he was no worse than Brougham, who voted for the Corn

[1] *Grounds*, &c., p. 46 n. [2] *Ibid.*, pp. 3, 11, 12.
[3] *Ibid.*, pp. 30, 33.

Law in 1815, and for the support of the Navigation Act in 1849,—and little worse than Ricardo, who would allow a temporary restriction for the sake of leaseholders.[1] A better is that he was advocating a policy that was against his private interests as a holder of a fixed salary and owner of three per cents.[2] But at the best the atmosphere of these two tracts is a little depressing.

The tract on Rent is more bracing. It was the first-fruits of the larger work on *Political Economy* (1820); and its substance had been delivered in the professor's lectures at Haileybury. It expounds the *Nature and Progress of Rent* with clearness and intelligibility, if without the liveliness of 1798. Malthus gives us to understand that, to explain this or any other economical notion, we must keep as closely as possible to the usage of ordinary language, the language of clear-thinking ordinary men.[3]

To them, rent does not mean, as by derivation, simply produce or profit; nor, as to a Frenchman now and to Bailie Nicol Jarvie in his days, interest on a debt. It means a certain price paid to a landlord for the use of his land. But such a definition is too wide. It might include the proceeds of a monopoly, or an interest on capital, or a Government tax, or a legal rate, or a toll, or a payment for service rendered. We must define the term a little more clearly.

There is a certain portion of a landlord's income

[1] Ricardo, *Works*, p. 385 (MacC.'s ed.). For remarks on this part of Malthus' tract see *ibid.*, p. 382.

[2] *Grounds*, &c., p. 36 n. Cf. Ricardo, p. 390. [3] See above, p. 211.

and of a peasant proprietor's earnings that has an origin and character distinct from the rest, and demands the economist's separate attention, whether it alone receives the name of rent or not;—this is, the excess of the produce of land beyond the cost of production and the current rate of profits. Represent these in money; and suppose the current profit five per cent. Suppose that a tenant lays out £500 on his farm, and gets by the harvest and farm produce not only £500 plus £25, but £600; the additional £75, which would if retained by him be over or extra profits as compared with the rate usual among farmers and men of like business, is the value of his rent; and the landlord can take that from him without impoverishing him. Rent is that portion of the produce which remains, after all the outlay of the cultivator has been repaid him together with the current profits. From accidental or temporary causes the money rents of land may be more or less than this; but this is the point to which actual rents will gravitate.[1]

So far as this account goes, it might seem that Malthus' description is too general; it would include the extra profits, for example, of any monopoly or a royalty for the use of a patent; and Ricardo's definition, "the price paid for the indestructible powers of the soil," might seem more definite. But Malthus is rather too specific than too general. He is thinking of agricultural land only, and that mainly as producing food for man. If his description of the

[1] *Pol. Econ.*, ch. iii. sect. i. p. 134 (1820).

Nature of rent adds little to that of Adam Smith,[1] his account of its Causes, which he himself was the first to grasp, is characteristic and peculiar.

First, he says, fertile[2] soils yield a produce that more than feeds the producer. This may be put more generally than Malthus has put it. If rent is to be paid, there must be wherewithal to pay it; and there cannot be so if production does no more than repay cost. There may, however, be a production beyond mere repayment of cost, not only in farming but in all trades. The very principle of the division of labour and the separation of trades implies that devotion to one occupation makes men so dexterous in production that, besides providing for themselves, they have an overplus wherewith to supply their other wants and the wants of others.[3] This overplus, where the facilities for trading were specially good, might be so much above the overplus of an ordinary profit that the granter of the facilities, who is usually the ground landlord, might get the lion's share of it, and still leave the user of the facilities as thriving as his neighbours. On the other hand, if no such overplus can be earned, no such rent can be paid. Rent, in short, when it is paid by men of business, either in town or in country, means over-profits, and ground-rents mean advantage of situation.

[1] *Wealth of Nations*, I. xi., beginning.

[2] He does not always prefix this qualification; but that he intended it appears clearly from the *Tract on Rent*, p. 3 n.: Not every land that yields food will yield rent. Cf. *Pol. Econ.* (1820), p. 141.

[3] Compare *Tract on Rent*, p. 16 n.

The second cause of rent, according to Malthus, who is considering, be it remembered, the cause of the Progress of rents as well as of their actual volume at any given time,[1] is the peculiarity belonging to agricultural land, that the demand increases with the supply; in other cases the demand is external to the supply, but in this case[2] the supply creates its demand. Where there is food there will be mouths. In the supply of food no over-production is possible.[3]

It is here that the *Essay on Rent* is connected with the *Essay on Population*. By the law of population the tendency is that where food enough for six is being produced by two, the other four will soon make their appearance; and so, thinks Malthus, the farmer makes his customers by simply making his wares. Something like this, we might add, would happen in a completely developed co-operative society, where the makers would sell to each other and buy from each other. It is even true, in a sense, of all manufacturers as things now are, in proportion as their articles come near to being necessaries;—if they supply that without which people cannot live, they go far to bring people into being. Malthus, however, regarded it as much more true of agricultural production than of any other. He regarded food as the chief necessary, and thought with Adam

[1] The title of the tract is, *An Inquiry into the Nature and Progress of Rent, and the Principles by which it is regulated.* It appears from a letter of Malthus to Sir John Sinclair on 31st Jan., 1815, that it was passing through the press in that month. Sinclair, *Correspondence*, i. 391 (1831).

[2] As, he might have added, in education.

[3] *Pol. Econ.* (1820), p. 142, but especially p. 187. Cf. *Tract on Rent*, pp. 8—12.

Smith, that "when food is provided it is comparatively easy to find the necessary clothing and lodging."[1] Against this we need only remember, how the *Essay on Population* showed that it was only in the lower stages of existence that increase of mere food involved increase of population; and so the tendency of the supply to create its own demand was, on the author's own showing, nothing more than a tendency.[2] His economical reasoning was swayed a little by his circumstances. The insularity of English life in his days prevented him from conceiving how a nation could safely derive half its food from abroad; what Adam Smith had thought too good to be likely,[3] he thought too dangerous to be desirable. Good or bad, it is our position now, and the result is, first, that the supply of food does not, in the same degree or way, produce its own demand as formerly, and, second, that our other productions are, even more truly than the agricultural, the supply that creates its own demand, for they give the power of buying the food that feeds new demanders. The production carried on, on the surface of the land, has come in this way to be a more potent cause of the Progress of rents than production from the soil itself. With this restatement the second of Malthus' causes of rent becomes perhaps a little more intelligible.

His third cause is that good land is scarce. Lands differ in fertility, and there is not, as in a new country, enough of the most fertile to supply all our

[1] *Rent*, p. 10. [2] Cf. also below, p. 294.
[3] *Wealth of Nations*, IV. ii. 307, 2; cf. IV. v. 240, 2.

wants. When the produce of the inferior begins to be absolutely necessary, the inferior will be cultivated at a price enough to repay cost and give ordinary profits to the farmer. But what is simply enough to do that for him will do much more than that for all the holders of superior lands, and all that is much more can be taken by a landlord as rent without placing the tenant at any disadvantage as compared with his neighbours. As soon as this happens in a country, the extra profits, which are called by economists rent, will appear in it; and the growth of population, by leading to an increased demand for food and to an increased price of it, will cause the cultivation of inferior lands, or else a more expensive cultivation of the old ones; and again, since the necessary new supplies cannot be permanently kept up without one or other of these two resources, the price, and with it the rent, will, in the absence of inventions, remain permanently higher. In other words, this third cause is the "law of diminishing returns."

It is this law of diminishing returns which bulks most largely in the tract of Sir Edward West, written in the same year as that of Malthus. West's theory of rent is simply, "that in the progress of the improvement of cultivation the raising of rude produce becomes progressively more expensive, or in other words, the ratio of the net produce of land to the gross produce is continually diminishing."[1]

[1] *Essay on the Application of Capital to Land*, with observations showing the impolicy of any great restriction of the importation of

He sees how near Adam Smith came to it when he said, that in the progress of cultivation the total amount of rent increased, but the proportion of it to the produce diminished, so that from being *e. g.* half the produce it became one-third.[1] He sees, as even in 1798 Malthus had seen,[2] that but for this law population might increase indefinitely on a few fertile lands instead of spreading over the globe (West, p. 13), whereas because of this law inventions in agriculture are not able to remove "the necessity of having recourse to inferior land, and of bestowing capital with diminished advantage on land already in tillage" (p. 50). He pushes the principle so far as to say broadly that whatever increases agricultural production increases cost, while whatever increases manufacturing production diminishes cost (p. 48), inferring that the former must tend abroad and the latter at home to prevent the displacement of English agriculture by foreign competition. As he had little or no influence on Malthus, his tract need not be noticed in detail; it is enough to say that, while West is superior in style and arrangement, Malthus is the more comprehensive. West is clearer and simpler because he includes less.

Looking at the three causes together, we see that the first and last relate to the statics, and the second to the dynamics of the subject. We need to remember that Malthus is having regard in the first instance

corn, and that the bounty of 1688 did not lower the price of it. By a fellow of University College, Oxford. (London, 1815.) Page 2.

[1] *W. of N.*, II. iii. 148, 1. [2] *Essay*, 1st ed., pp. 90, 107. &c.

not to the value but to the quantity of the produce. Now, apart from questions of value, it is possible there might be, in a country, land yielding to the sower more than he sowed; but it might be an ordinary excess, secured by all producers in that country, for the land might be all equally fertile, and production from land might be the most fertile of industries. In that case, even if the land was a State monopoly and the producer's gains could be taken from him by a tax, there would be nothing corresponding to rent, in the received sense. But, as soon as there were differences in the fertility, and therefore differences in the quantity produced at the same cost, the farmer who had the difference on his side could be said to have a rent. It is this surplus, conjoined with the institution of private property, that, according to Malthus, makes leisure and mental progress, and even great material prosperity, possible.[1] The rent is properly the extra profits, and not the equivalent paid over for them to a landlord; rent can easily exist without a landlord. "It may be laid down, therefore, as an incontrovertible truth, that, as a nation reaches any considerable degree of wealth, and any considerable fulness of population, which of course cannot take place without a great fall both in the profits of stock and the wages of labour, the separation of rents, as a kind of fixture upon lands of a certain quality, is a law as invariable as the action of the principle of gravity. And that rents are neither a mere nominal value, nor a value unnecessarily and injuriously

[1] *Tract on Rent*, p. 16; *Essay on Pop.* (7th ed.), p. 327. Cf. above.

transferred from one set of people to another, but a most real and essential part of the whole value of the national property, and placed by the laws of nature where they are, on the land, by whomsoever possessed, whether the landlord, the crown, or the actual cultivator."[1]

It is the second cause that brings the first and third into operation in such a way as to produce the rents that we actually know in an old country. The fertility which secures a produce beyond cost makes extra profits possible; the growing population, which gives the produce a value, makes them actual; and the gradations in fertility, whereby a uniform increase in the value of produce creates far from uniform extra profits to different cultivators, give the extra profits the peculiar graduated character, which is characteristic of rent in the economical sense of the word.

Malthus believed himself to have included, in this theory of rent, what truth there was in the view of the French economists and of Adam Smith, when they spoke of rent as due to the qualities of the soil and not to an ordinary monopoly. His contemporaries admitted him to have been the first clear expounder of the subject. But his most eminent brother economist found general agreement quite consistent with emphatic divergence in details,[2] not wonderful in a writer who regarded every economical question as a particular case of the problem of value rather than of wealth.

[1] *Rent*, p. 20; cf. pp. 18, 57. *Essay on Pop.*, 2nd ed., p. 433; 7th ed., p. 327. "If we look only to the clear monied rent," &c.

[2] Ricardo, Preface to *Principles of Pol. Econ. and Taxation*.

Ricardo admits that his own theory of rent is simply a farther development of the Malthusian. In an essay on *The Influence of a low price of Corn on the Profits of Stock, showing the inexpediency of Restrictions on Importation* (1815),[1] published in answer to the two tracts of Malthus above mentioned, he makes this quite clear, and, unlike his disciples, is warm in praise of his rival's powers as an economist.[2] He agrees with the definition (of the *Tract on Rent*) that rent is "that portion of the value of the whole produce which remains to the owner after all the outgoings belonging to its cultivation have been paid," including an ordinary rate of profits for the employed.[3]

But, whereas Malthus regards rent as increased by whatever lessens the outgoings in any shape or form, Ricardo considers that can happen in one way only, namely, by the increased cost of raising the last part of the necessary supplies. Arithmetically it was clear that, if you had four items making up the total expense of cultivation, whatever reduced any one of the items *pro tanto* reduced the total.[4] Accordingly, Malthus said that rent could be increased by such an accumulation of capital as will lower the profits of stock,—such an increase of population as will lower

[1] Reprinted by MacCulloch in his edition of *Pol. Econ. and Taxation*, pp. 367—390.

[2] MacCulloch ed. of *Pol. Econ. and Taxation*, p. 374 n.

[3] *Ibid.*, p. 371.

[4] So Prof. Rogers ascribes the high rents of the seventeenth and eighteenth centuries very largely to the low wages; higher ones would have "reduced rent first, and profits afterwards."—*Six Centuries*, p. 482; cf. pp. 480 and 492.

the wages of labour,—such agricultural improvements or such increase of the cultivator's exertions as will diminish the number of labourers needed,—or such an increase in the prices of produce from increased demand as will increase the difference between the expense of production and the price of produce.[1] Ricardo, on the other hand, says that profits can never be reduced by mere accumulation of capital or competition of capitals, but only by the progressively less fruitful character of the investments to be found for capital as accumulation goes on. As long as there is fertile land to be had, yielding a rich return to capital, no one will accept a poor return. "If in the progress of countries in wealth and population new portions of fertile land can be added to such countries with every increase of capital, profits would never fall nor rents rise."[2] In things as they are, capital soon accumulates beyond the rich investments and has to take the poorer. Sooner or later, even in a new colony, a point is reached where fertile land will not supply food enough for the growing population except at an increased cost.[3] Now, if the supply is absolutely required, the most costly portion of it, whether it be got by an extension of cultivation to poorer lands, or by a more thorough cultivation of the richer, will determine the price of all the rest,

[1] *Pol. Econ.* (1820), p. 161 (ch. iii. sect. iii.).

[2] *Pol. Econ. and Taxation*, pp. 373, 375, 379-80; cf. pp. 71 and 72, but especially 68 ft. Malthus on the whole follows Adam Smith, I. ix.; Mill has followed Ricardo.

[3] So far as the account is meant to be historical, it must be corrected by Carey. See above, p. 65.

for there cannot be two prices in the same market; and the profits of the producer of it will determine the profits of all his fellow-cultivators, for there cannot be two rates of profit in the same business. Furthermore, the agricultural profits will determine the rate in other businesses, for in a full-formed society the rate in the others must bear a fixed relation to the rate in this business, so that the one cannot materially vary without the other.[1] Therefore the greater cost of the last portion of the necessary supply of food will lower profits generally, will thereby increase the range of extra profits from the richer soils, and will thereby raise rents.

The difference between the two men is, that what Malthus makes only one cause, Ricardo makes the only one, the increased cost of cultivation.[2] Ricardo and his friends have certainly put cause for effect.[3] It is of course in the first instance the high prices that lead to the costly cultivation, and not *vice versâ*, for without the high prices the produce of the costly cultivation would not be profitable.

Malthus was asked by the Committee on Emigration: "Among other effects of resorting to a soil inferior to any now in cultivation, which is involved in the proposition of cultivating waste lands, would not one be to raise the rents of all the landlords

[1] Ricardo, *l. c.* p. 372 and n. Cf. below. He appeals to Adam Smith's principle of compensation (*Wealth of Nations*, I. x.).

[2] Rogers (*Six Centuries*, p. 352) goes so far the other way as to make improvements the only cause of an increase of rent, though the passage should be read with p. 480, and especially pp. 482 and 492.

[3] *E. g.* Mrs. Fawcett, *Pol. Econ. for Beginners*, pp. 65, 66; and even West, on *Rent*, p. 50.

throughout Great Britain and Ireland?"—He answered: "I think not. The cultivating of poor lands is not the cause of the rise of rents; the rise of the price of produce compared with the costs of production, which is the cause of the rise of rents, takes place first, and then such rise induces the cultivation of the poorer land. That is the doctrine I originally stated, and I believe it to be true; it was altered by others afterwards." [1]

On the other hand, what makes the high prices permanent instead of temporary, is the fact that the cultivation essential to the completeness of the supply cannot be other than costly.[2] It is, therefore, not wrong to consider costly cultivation as one cause of the permanence of high prices, and therewith of high rents. But Ricardo goes further, and counts it the only cause.

Through the whole progress of society, he says, profits are regulated by the difficulty or facility of procuring food; and, "if the smallness of profits do not check accumulation, there are hardly any limits to the rise of rent and the fall of profit." Nothing can increase the general rate of profit but the cheapening of food;[3] as by improvements in agriculture, which, by securing the same production with less labour, for the time increase the profits and lower the rents.[4] The landlord's interest is therefore at all

[1] *3rd Report*, 1827, p. 321, qu. 3341. Cf. Perr. Thompson, *True Theory of Rent*, pp. 8, 12, 34, &c. (1832, 9th ed.).

[2] *Tract on Value*, p. 6.

[3] Ricardo, *Low Price of Corn*, &c., *Works*, pp. 373, 380, 381, &c.

[4] *Ibid.*, pp. 377, 379.

times opposed to that of every other class in the community,[1] for it means dear food, low profits, and high rents. Still, high rents are not the cause either of the dear food or the low profits, but are, equally with them, the effect of a common cause, more costly cultivation. The effect of a costly cultivation on wages might seem *vi terminorum* to be a raising of them, for wages depend on the proportion of the supply of labourers to capital's demand[2] for them, and by assumption there was a greater demand. But since the cause of the rise of price was in the first instance an increase of population, it follows that the increased cost of raising the most costly supplies of corn will be incurred not by higher payment of old labourers, but by employment of new. Wages again will buy less corn, for corn has risen. "While the price of corn rises ten per cent., wages will always rise less than ten per cent., but rent will always rise more; the condition of the labourer will generally decline, and that of the landlord will always be improved."[3] In his statement of the doctrine of wages, Ricardo is perhaps more careful in 1815 than he is in 1817, saying that, "as experience demonstrates that capital and population alternately take the lead, and wages in consequence are liberal or scanty, nothing can be positively laid down respecting profits as far as wages are concerned."[4] But even in 1817 his exposition is hardly more rigid than that of Malthus

[1] Ricardo, *Works*, l. c. p. 378.
[2] *Pol. Econ. and Tax.*, ibid. pp. 50 *seq.*, esp. pp. 54, 55.
[3] *l. c.* p. 55 ft.
[4] *Low Price*, &c., *ibid.*, p. 379.

himself. So far is he from recognizing an iron law driving wages down to "the natural price" or bare necessaries, that he thinks the market rate may be constantly above the natural for an indefinite period, and he regards the natural itself as expansive. The whole chapter on wages[1] shows a just understanding of the *Essay on Population*. Nevertheless, if Ricardo in one sense made too much of the principle of population in relation to Rent, in another sense he made too little of it. He does not see that in a progressive country it counteracts the tendency of improvements in agriculture to cheapen produce, and thereby reduce rents;[2] agricultural rents have risen since 1846 largely because of high farming. He does not grant that high or low wages can affect rent, because he regards them as purely relative to profits, and making with profits a total amount, of which only the proportions vary; but it is difficult to believe that the rise in agricultural wages since 1873 or so can have failed to play a part in keeping down farmers' rents since that date. As, however, our view of the power or powerlessness of lowered profits or lowered wages to increase rent will be found to depend on our view of the causes of value, and as the difference of the two economists on the relation of wages to profits might have the appearance of a technical subtlety, these two items of the total may be passed by for the present.

In regard to agricultural improvements the issue seemed plainer, and the evidence seemed all for Ricardo

[1] *Pol. Econ. and Tax.*, ch. v.; cf. Malthus, *Pol. Econ.* (1820), p. 230.
[2] But cf. *Works*, p. 377 n.

and against Malthus. In a country depending chiefly on itself for grain, a general adoption of improvements would seem to make supplies cheaper because less costly, and therefore to lower rents because forcing farmers to lower prices. Even Mr. Mill did not break away from Ricardianism at this point,[1] though he speaks less unreservedly than Ricardo upon it. Malthus, on the other hand, who regards rent as depending largely on the ability of the agricultural supply to create its own demand, regards rent, accordingly, as at all times keeping pace with the increase of grain caused by improvements, unless the improvements outrun population. What cheapness does in other cases is to make an article accessible to a circle of buyers previously excluded from it. Every one is a buyer of agricultural produce and no one is excluded; but the temporary cheapness of grain creates new buyers by making marriage accessible to a wider circle.

The progress of rents in fact results from the conflict of two economical tendencies—the tendency of economical expedients to lower prices, and the tendency of an increasing population to raise them. If Malthus' ripest view of population be true, then a cheapening of food among a civilized people by no means leads to a corresponding increase of their numbers, and therefore the course of improvement would tend so far towards a diminution of price, and

[1] *Pol. Econ.*, IV. iii. § 4. Cf. Walker, *Land and its Rent*, pp. 177-81, though it has been pointed out that on p. 178 that writer omits Mill's qualifying phrase, (improvements) "suddenly made."

therewith of rent. If rents depended on the price of corn alone, economical expedients (including not only the direct aids to tillage, mechanical and chemical inventions directly applied to it, but the indirect aids, free trade, railways, and steamers) must certainly have lowered rents in the last hundred years. But the reverse is true,[1] chiefly because the produce of a farm is ceasing to mean wheat, and coming more and more to mean cattle and dairy produce, which have not fallen but risen in price in one hundred years, while corn has actually fallen. This variety of productions has proved financially an equivalent to what Malthus (seventy years ago) considered the main cause of greater extra profits to the farmer and greater money rents to the landlord—the increased fertility of the soil in the matter of grain, and an increased price keeping pace with it.

The commercial policy of England has become what Malthus describes in the latter part of the *Essay on Population* as a combination of the agricultural and the commercial systems. His views on this subject became modified as he grew older. In the second edition he says:[2] "Two nations might increase exactly with the same rapidity in the exchangeable value of the annual produce of their land and labour; yet . . . in that which had applied itself chiefly to agriculture, the poor would live in greater plenty, and population would rapidly increase; in that which

[1] See Sir James Caird's table appended to *Landed Interest* (1878). Cf. Cairne's *Essays in Pol. Ec.*, vi. p. 216.

[2] Bk. III. ch. vii. p. 429.

had applied itself chiefly to commerce, the poor would be comparatively but little benefited, and consequently population would either be stationary or increase very slowly." "In the history of the world the nations whose wealth has been derived principally from manufactures and commerce have been perfectly ephemeral beings compared with those the basis of whose wealth has been agriculture. It is in the nature of things that a state which subsists upon a revenue furnished by other countries must be infinitely more exposed to all the accidents of time and chance than one which produces its own."[1] It is not, he thinks, because of her trade, but because of her agriculture that England is so rich in resources; it is not without danger that our commercial policy has diverted capital from agriculture into manufacture and commerce. About the middle of the eighteenth century we were strictly an agricultural nation, and we were safe, for in a country whose commerce and manufacture increase from and with the improvement in agriculture there is no discoverable germ of decay. But all is changed now; and there is reason to fear that our prosperity is temporary, and we have only risen by the depression of other nations.[2] When the nations that now supply us with cheap corn shall have prospered like ourselves and increased their population till corn is dear among them, then we shall be ruined. The evils of scarcity are so dreadful that it is worth our while to give special encourage-

[1] *Essay*, 2nd ed., Bk. III. ch. viii. p. 437.
[2] *Ibid.*, l. c. ch. ix. pp. 443 *seq.*.

ments to agriculture, and, in order to be certain to have enough, to have in general too much.[1] Otherwise "we shall be laid so bare to the shafts of fortune that nothing but a miracle can save us from being struck."[2] "If England continues yearly her importations of corn, she cannot ultimately escape that decline which seems to be the natural and necessary consequence of excessive commercial wealth; and the growing prosperity of those countries which supply her with corn must in the end diminish her population, her riches, and her power,"—not indeed in the next twenty or thirty years, but "in the next two hundred or three hundred."[3] In 1803 Malthus had much in common with the author of *Great Britain independent of Commerce*, to say nothing of the French economists. He cannot be said to have entirely lost the bias in favour of Agriculture in later years. In the *Political Economy*, reviewing the last five centuries of English work and wages,[4] he tries to explain away the instances where rising prices of corn and an "influx of bullion" seem to have injured the condition of the labourer; and there can be little doubt he was indirectly answering an objection to Corn Laws. When depreciation of the currency, whether through American discoveries or suspensions of cash payment, has occurred, the rebound from it (he says) has made prices fall much more than wages, and so (we are to infer), when prices

[1] *Essay*, Bk. III. ch. ix. p. 450. [2] *Ibid.*, ch. x. p. 465.
[3] *Ibid.*, Bk. V. ch. x. p. 468 n.
[4] *Pol. Econ.* (1820), pp. 227 *seq.*, (1836) pp. 240 *seq.*

are kept high, wages will follow. It may be doubted if he had weighed the full consequences of such a contention in the light of his own principles of free trade. Professor Rogers[1] has had the valuable aid of old College accounts. Malthus had little besides Eden, Arthur Young, and the Reports to the Board of Agriculture; and it is doubtful if he fully understood the effects on the labourer of Henry VII.'s debasement of the currency, or could apply the analogy to the depreciation in his own day.[2] But on the whole, as years went on, he became less physiocratic. He came to acknowledge that, if a purely agricultural country might in some cases, like America, be the best possible for the labourer, it might in other cases, like Poland or Ireland, be the worst possible for him.

[1] *Six Centuries of Work and Wages*, ch. xii., esp. p. 345.

[2] The facts of Malthus' "review" may be roughly given in the following diagram, where the bar indicates the wheat earned per day by the agricultural labourer. The amount for 1350 assumes that the Statute of Labourers was successful.

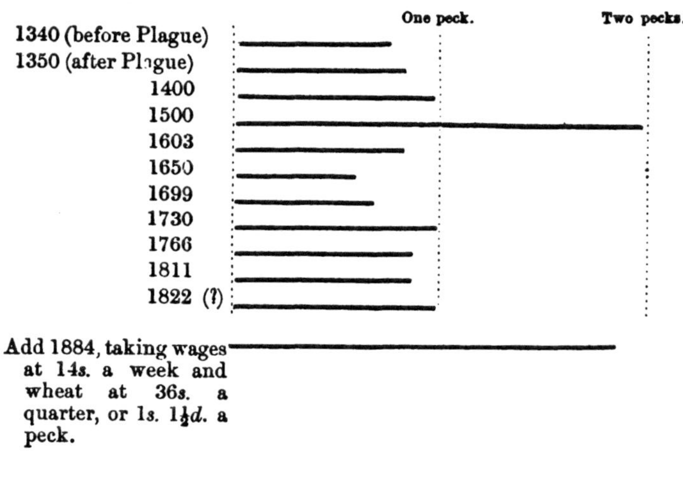

If we hear that the labourer in one country earns in a year fifteen and in another nine quarters of wheat, we cannot be sure that the former is the better off till we know the value of other things in the country in comparison with wheat. If manufactures were very dear in comparison, then the labourer's wages except in food would go very little way, unless in a case like America, where the quantity is so great that it makes up for the little value of corn wages. In Poland the value of corn is so low, and there is so little capital in the country, that the high corn wages mean low real wages, and the population is either stationary or very slow in its increase. The prosperity of an agricultural country, then, depends on other causes than the direction of its attention to the one industry of agriculture, and without knowing these we could not infer or predict it.[1]

Malthus in fact reached the point at which he was always glad to arrive, the medium between two extreme views.[2] He would neither approve of a purely agricultural nation, whose danger was want of capital, nor of a purely commercial, whose danger was want of food. In a purely commercial, everything depends on a superiority in industry, machinery, and trade, which from the nature of things cannot last. Not only foreign but domestic competition will

[1] 7th ed., pp. 321 *seq.* (Bk. III. ch. viii.), first in 1817.

[2] Cf. above, p. 225 n. In *Pol. Econ.* (1820), p. 432, he says, "All the great results in *Pol. Econ.* respecting wealth depend upon proportions." 2nd ed. added (p. 376), "not only there, but throughout the whole range of nature and art." So he thinks a peck of wheat a good "middle point" of daily wages. *Pol. Econ.* (1820), p. 284, (1836) p. 254.

bring down profits, and thereby, by discouraging saving and enterprise, diminish the demand for labour and bring the population to a standstill. Christendom has seen Venice, Bruges, Holland lose their trade by their neighbours' gain.[1] To say that the nations of the world ought to be allowed to develope their trade as freely as the provinces of a single empire, is, in his opinion, to overlook the reality of political obstacles. If England were still separated into the kingdoms of the Heptarchy, London could not be what it is. The interest of a province and the interest of an independent state are never the same.[2] To one who believes political divisions inevitable, there can be little hope for universal free trade. Malthus is unable to rise to the cosmopolitan view of Cobden, and he never seems to see that by ignoring political barriers free trade may really weaken them. His ideal is a state which combines agriculture and commerce in equal proportions.[3] The prosperity of the latter implies the decay of feudalism and the establishment of secure government; with security comes the spontaneous extension of enterprise and a steady demand for labour. Since the two great classes of producers provide a market for each other, wealth will constantly grow, and without risk of sudden check by a foreign influence. The prosperity of such a country may (he thinks) last practically for ever, and we might answer in the affirmative for our own country the query of Bishop

[1] *Essay*, 7th ed., Bk. III. ch. ix. pp. 328 *seq.* Cf. pp. 334, 338.
[2] *Ibid.*, p. 332.
[3] *Ibid.*, Bk. III. ch. x. pp. 334 *seq.*

Berkeley about his.[1] "The countries which unite great landed resources with a prosperous state of commerce and manufactures, and in which the commercial part of the population never essentially exceeds the agricultural part, are eminently secure from sudden reverses. Their increasing wealth seems to be out of the reach of all common accidents, and there is no reason to say that they might not go on increasing in riches and population for hundreds, nay almost thousands of years."[2] They would go on in fact till they reached the extreme practical limits of population, which under the system of private property would mean such a state of the land as would "enable the last employed labourers to produce the maintenance of as many probably as four persons," the man, his wife, and two children. As soon as the labour ceases to produce more than this, it ceases to be worth the employer's while to give the wages and employ the labour. These practical limits are far from the limits of the earth's power to produce food, and a Government which compelled every member of society to devote himself wholly to the raising of food and necessaries, would succeed in coming nearer to those farther limits, though at the expense of everything we mean by civilization.[3] As a matter of fact, even the practical limit is not approached by way of a uniform decline of profits and of population. Various causes, acting at irregular intervals, stave off the event. The decline of general

[1] See above, p. 201 n. Cf. *Essay on Pop.*, 7th ed., p. 337.
[2] *Essay*, l. c. p. 338.
[3] *l. c.* Bk. III. ch. x. pp. 338-9.

profits, the introduction of long leases and large farming, would bring more capital to the land; improvements in agriculture will increase the produce, inventions in manufacture will lessen the cost of the agriculturist's comforts, and make his wages and profits go farther; the opening of a foreign market may raise home prices; a temporary rise in the value of agricultural produce may stimulate the investment of capital in farming. So Malthus concludes, for reasons not unlike Cliffe Leslie's,[1] that, though there is a tendency of profits to fall, yet the tendency is often defeated. Though there is much truth still in many of his statements, the conclusion he draws from them,[2] that we ought by a judicious system of corn duties and corn bounties to keep the price of food steady and secure a large home supply, is quite out of court now. The variations in price have been under free trade very moderate; and the supply from one quarter or another has never failed us. Free trade is no longer among our problems.

It must be added, however, that there is no reason why the "practical limits" should not exist under a paternal or fraternal socialism as well as under the present social system. Even if industry were initiated and directed not by individuals but socialistically by Government, the sole motive need not be to increase the mere numbers of the people, and therefore the mere total quantity of food needed for

[1] *Fortnightly Review*, Nov. 1881, his last writing. Cf. *Essay*, l. c. pp. 340—342.

[2] In two long chapters on Corn Laws and Bounties, *Essay on Pop.*, Bk. III. ch. xi. pp. 343—367. Cf. above, pp. 226 *seq.*

a bare life. The motive of socialistic government would be to secure a high degree of comfort, not a bare subsistence, for all; and therefore, at the cost of a limitation of numbers, society would still remain at a distance from its greatest possible production of food. Whether such a limitation of numbers is likely to take place in the reconstituted society is discussed elsewhere.[1]

[1] See below, Bk. IV.

CHAPTER II.

THE WORKING MAN.

Measure of Value, 1823—In what sense Labour a Measure—Difficulties—Arguments of the Tract on Value—Measure in the same Country—Measure in different Countries—Measure at different Periods in the same—Measure as applied to varying Value of Currency—The Royal Literary Society—The *Definitions*—Wages—The Minimum of Social different from the Minimum of Physical Necessaries—High Wages, how made Permanent—The "Wages Fund," whose Invention, and how far a Reality—"The New School of Political Economy," its three Tenets—A General Glut in what Sense possible.

As the Rent and Corn pamphlets deal chiefly with Mother Earth, the tract on the Measure of Value[1] deals chiefly with Father Work. The search for a common measure of value is not, to Malthus, a purely academical problem. He considers such a measure desirable because in any inquiry into the wealth of nations it is important to distinguish between the rise of one commodity and the fall of another. The former is an intrinsic alteration of value which will affect every exchange in which the object is concerned; the latter an extrinsic which affects only the one exchange, of the object in

[1] *The Measure of Value stated and illustrated, with an application of it to the alteration in the value of the English currency since* 1790. (April) 1823.

question with the foreign object that has been altered. By value of course is to be understood economic value, or "the power of commanding other objects in exchange," not value in the (not uncommon) wider sense, of usefulness in supplying wants.[1] The economic value of anything, taken in relation to some object which never changes its value from intrinsic causes, may be called the "natural or absolute value" of that thing, and the object with which it was compared may be called the "measure" of absolute or natural value, in other words, of the value which a thing must fetch if its supply is to be continued. While not only money but any and every object may be such a measure of value for a limited place and time, even money itself is not a good measure for widely different places or for long periods of time; and corn, which is better for long periods, is worse for short.

Labour is better than either, but Labour is ambiguous. We may measure the value of anything either by the labour it has cost us in the making of it, which gives us Ricardo's sense of natural value, or by the labour it will purchase after it is made. Adam Smith,[2] who preferred labour both to money and corn as the measure of value, wavered between these two meanings of the terms. Malthus declares at once against the first sense. Labour, he says, in the sense of cost does not altogether determine value and

[1] So *Tract on Value*, p. 1. But in *Definitions* value is "the relation of one object to some other or others, in exchange, resulting from the estimation in which a thing is held" (def. 40, 41; cf. with def. 5).

[2] Adam Smith, *Wealth of Nations*, I. v.

therefore cannot measure it, even for similar places and times. In 1820 Malthus had been of opinion that a mean between corn and labour was a better measure of value than labour itself; but since 1823 he recurred to the view of Adam Smith,[1] and held that the amount of the unskilled common day labour of the agricultural labourer, which a thing will purchase or command, is a good measure of the value of it even at widely different places and times. "Agricultural labour is taken for the obvious reasons that it is the commonest species of labour, that it directly produces the food of the labourer, and that it is the most immediately connected with the gradations of soil and the necessary variations of profits. It is also assumed with Adam Smith, Mr. Ricardo, and other political economists, that, on an average, other kinds of labour continue to bear the same proportions to agricultural labour."[2] The bodily exertion of the labourer does not change; it is the same sweat of the brow, the same sacrifice of physical force. When corn, for example, will command a less amount of labour than it would have done a century before, we may be sure it is because of a change not in the labour but in the corn; and we ought therefore to say not that labour has risen in value, but that corn has fallen. Malthus' search for a permanent element in the changeable has led him to individual human labour as the economical unit. If

[1] *Measure of Value*, p. 23. Cf. *Pol. Econ.* (1820), pp. 126 *seq.*; (1836), pp. 84, 93 *seq.*

[2] *Measure of Value*, p. 20 n. On pp. 23-4 he adds, "taking the average of summer and winter wages."

the Chinese labourer has lower wages than the English, it is not because his labour is of lower value, but because his necessaries are of higher. Wages are higher in the United States not because labour is of higher value, but because necessaries are of lower.[1] Of course when skill enters into the labour, the unit is not the same; but, when we look only at unskilled, we find confirmation of Malthus' view in the experience of the elder and the younger Brassey as employers of labour, that quantity for quantity "the cost of the labour [the expense of it to the employer] is the same everywhere" over the world.[2] The measure, however, is by no means out of court as regards skilled labour; the difference in kind may be stated in terms of a difference in degree. If the watchmaker's labour be paid at the rate of 10*s.* a day, and the common agricultural labourer's only at 1*s.* 8*d.*, the former may be stated as equivalent to six days' common labour.[3] Malthus has in his mind a scale of compensation such as is drawn out by Adam Smith in the tenth chapter of the first book of the *Wealth of Nations*.[4] Disagreeableness, difficulty, inconstancy, responsibility, risk of failure, are so many disabilities, for each of which a compensation must be made to the workman in the scale of his wages, as adding in effect so many more hours' labour; and each higher class of workman must be

[1] See below, p. 268. *Pol. Econ.* (1820), p. 125; (1836) p. 102, &c.; *Tract on Value*, passim.

[2] *Work and Wages*, ch. iii. p. 75. Malthus, *Pol. Econ.*, 2nd ed., pp. 108 *seq.*

[3] Cf. Marx, *Kapital*, pp. 19, 21, &c.

[4] MacC.'s ed., pp. 45 *seq.* Cf. *Tract on Value*, p. 20 n., above quoted.

paid the unit of common labourer's wages, with the compensations superadded. In practice this means that men will not be found in sufficient numbers to do the higher class work unless the wages are sufficient to make it worth their while to undergo the disabilities. It is assumed that this scale has been adjusted by custom and the "higgling of the market" from generation to generation, till in any given neighbourhood each of the several skilled trades has a definitely recognized place in the series.[1]

This reasoning seems less convincing when we consider that the translation of skill into terms of hours would be different in different localities, and that the common labour, which is the unit, would vary in the same way. The measure of value would hold only for a given place, time, and people. To escape from the difficulty, we must consider the difference between the common labour at one time and place and the common labour at another as itself measurable, and allow for it; or else we must consider it as too small to disturb our conclusions, and so neglect it altogether. To reduce common labour to its theoretically simplest terms is to reduce it to something below our experience; and to reduce it to its actually simplest in the given cases is to reduce it to one thing in England, a second in France, a third in India, a fourth in America. There are differences of quality which cannot be with any certainty resolved into differences of quantity; such are the differences of individuals, the differences of nations, the differences

[1] Cf. Ricardo, *Pol. Econ.*, *Works* (ed. MacC.), p. 15.

of races. It will be found, also, that the part played by common as opposed to skilled labour, and by agricultural as opposed to manufacturing labour, differs so much between country and country that, in order to use labour as a measure, we should need other measures in addition to it. In short, if we had data enough to apply this measure, we should have data enough to dispense with it.

It was possibly the force of these considerations that led Malthus, as time went on, to approach somewhat nearer to Ricardo, whose measure, so far as he had one, was not the labour purchased but the labour that entered into cost. But he adhered to the substance of his doctrine as expressed in the tract; and his positions, in detail, were as follows:—

The power of one object to command another in exchange is influenced either by a change in the object itself, or by a change in the other. If we found a case where there was never a change in the first object itself, then we should have, in that first, a measure of natural or absolute as opposed to nominal or relative value, *i. e.* a measure of that value of an article which satisfies the "conditions of the supply" of it, and enables its production to be continued without loss to the producers. By "conditions of supply" is meant Ricardo's "cost of production" with the addition of ordinary profits. No measure of market or relative values is possible; and to have a measure of natural value itself we must make two postulates,—that natural value depends on "labour and profits" (*sic*), on rent little if at all, and that the "wages" of labour are also the "value" of labour,—what labour is paid is also what labour will fetch. It is easy to apply the measure where *only* labour is concerned, for then the labour that the things *cost* is a sufficient measure; it would be evident, at any change, that the things had become cheaper, not the labour dearer. But in present society value is more complicated; labour is no doubt the chief source of it, but profits are a very considerable one.[1] The natural conditions of supply, however, may be stated in terms of labour, just as if labour had been the sole ingredient. This would give us a measure for the *same* country at the same place and time. The total quantity of labour that an article cost, with the addition of ordinary profits stated in terms of labour, would be the same as that quantity of labour which an article would purchase at its natural value.

In the case of *different* countries, at the same time, the difficulties are not quite the same. Exchange is there determined not by labour but by money prices; and money is of very different value in the one country and in the other. But the differences in the value of money in different countries are in proportion to the different prices of agricultural labour—1500 days' labour at 4*d*. a day in India, at 2*s*. in England, meaning £25 and £150 respectively; and, if fixed capital to the value of 300 days' labour were advanced to each of them, while profits calculated in days' labour were twenty per cent. in the one case, ten

[1] *Meas. of Value*, pp. 8—12.

in the other, the result would be an article whose conditions of supply would require in the one case a money price of £31, in the other of £168. The difference is no doubt due to the superior efficiency of English industry and skill which enables England to purchase the precious metals more cheaply,[1] but the cost of getting the money would not tell us the true present value of the money in England or in India. It is not the labour spent on the gold, but the labour purchased by it, that will help us here. In each country within itself we would measure the natural value of money as well as of anything else by what labour it will purchase; know the difference between the value of money in the one and its value in the other by the difference between the amount of labour it will purchase in the one case and the amount it will purchase in the other.[2]

In the case of *different periods in the same country*, though we have not, as in the case of two different countries, the test of an actual exchange, we can still use labour as the measure. We must allow for the higher profits of the earlier period; and on the (Ricardian) principle that profits and wages vary inversely, though corn wages have risen, profits have in proportion fallen, and the total value of the produce measured by its power of purchasing labour must be the same,[3] the purchased labour then representing the producing labour plus

[1] *Meas. of Value*, pp. 22, 65. Cf. Cairnes, *Australian Episode*, in *Essays in Pol. Econ.* (pp. 92 *seq.*; cf. pp. 37, 61), (1873),—first published in *Fraser's Mag.*, Sept. 1859.

[2] *Meas. of Value*, p. 23.

[3] *Ibid.*, pp. 27—29.

the then rate of profits. From Ricardo's dogma it seems (to Malthus) to follow directly that the value of labour is constant.[1] Taking the labour they will purchase as the best measure of the value of the precious metals, as of anything else, we have light on one of the pressing questions of the day (in 1823), the causes of the changing value of money. The causes affect not the labour but the money, and they are of two kinds. The first Malthus describes as a primary or necessary cause, namely, the variation in profits depending on the (Ricardian) theory of the interlocking of wages and profits, and the (Malthusian) theory of the relation of profits to rent. Dear corn due to difficult cultivation would lower profits, and would alter the value of money, but only in relation to raw, not in relation to manufactured produce, or at least (from the effects of Ricardo's principle of the inverse variation of wages and profits) not to the same extent. But the second, which is a "secondary and incidental" class of causes, affects both raw and manufactured goods, and is often enough to completely dwarf the effects of the primary cause;[2]—it is the general commercial situation of a country,—"the fertility and vicinity of the mines, the different efficiency of labour in different countries, the abundance or scarcity of exportable commodities, and the state of the demand and supply of commodities and labour compared with" the precious metals.[3] The

[1] *Meas. of Value*, p. 29 n.

[2] He might have said simply that the one is intrinsic, the other extrinsic, in relation to the agricultural products themselves.

[3] *Meas. of Value*, p. 63.

efficiency of labour and a prosperous commerce, with a great consequent demand for corn and labour, are often more powerful in making bullion cheap than agricultural productiveness and high profits in making bullion dear and corn cheap. During the war—say from 1790 to 1814—we had an instance of this, and since the war—say from 1814 to 1823—we have had a clear instance, he thinks, of the converse.[1]

Two elaborate papers on the measure of value, written in 1825 and 1827, show that Malthus was becoming inclined to make less of his differences with Ricardo.[2] They were intimate friends; their discussions had no bitterness; and, to use the words of one of them, "both were so anxious for the truth that sooner or later they would have agreed."[3] These papers are a fulfilment of his duty not (as we might guess) as a fellow of the Royal Society or a member of the Political Economy Club,[4] but as an associate of the Royal Society of Literature.[5] "That branch of literature" [*sic*] "on which it shall be his duty to communicate with the Society once a year at least" is described as "political economy and statistics."[6] He does little credit in these papers to his literary faculty. Their composition is laboured and devoid

[1] *Meas. of Value*, pp. 67 *seq.* Cf. below, pp. 283 *seq.*

[2] Who allows cost to play a greater part in value. Cf. below, pp. 278-9. But Ricardo, *Pol. Econ.*, sect. vi. p. 28, disclaims belief in *any* universal measure of value.

[3] Malthus, quoted by Empson, *Edin. Rev.*, Jan. 1837, p. 499.

[4] He was F.R.S. 1819, and a member of Pol. Econ. Club at its foundation in 1821.

[5] 4th May, 1825; 7th Nov., 1827. *Transactions of R. S. L.*, vol. i. part i. p. 171.

[6] *Report of R. S. L.*, 1824, p. 21.

of ornament. The first is *On the Measure of the Conditions necessary to the Supply of Commodities;* and the thesis is, that "the natural and necessary conditions of the supply of all commodities," that are not monopolies, are represented and measured by the labour which they will on an average command, and by nothing else. The second is *On the Meaning which is most usually and most correctly attached to the term, Value of Commodities;* and the thesis is, that, when value is used without a qualifying adjective or reference to any special equivalent in a possible exchange,[1] the term refers to the "conditions of supply." When we say, for example, anything is sold at a price far above its true value, we mean far above its cost price, including under "cost" the average rate of profits that must go to the maker if he is to live by his trade. The two papers taken together form a sort of indirect proof of the position taken up in the tract on the *Measure of Value* (1823), and the relevant parts of the second edition of the *Political Economy* (1836), and may be stated briefly thus:—The labour commanded by an article is generally the measure of that article's cost;—but that article's cost is what people generally mean by its value;—therefore the labour commanded by an article is the measure of that article's value in the ordinary sense of the word.

The second paper was written at the same time as the *Definitions in Political Economy*, and illustrates

[1] We might expressly wish to know a coat's value in money or its value in cutlery or coals. The Professor at the Breakfast-table talks of "Madeira worth from two to six Bibles a bottle."

the rule laid down there, prescribing adherence, when possible, to the meaning which economical terms bear in the mouths of ordinary folk.[1] The *Definitions*, for example, repeat from (or with) the second paper, "when no second object is specified, the value of the commodity naturally refers to the causes" which determine "the estimation in which it is held" "and the object which measures it."[2] "The natural value of a commodity at any place and time" is "the estimation in which it is held when it is in its natural and ordinary state," as "determined by the elementary costs of its production," or in other words, by "the conditions of its supply." And the measure of the natural value of a commodity at any place and time is "the quantity of labour for which it will exchange at that place and time when it is in its natural and ordinary state."[3]

As a literary production the book written for the public is superior to the papers prepared for the men of letters. Next to the first *Essay on Population*, the critical parts of the *Definitions* give the most pleasant examples of the author's style. The two papers above mentioned are chiefly important as showing the importance which Malthus, unlike Ricardo, attached to the question of a measure of value.[4] A contemporary writer said very happily that the fault of Ricardo was

[1] *Definitions* (1827), p. 235.

[2] I. e. *to* the object which measures that *cost-value*.

[3] *Ibid.*, p. 243.

[4] See above, p. 254. Ricardo's long correspondence with Malthus on the subject is mentioned by Empson, *Edin. Rev.*, l. c. p. 469. Empson's extracts from it are the most valuable part of his article.

to generalize too much, and of Malthus to generalize too little. Malthus, he added, is a keen observer but poor in analysis; he is "so occupied with particulars that he neglects that inductive process which extends individual experience throughout the infinitude of things," and converts knowledge into science. "As presented by Mr. Ricardo, political economy possesses a regularity and simplicity beyond what exists in nature; as exhibited by Mr. Malthus, it is a chaos of original but unconnected elements."[1] On the other hand, the testimony of a recent German writer is very different. Malthus, he tells us, resembles Ricardo in his sombre view of human life and frank statement of unpleasant facts. Their names are often associated, and no doubt both are children of their times. But their leanings were really unlike. Ricardo took up certain ideas of his time in their narrowest, clearest, and harshest form, and applied them wholly in the interest of capital. Malthus is far less narrow. His influence on economics has been much smaller than Ricardo's; but he will be found "by far the more suggestive and less prejudiced of the two," and, if he found more opponents, it is because he was less understood and less read.[2] The sprightly *Dialogues*[3] of De Quincey contribute nothing to the discussion on value; but they show

[1] R. Torrens, *Production of Wealth*, 1821, pp. iv, v.

[2] Held, *Sociale Geschichte Englands*, p. 205.

[3] *Dialogues of Three Templars on Political Economy*, 1824 (*Works*, Black, 1863, vol. iv.). All depends on the assumption in the middle of Dialogue I. p. 196, ("it is Mr. Ricardo's doctrine that," &c.), and on the confinement of the discussion to natural value (p. 198).

how completely Ricardo had won the ear of the literary world, and how little pains the opponents of Malthus took to do him justice. Malthus reduced the problem to many elements; Ricardo to few; and the latter, as certainly easier to understand, was readily represented as the likelier to be true. Simplicity in such a case is a treacherous virtue; and the apparent chaos may have been much nearer the truth than the apparent cosmos, if there was a hidden flaw in the latter and a latent principle of union in the former. Sound or unsound, such a principle may be traced in the most abstract discussions of Malthus. We shall find this true when we compare his views with Ricardo's on the nature and causes of value itself, and the movements of prices. We may recognize it even in these discussions on the measure of value. The measurement of all value by individual human labour is of a piece with the author's final view of population, where all is made to depend on individual responsibility. The main weakness of the position is perhaps that by unskilled labour he means always agricultural, and does not sufficiently recognize how in manufacturing England it has perhaps become easier to measure unskilled by skilled than the latter by the former. The difficulty met Robert Owen, when in his *Labour Exchanges*[2] he not only tried to reduce all values to a common measure in labour, but to make labour a means of

[1] *Measure of Value*, p. 20 n.

[2] London, 1832; Birmingham, 1833. The Constituent Assembly applied the same measure, but in a different way, in 1791. See Roscher, *National ökon.* (1879), p. 298.

exchange, for which it is certainly worse suited than money.

Labour as something to be rewarded by Wages has a more evident connection with the principles of the *Essay on Population* than labour as the measure of all values. In this case unskilled agricultural labour is again the unit. The first "condition of the supply" of this labour is the necessaries of life, in such quantities as will enable the labourers to maintain their numbers or to increase them,[1] as the case may be. If the former only, the price of labour is not, as Ricardo says, the "natural," but really a most unnatural price, for it would mean that the country giving it had arrived at the final limit of its resources.[2] Necessaries, however, are not a simple or even a fixed element. We can of course measure them in corn if we like; but they consist not only of the prime necessary, the staff of life, but of other absolute necessaries, of shelter and clothing, and many "conveniences" which have become necessaries, inasmuch as they are essential to healthy life, such as soap and shoes and candle-light. It has happily become a truism that the necessaries of life are not a fixed but an expanding factor. Even if competition were always to drive wages down to a "minimum of social necessaries,"[3] social are always beyond animal necessaries; our basest beggars are in the poorest thing

[1] The words are, "enable the labourers to maintain a stationary or an increasing population" (*Pol. Econ.*, 1836, p. 218). The awkwardness of the sentence may be due to bad editing; but we read elsewhere of the "*price* of *wages*."

[2] *Pol. Econ.*, 1836, pp. 218, 223.

[3] See Lassalle and Marx.

superfluous; and "the barest social necessaries" seem likely in process of time to mean a high standard of comfort. To raise the minimum of social necessaries is the way to raise wages really, universally, and almost irrevocably.[1] Malthus himself declares that "it is the diffusion of luxury" in this sense of the word, "among the mass of the people, and not an excess of it in a few," that seems to be advantageous, both for national wealth and national happiness. Paley's ideal of national prosperity, "a laborious frugal people ministering to the demands of an opulent luxurious nation," is heartily scouted by him. The luxuries of the few rich, he says, harass the industry of the poor by varying with the fashion; but the luxuries of the poor, when embodied in their general standard of living, are not only the best kind of check to population, but the steadiest encouragement to general trade.[2] He seems to have supposed the elevation in the standard of living to have been effected, like the progress of nations in civilization, by the happy improvement of an accidental advantage, by the retention of high wages, when once secured in a time of brisk trade in the ordinary way of competition; the workmen, in short, succeeded in making permanent and *de jure* a change once *de facto* for the time effected.[3] "When our wages of labour in wheat

[1] Cf. Malthus, *Pol. Econ.* (1836), pp. 224, 225, &c. *Essay on Population*, 7th ed., III. viii. 323, but especially IV. xiii. 473. See also Rogers, *Six Centuries*, ch. viii., 'The Famine and the Plague,' especially pp. 233—242.

[2] Malthus, *Essay on Pop.*, IV. xiii. 473; cf. pp. 373 and 434.

[3] Cf. especially *Essay on Pop.* (2nd ed.), III. ix. 444. "The price of labour has been rising—not to fall again."

were high in the early part of the last century, it did not appear that they were employed merely in the maintenance of more families, but in improving the condition of the people in their general mode of living."[1] Malthus, without knowing it, was certainly father of the theory of a Wages Fund. The theory is that the average wages of the labouring classes at any given time are high or low in proportion to the great or small amount of circulating capital devoted to the payment of wages, or, as it is sometimes expressed (more tersely and inexactly), wages depend on "the ratio of population to capital." This might mean no more than the arithmetical truism that we may always find the average wages by dividing the total sum received by the total number of recipients; and the quotient would be unalterable only in the sense in which all other facts might be said to be so, in retrospect. But it is usually taken to mean that the first total could not at any given time have been greater or less than it actually was, being fixed unalterably by circumstances,[2] and so "devoted" or "determined" to the payment of wages. The simplest test of this theory is the application of it to the case of a single individual capitalist and his payments in wages. Suppose he has a capital of £10,000, £5000 fixed and £5000 circulating; and suppose that the latter means wages only (instead of chiefly), and is

[1] *Emigr. Comm.* (1827), p. 326, qu. 3411; cf. 3408, 3409. Cf. above, p. 197.

[2] The chief of them being the rate of profits which is at the given time enough to induce the "undertaker" (or "enterpriser") to continue business.

paid to one hundred men ;—£50 a year will be the average wages of the hundred men ; and, by the theory, given the rate of ordinary profits and given the "desire of accumulation" at the time and place, it could not possibly have been either more or less. But, as the profits are not unconditional, neither are the wages ; the capitalist might conceivably, to save his business, keep it up in bad times at a loss, and pay wages at the expense of profits and at the expense of his personal pleasures.[1] He has often the choice before him to spend more on fixtures, or more on new hands, or more on further employment of the old hands. In truth, too, though wages, especially in England, are often in the first instance advanced out of capital, they are always meant to be paid out of the gross returns, and in every sound business really are so. The workman and employer make their contract beforehand, and expect each other to abide by it, be the profit much or little ; the wages depend, therefore, directly on this contract, and indirectly on that which is the means of fulfilling the contract on the master's side, the price of the article made. The price of the article is the real wages fund ;[2] and therefore the wages fund must be as flexible as market prices, and the actual wages as changeable as are the powers, habits, and desires of the two contracting parties.

[1] See Mill on Thornton's 'Labour,' *Fortnightly Review*, May 1869. Cf. Walker on *The Wages Question*, pp. 140 *seq.*

[2] So in *Quarterly Review*, Jan. 1824, p. 315, Malthus says profits depend rather on the demand for produce than on the demand for labour.

The theory of a wages fund was formed from the facts of a perfectly exceptional time, and on the strength of two truths misapplied, the doctrine of Malthus (on Population) in its most unripe form, and of Ricardo (on Value) in its most abstract. J. R. MacCulloch seems to have been the first who put the two together to deduce a rigid law of wages. "The market rate of wages," he says, "is exclusively dependent on the proportion which the capital of the country, or the means of employing labour, bears to the number of labourers. There is plainly, therefore, only one way of really improving the condition of the great majority of the community or of the labouring class, and that is by increasing the ratio of capital to population," which the labourers for their part can only do by diminishing the supply of labour.[1]

Even Mrs. Marcet, a docile Ricardian, had put the case more carefully. "*Work* to be performed is the immediate cause of the demand for labour; but, however great or important is the work which a man may wish to undertake, the execution of it must always be limited by the extent of his capital, *i. e.* by the funds he possesses for the maintenance or payment of his labourers."[2] She professes to be expounding the received doctrine of her day. MacCulloch's exposition is much more rigid. When he speaks of the "funds devoted to the payment of

[1] *Discourse on Pol. Econ.*, by J. R. MacCulloch, pp. 61, 62 (1st and 2nd edd.), 1825.

[2] *Conversations on Pol. Econ.*, 1817 (1st and 2nd edd.), p. 137. Mrs. Marcet's memory is preserved for latter-day readers by Macaulay's reference to her in the essay on Milton.

wages," he means "that portion of the capital or wealth of a country which the employers of labour *intend* or *are willing* to lay out in the purchase of labour." It "may be larger at one time than at another. But, whatever be its magnitude, it obviously forms the only source from which any portion of the wages of labour can be derived. No other fund is in existence from which the labourers as such can draw a single shilling. And hence it follows that the average rate of wages or the share of the national capital appropriated to the employment of labour falling, at an average, to each labourer, must entirely depend on its amount as compared with the number of those amongst whom it has to be divided."[1] Neither MacCulloch, nor James Mill, nor John Mill in his early writings, nor apparently any of the expounders of the theory, were in the habit of describing the fund as "unconditionally" devoted to the payment of wages, though John Mill, in restating the position after he abandoned it, gives us so to understand.[2] Something like unconditional determination, however, is assumed in all the reasonings of the school. Adam Smith's frequent use of the words "funds devoted" or "funds determined" to this or that purpose may easily have been misunderstood. Certainly in his pages they mean no inflexible compulsion. He says the demand of those who live by wages can only increase in proportion to the

[1] *Discourse*, l. c. Cf. MacC.'s *Pol. Econ.*, Pt. III. ch. ii. p. 378 (ed. 1843); Prof. Fawcett's *Manual of Pol. Econ.*, p. 131 (1876).

[2] James Mill, *Elem.* (1821), p. 25; John Mill, *Principles*, II. xi. § 1. Cf. *Fort. Rev.*, 1869, May; Thornton, *Labour*, II. i. p. 83.

increase of the "funds" which are "destined" for the payment of wages, these funds being (he adds) either the surplus revenue of an idle monied man who will "naturally" use any addition to them in increasing his staff of domestic servants, or the increased capital of the capitalist who will just as "naturally" use them in employing more workmen.[1] The word "destined" is so far, with him, from implying any iron necessity that it means simply "intended"; and the intention is one that can be foiled or altered. He speaks of the "funds destined for the consumption" of the manufacturing class,[2] and of the townsfolk's "fund of subsistence,"[3] meaning simply their food; he even speaks of the funds destined for the repair of the high roads in France.[4] Even the strong passage in Book I. chap. viii., "the demand for those who live by wages necessarily increases with the increase of the revenue and stock of every country, and cannot possibly increase without it," stops considerably short of the doctrine of a rigid wages fund. It is never suggested by Adam Smith that the wages fund is inelastic, and that wages could not at any given time have been greater or less than they actually were. The doctrine is seldom traced further back than to Malthus; and Malthus cannot be shown to have held the doctrine. With express reference to the passage last cited from the *Wealth of Nations*, he says that "it will be found that the funds for the maintenance of labour do not

[1] *Wealth of Nations*, I. viii. p. 31, 2.
[2] *Ibid.*, IV. ix. 306, 1.
[3] *Ibid.*, IV. ix. 310, 2.
[4] *Ibid.*, V. i. 327, 2.

necessarily increase with the increase of wealth, and very rarely increase in proportion to it, and that the condition of the lower classes of society does not depend exclusively upon the increase of the funds for the maintenance of labour or the power of supporting a greater number of labourers" (*Essay*, 7th ed., III. xiii. 363). The condition of the working classes depended, he thought, partly on the rate at which the "funds for the maintenance of labour,"[1] or, as he expressed it at first, "*the resources of the country*"[2] and the demand for labour are increasing, and partly on the "habits of the people." Among their habits we should need to put their education and their power of union among themselves, and consequent strength in a struggle with the masters, to obtain or to raise the market rate of wages. From Ricardo he differed on the subject of wages very much as on the subject of value. Ricardo looked at cost price as the natural value of an article, and mere subsistence as the natural wages of labour. Malthus could do neither.

The issues between the two economists are nowhere so well or so calmly stated as in a paper written by Malthus (a few months after Ricardo's death) in the *Quarterly Review*,[3] where he deals with MacCulloch's treatise on *Political Economy*.[4] In that article Malthus professes to regard the political economy of Ricardo,

1 *Pol. Econ.*, ed. 1836, ch. iv. sect. ii. p. 224.

2 *Ibid.* ed. 1820, ch. iv. p. 248.

3 *Quarterly Review*, Jan. 1824. Cf. below, p. 288.

4 Supplement to *Encyclopædia Britannica*. Cf. above, p. 71.

James Mill, and most of the economical writers in the *Encyclopædia*, as a new and wrong departure. It is said to have been regarded by the writer as one of the best economical papers he ever wrote;[1] and, among other virtues, it has the merit of perfect courtesy and respect towards the persons criticized. Their system, he says,[2] is remarkably like that of the French economists. They "were equally men of the most unquestionable genius, of the highest honour and integrity, and of the most simple, modest, and amiable manners. Their systems were equally distinguished for their discordance with common notions, the apparent closeness of their reasonings, and the mathematical precision of their calculations and conclusions founded on their assumed data. These qualities in the systems and their founders, together with the desire so often felt by readers of moderate abilities of being thought to understand what is considered by competent judges as difficult, increased the number of their devoted followers in such a degree, that in France it included almost all the able men who were inclined to attend to such subjects, and in England a very large proportion of them.

"The specific error of the French economists was the having taken so confined a view of wealth and its sources as not to include the results of manufacturing and mercantile industry.

"The specific error of the new school in England is the having taken so confined a view of *value* as not to

[1] Empson in *Edin. Rev.*, Jan. 1837, p. 496.
[2] *Quart. Rev.*, Jan. 1824 (no. lx.), pp. 333-4.

include the results of demand and supply, and of the relative abundance and competition of capital.

"Facts and experience have, in the course of some years, gradually converted the economists of France from the erroneous and inapplicable theory of Quesnay to the juster and more practical theory of Adam Smith; and, as we are fully convinced that an error equally fundamental and important is involved in the system of the new school in England as in that of the French economists, we cannot but hope and expect that similar causes will, in time, produce in our own country similar effects in the correction of error and the establishment of truth."

The new school has, according to Malthus, three main principles. The first is, that what determines value is the quantity of labour that a thing costs to make,—the second, that supply and demand do not as a rule affect values,—and the third, that fertility of soil and not competition regulates the rate of profits. The new school thinks that profits enter so little into the price of an article that they may be neglected altogether in the computation of the causes of value. But (says Malthus) the value of a stone wall would be due, nearly all of it, to labour, and the value of a cask of old wine kept for twenty or thirty years would be largely due to profits. £50 worth of stone wall would have much more labour "worked up in it" than £50 worth of old wine. It is not sufficient to answer that profits are simply accumulated wages. As well say that five is another name for four. Ricardo himself introduced many qualifications into his own statement that value is due to labour. The principle (he confessed) was modified by the use of machinery and by the unequal durability of capital.[1]

Malthus admits the truth of Ricardo's dogma that profits and wages can only increase at each other's expense, and he even applies this principle of Ricardo's in a new way to the facts of the commercial depression that had prevailed since the peace.[2] It was universally allowed there had been a less demand for labour and a great fall in wages, but, it was also allowed, a much greater fall in profits; so that wages while lower in gross amount bore a higher proportion to profits than before. The reason was that, while the competition of labourers was great, the competition of capitalists with capitalists was still greater. The result was a universal fall of prices; the wages, though relatively greater, were absolutely less in amount, and the demand for labour would have been greater if prices had risen and the capitalist had got greater returns to his capital. Malthus would not go farther than this, and the Ricardian doctrine needs to be otherwise applied to yield the doctrine of a wages fund. It was applied in some such way as follows:—Competition drives prices down to the cost of production; this means that at any given time the sum total of profits and wages cannot be more than they actually are, and

[1] Ricardo, *Pol. Econ. and Tax.*, ch. i. sections iv., v.; *Works*, pp. 20, 25. Cf. Malthus, *Pol. Econ.*, 1820, p. 104, and the whole of section iii. pp. 72 *seq.*

[2] *Quart. Rev.*, l. c. p. 324; cf. p. 315. Cf. above.

both are kept down by competition to their minimum; the masters could not give higher wages without cutting down their profits, the men could not get less wages without either starving or being driven to seek other employments. Malthus does not so apply his doctrines. To him, what fixes the sum total of wages and profits is not the cost of production, but the demand for the thing produced; not the labour spent on a thing, but the labour that others are willing to give for it; and the cause of value is not cost, but demand acting with supply. Ricardo, who prefers to confine his theories to natural value, allows that the state of the demand and supply raises market value above or depresses it below cost price; and he does not see how seriously his own qualifications[1] impair the truth of his theory of value even when the value is "natural."[2] It is true, on the other hand, that the supply at any given time is a supply that will not be kept up unless the cost price be paid back. The cost price would certainly be the minimum below which prices could not permanently pass. But to Ricardo the cost in labour is the formal as well as the material cause of a value; to Malthus it is only the material, and only part of that, a mere *sine quâ non*, while the efficient is the demand, and the final is the consumption of the article by its last buyer or user.

The third leading tenet of the new school, says

[1] *Pol. Econ. and Tax.*, ch. i. sections iv. and v.

[2] Any given value, it might be added, is influenced by custom as well as competition.

Malthus, is that the rate of profits in a country depends on the fertility of the soil there, and not, as Adam Smith thought, on the competition of capital with capital for employment. Against them Malthus maintains that there is no necessary (though there is a frequent) connection between the productiveness of industry and the rate of profits, still less between the latter and the productiveness of any one single industry, such as agriculture. Profits depend on the proportion of the whole produce which "goes to replace the advances of the capitalist"; but this proportion may remain the same when the productiveness of industry is very various. In the previous eight or nine years, say from 1815 to 1824, there had certainly been no costliness in production. Corn had been cheap, and farmers' losses had led to the discontinuance of high farming, and especially of the forced cultivation of the dear years. The production, therefore, was at the cost of much less labour. But profits, instead of higher, were much lower. Abundance of produce and competition of producers had caused a fall in the value of produce, so that it was possible for the labourer to receive a greater share of what he made, though his labour had not become more productive. Ricardo does not take sufficient account of the influence of prices, both on wages and on profits.

There had in fact been over-production and a general glut. James Mill's *Elements of Political*

Economy[1] contain a careful demonstration that general gluts are impossible. It was emphatically a controversial passage, and in the pages of John Mill it has the look of an anachronism.[2] All depended on the meaning of "general." If it meant universal, the case was impossible. It is incredible that all without exception should have something to sell and no wish to buy. To offer anything for sale must of itself imply a desire to buy something else with it, either directly or by means of money. Even a very near approach to universality is not easy to understand; and it would mean simply that a bad organization of the world's markets had prevented buyers and sellers from reaching each other, and prevented goods from going where they are wanted, at the time when they are wanted; it would mean that not the malady but the scale and degree of it had passed belief.

[1] 1821, p. 186, ch. iv. sect. iii. "That consumption is coextensive with production."

[2] *Pol. Econ.*, III. xiv. "Of excess of supply." Cf. I. v. § 3, p. 42.

Note (on p. 263).

Malthus was one of the founders of the Statistical (now Royal Statistical) Society, March 1834. The "Journal" of the Society began in 1838, but there are two volumes of earlier "Proceedings," and the first of them (Vol. I. 1835–6, No. 4, pp. 87–96) contains a paper, 8th January, 1836, by Henry Hallam, the historian, on the Geometrical Ratio of Malthus, in relation to figures compiled for Wiltshire, Essex, and Kent by Sir Francis Palgrave. Hallam suggests diagrammatic illustrations, perhaps among the earliest of their kind.

CHAPTER III.

GENERAL GLUTS.

French War and English Trade—English Currency—Bullion Committee—Restriction not the only Cause of High Prices—Ricardo on Currency—Tooke on Prices—Say on Gluts—English Trade from 1824—High and Low Wages—Some Fallacies of Malthus.

THE discussion on General Gluts was simply a phase of the discussions on Value; and the prominence of such discussions in the political economy of sixty years ago was largely due to the peculiar effects on trade and prices of a twenty years' war with France. The theories of economists were becoming most abstract precisely at the time when the justest generalizations were most severely tested by abnormal conditions. Even if the Industrial Revolution heralded by the *Wealth of Nations* had been allowed a free course, the new conditions of manufacture would have raised new economical questions; and they could not have failed to turn, to some extent, on the subject of value, which Adam Smith had by no means exhausted. But there was no free course. War was declared against England by France in 1793. In the same year Pitt was forced to offer English merchants a loan of public money, to cure a financial crisis. Then followed, under the long Tory supremacy, heavy taxes, repressive laws, and something more nearly approaching a war of classes than anything known in England before or since.

The effects of the first ten years of the French war (1793 to 1802) were to all appearance rather good than bad. Britain itself, unlike the other belligerent countries, was always intact, and the labours of British manufacturers could go on as if nothing unusual was happening on the Continent. Our command of the sea, to say nothing of the conquest of new countries, gave us trade which others lost, and made amends for the annulment of the French treaty of commerce, and the loss of the Dutch trade. In 1806 the situation became less pleasant. The Berlin and Milan decrees excluding us from almost every country in Europe, the retaliatory Orders in Council and consequent alienation of America did real damage to English commerce. The very expectations they caused of a probable scarcity of particular goods sent up prices; and, with the real scarcity, contributed to an acute disturbance of trade, which lasted about five years for the Continent and three years more for America (1807-12, 1807-15). New markets were opened to us in South America; and the pent-up commercial enterprise of our countrymen vented itself in that direction, with wild disregard of the needs of consumers in that quarter.[1] The same happened, with more reason, in 1814 and 1815. When peace was restored, it was thought that the whole Continent must be eager to

[1] A cargo of skates was sent to Rio Janeiro in 1808.

have our goods, after being so long without them; and we sent them lavishly everywhere without waiting for orders. Unhappily the rest of Europe was exhausted by the war, which had lessened their production; and such products as they could offer us in exchange for our manufactures we seldom took without taxing. The very food that we most wanted from them we were careful to keep out till the last moment.[1] Anything more unlike the "simple system of natural liberty" could not be conceived; and the result certainly seemed to be an over-production on our part;—it was at any rate a reign of low prices and deep commercial depression. This was not all. Since 1797 we had had a paper currency of uncertain value. In that year the Bank of England, whose department of issue was not then separated from its department of banking, gave advances to Government, in return for which it was relieved of immediate obligation to pay gold to the holders of its notes. As long as the issues were moderate, the notes kept their value; but this was a time when economical substitutes for the currency, cheques and bills and County notes, were lessening the proportion of the Bank's notes to the total transactions of trade; and the Bank's power of calculating the public need without the natural safety-valve of convertibility became more and more fallible; the circulation soon contained superfluous paper, which dragged down the

[1] The intention of the new Corn Law of 1815 was to keep out all foreign grain till the home price should reach 80*s.* a quarter, *i.e.* the loaf 1*s.* See above, p. 221.

whole currency. In these circumstances, discussions on currency gained an interest they could never have had in the abstract; and they led to measures of the most practical and permanent usefulness. Ricardo's tract *The High Price of Gold Bullion a Proof of the Depreciation of Bank-Notes* (1810) prepared the way for the Bullion Committee of the House of Commons (1810), and through them for our own Bank Charter Act (1844). Malthus played a more quiet part. His chief writings on the subject of the currency were two magazine articles, one in the *Edinburgh Review* of February 1811,[1] and another in the *Quarterly Review* of April 1823.

The first treats of *The Depreciation of Paper Currency*, and is a review of pamphlets by the leading advocates and assailants of the principles of the Bullion Committee's Report. The Committee had inquired into three subjects: the high price of gold bullion, the state of the currency, and the state of the foreign Exchanges. As to the first, they found that, while an ounce of standard gold was converted at the Mint into £3 17*s.* 10½*d.* (which sum was therefore the Mint price of gold bullion),

[1] The article on the Bullion question, in August of the same year, might be his, if it was not Francis Horner's. Cf. Horner's *Life*, vol. i. ch. vi., dates April and Sept. 1805, from which it appears that Horner was working hard at the question and meant to write on it, as he might have done better in 1811, fresh from his experience on the Bullion Committee. As to the February article, the authorship is shown partly by internal evidence, partly by Horner's *Life*, vol. ii. p. 68 (Jan. 1811): "I received Malthus' MS. from you [Jeffrey] and have since transmitted it to him with such remarks as occurred to me in perusing it," &c. MacCulloch did not begin to write the economical articles for the *Edin. Rev.* till 1818. See *Notes and Queries*, 5th Oct., 1878.

the said ounce could not in the years 1806-8 be bought by the Mint for less than £4 in bank-notes, or in 1809 for less than £4 10*s*. The market price had risen to that extent above the Mint price, of gold bullion. As to the second, they found that guineas had gone out of circulation, and were practically replaced by small notes between £1 and £5. Finally, as to the third, they found that from the end of 1808 the Exchanges had become more and more unfavourable to England, till in 1809-10 they were with Hamburg nine, with Amsterdam seven, with Paris more than fourteen per cent. below par. After examination of witnesses and consideration of their evidence, the Committee resolved "that there is at present an excess in the paper circulation of this country, of which the most unequivocal symptom is the very high price of bullion, and next to that the low state of the Continental Exchanges; that this excess is to be ascribed to the want of a sufficient check and control in the issues of paper from the Bank of England, and originally to the suspension of cash payments, which removed the natural and true control." The effects had been very serious, especially on the wages of common country labour (*Report*, p. 73); and the Committee recommend a speedy return to the principle of cash payments, whether the nation be at peace or war, though caution demands that this take place gradually, in the space of two years. It took place, not in two years, but in more than ten, namely on 1st May 1821,[1] Parliament

[1] For the history of the currency in the interval see Miss Martineau's

not agreeing to the change till 1819.[1] Cobbett's venture (to be broiled on a gridiron when the Bank paid in gold) seemed a perfectly safe one.

Both Malthus and Ricardo agreed with the Report of the Bullion Committee. Ricardo indeed is in a sense the father of it. Malthus (in the *Edin. Review*) speaks strongly of the bad policy and injustice of continuing the suspension, and he does not spare the Bank of England and its mischievous monopoly,[2] or the "practical men" and their narrow views.[3] Yet he finds fault with Ricardo here as elsewhere for making his statements too absolute. Malthus' fault is in the contrary direction; he qualifies too much.[4] He thinks that Ricardo has gone too far in attributing all the movements of the Exchanges to excessive or defective currency; a purely commercial excess of imports over exports might, he thinks, cause the same effects, and even in the high price of bullion it was the commercial difficulty that began what the depreciation of currency continued. Ricardo, who replies in a long appendix,[5] answers, in substance, that in any and every case money goes from where it is cheaper to where it is dearer, and therefore from

Introd. to Hist. of Peace, Bk. II. ch. iii.; *Hist. of the Peace*, Bk. I. ch. iii. and ch. xv.; Cobbett's *Paper* v. *Gold*; Macleod's *Banking*, vol. ii., end of ch. ix. pp. 174—221, much the completest account.

[1] Peel changed his views then on Currency, as he did later on Catholic Emancipation and the Corn Laws.

[2] p. 370. He speaks approvingly of the American free trade in banking in a way that would have pleased Cobden.

[3] p. 371.

[4] *E. g.* Horner complains of this even in so clear a paper as that on Newenham. See Horner's *Life*, vol. i. pp. 436-7 (*sub dato* 1808).

[5] *Works* (ed. MacC.), pp. 291—296.

where the currency has lost value to where it has gained it. But this hardly meets the contention of Malthus, that the efficient cause, though it affects the currency, is not in all cases the currency itself, and in the case of an unequal balance of trade, however temporary, the cause of the exportation of the money is rather the superfluity of the goods in the foreign country than the deficiency of the money there;—it would be otherwise when the first cause was in the currency itself. The rest of the article contains little that is new to readers of the *Political Economy*, and the reference to a possible over-production is chiefly valuable as a sign of the authorship, and as showing that the views of the author were becoming fixed. The personal acquaintance of Malthus with Ricardo had begun before the appearance of this article;[1] and they continued to discuss and correspond, in perfect friendship, till the death of Ricardo in Sept. 1823.[2]

His friendship with the Edinburgh Reviewers remained unbroken; and, when he wrote in the *Quarterly Review*, it was the *Review* not the writer that had changed. On finance, indeed, the *Quarterly Review* had been saved from unsoundness by Canning's influence,[3] and an article on Tooke's *Prices* need have no politics.

There can be little doubt that Thomas Tooke[4] was right in holding the difference between the Mint

[1] Ricardo, *Works* (MacC.), p. xxi. [2] Cf. below, Bk. V.

[3] Horner's *Life*, vol. ii. p. 68 (Jan. 1811).

[4] *Thoughts and Details on High and Low Prices during the last Thirty Years*, 1793—1823. The later ed. of 1838 in three vols. is more valuable.

price and the market price of gold bullion to be the full measure of the effect of this depreciation upon prices, the rest of the increase being due to great demand with small supply, being as a rule much exaggerated and in its worst forms purely local. He pointed out that there was, as a matter of fact, no coincidence between the Bank's contraction or extension of its issues and the fall or rise of prices in the market outside. Prices rose, for example, in 1795 and 1796, when the Bank's circulation had been not extended but contracted to meet the commercial crisis; and in 1798, when the Bank's issues were larger, prices actually fell to what they had been in 1793. Moreover, when some prices went up, others went down. When the prices of provisions went up in 1799 and 1800, the prices of colonial wares went down. The ruling cause (Tooke argues) was not the issue of many or few bank-notes, but scarcity and plenty, especially the plenty of a good harvest and the scarcity of a bad one. Wages in the same way fluctuated rather by the harvests than by the currency, but not by either so much as by the changes in general trade; it would not be true to say that the high or low prices produced high or low wages, but what produced the one produced the other. The recoil of the speculation that followed the Peace brought down both together; there was a glut not only of goods but of hands; and there were the discarded men of the army to swell the numbers of the unemployed. The Luddite outbreaks against machines, as taking work away from the hands, had made a notable beginning in 1812 during the war; in 1816, the year after the Peace, they began again with greater violence. The discussions of Say and Malthus on Over-production, and the reasonings in Ricardo (1817) and James Mill (1821) on Wages and the Wages Fund, are as truly commentaries on these events as the Letter of Cobbett to the Luddites[1] or the volumes of Tooke on Prices.

Malthus has adroitly used the work of Tooke to support his own economical positions. In a review in the *Quarterly* for April 1823[2] (pages 214 *seq.*) he tries to show that Mr. Tooke's conclusions as to the high and low prices of the past thirty years prove the following general statements:—First, that values and therefore prices depend on the supply compared with the demand, and are only affected by the labour required to produce goods (*i. e.* by what Ricardo counts the main cause of value) so far as this labour is the main condition of their supply; second, that the supply and demand are chiefly affected by the seasons, and, of the other causes, war may limit the supply but can hardly cause a demand; third, that when demand outruns supply trade is brisk, when supply outruns demand trade is dull; and that, finally, a long-continued deficiency or a long-continued excess of this kind brings with it a fall or a rise in the value of the precious metals.[3] Malthus, however, goes further than

[1] *Political Register*, 30th Nov., 1816.

[2] Internal evidence, *e. g.* p. 237 of the *Quarterly*, compared with p. 65 of *Measure of Value*, would show his authorship, and the article is ascribed to him by Tooke, *Prices*, ed. 1838, vol. i. p. 21.

[3] *l. c.* pp. 215-16.

Tooke with the Bullion Committee. Though on the bullion question the opposing parties, Bosanquet and Ricardo, seemed to him to be devoted to a preconceived theory,[1] the Report itself was "more free from this error of preconception than any work that had appeared on the subject;"[2] and he agreed with it that there had been a greater rise of prices and of wages at the end of the period of restriction, than could be explained by the bad seasons, and demand for men, and the difference between paper and gold. He is old-fashioned enough to think that even with convertibility there might be over-issue and depreciation, and speculation on a basis of paper. His reasoning on this point is hardly sound. It depends on a misapplication of the axiom that, in the case of necessaries, a very small deficiency in the supply will cause a very great increase in the price,—*e. g.* that wheat may rise from 100 to 200 per cent. when the deficiency of the crops is not more than 15 or 30.[3] The profits of English farmers between 1793 and 1815 must therefore have been enormous; and Malthus, though he loves agriculture above manufacture, has taken account of these high gains of individuals in judging the cause of the Agricultural Interest against the public.[4] But in connection with currency he actually speaks as if those gains were

[1] Bosanquet, *Practical Observations on the Report of the Bullion Committee* (1810); Ricardo, *The High Price of Bullion a Proof of the Depreciation of Bank-Notes* (1809), and his *Reply to Bosanquet* (1811).

[2] l. c. *Pol. Econ.*, Introd. (1820), pp. 6 and 7 n., (1836) p. 5 n. Cf. Tooke, *Prices*, Part I. p. 6 (ed. 1823).

[3] Tooke, *Prices*, Part III. p. 91.

[4] See *Tract on Value*, p. 18.

a public advantage; he does not see they were a mere transference of public wealth, not an addition to it. The farmer, he says, is obviously "able to set in motion a much greater quantity of industry than before," at least till wages have risen. "The specific funds destined for the maintenance of labour, though diminished in quantity, are by this happy provision of nature increased in their efficiency;" labourers get more employment, and there is "a burst of prosperity to the producing classes."[1]

This is a near approach to a worse fallacy than the Wages Fund. The archaic reasoning is the more unhappy, because the reasoner proceeds to use it in a good cause. Jean Baptiste Say[2] had taught that all increased or diminished demand depended on increased or diminished supply, and argued thence, with James Mill and Ricardo, the impossibility of general or rather universal gluts. Goods[3] being always meant to be exchanged with goods, one half will furnish a market for the other half; and thus, as production (which gives the means of buying) is the sole source of demand (so far as demand is effective), an excess in the supply of one article merely proves a deficiency in the supply of another, and is improperly called over-production. Indeed, whereas consumption takes an article away from the market, production brings one into it, and thereby increases, *pro tanto*, the demand by increasing the means of buying. James

[1] *Quarterly*, April 1823, p. 230.
[2] *Econ. Pol.*, Part III. ch. ii., 2nd ed., 1842; 1st ed., 1802.
[3] "Products" is Say's word, however.

Mill's neat demonstration of this doctrine[1] would be quite conclusive if we, first of all, defined demand and supply so as to include each other, and, second, supposed general to mean universal. The reply of Malthus himself is that goods are not always exchanged for goods, but frequently, perhaps most frequently, for labour. Say rejoins that he for his part used a term ("products") which includes both goods and services, and that the latter are always the real object of an exchange.[2] Malthus makes a better point when he accuses his opponents of treating goods as if they were mathematical symbols, instead of objects of human consumption owing their whole character to human wants.[3] But his case could be made convincing even on his opponents' premises. Division of labour, all admitted, is limited by the extent of the market;[4] allow that the most satisfactory cure for the limitation is to widen the market, not to lessen the division of the labour—still, *given* the limitation of the market, the extension of the division of the labour will cause an over-production. All that Malthus maintained was that this might happen in a great many cases as well as in a few; Say went as near as he dared to the assertion that it could not happen at all.

[1] *Elements* (1821), ch. iv. sect. iii. pp. 186 *seq.* "That consumption is coextensive with production." Mill taught this as early as 1808 in his tract (against Spence) *Commerce defended.*

[2] *Lettres à M. Malthus sur différents sujets d'écon. pol., notamment sur les causes de la stagnation générale du commerce* (1820), pp. 26 *seq.*

[3] *Pol. Econ.* (1820), p. 355, (1836) p. 316. Against Say's general position see *Definitions*, p. 56 n.

[4] *Wealth of Nations*, I. iii.

The question of a market, again, is not a mere question of numbers but of wants. A carpet factory, for example, among a people who preferred bare floors would have no market, whatever the numbers and even the wealth of the people. Say does not do full justice to Malthus in this connection. He thinks that the author of the *Essay on Population* cannot consistently believe in the possibility of a great abundance of products together with a stationary number of parsimonious consumers. But Malthus had allowed that in one case, the case of food, there could be no over-production,[1] the want in that case being constant, whereas, curiously enough, Ricardo thinks that food is the one object of which there might be a glut. "If every man were to forego the use of luxuries and be intent only on accumulation, a quantity of necessaries might be produced for which there could not be any immediate consumption. Of commodities so limited in number there might undoubtedly be a universal glut, and consequently there might neither be demand for an additional quantity of such commodities nor profits on the employment of more capital. If men ceased to consume they would cease to produce. This admission does not impugn the general principle," for there is no likelihood of such a contingency as it supposes;—there is a limit to the desire of food, but there is no limit to the desire of other good

[1] See above, p. 232. A curious footnote in *Essay on Pop.*, 3rd ed., vol. ii. p. 264, suggested that there might be over-production in the case of high farming when its cost made the farmers charge more than the public could bear. But this note disappeared afterwards.

things.[1] The insatiableness of human desires is here assumed by Ricardo to be always full-grown, instead of what it is, in perhaps three-fourths of the world, an undeveloped possibility. Till we know that the possibility has become actual, we cannot take for granted that all we produce will be wanted. Malthus did not enter with sympathy or even with full intelligence into the spirit of modern trade. But he sees that large manufacture, with its complement of speculative trading, must succeed or fail precisely as it has judged rightly or judged wrongly of its markets, for it no longer, like the old English small production, waits for orders—it anticipates, woos, and coaxes them. He believes that the awakening of man's insatiable wants will tend to secure us against both over-population and over-production, by creating a high standard of living. The taste for luxuries, whatever its positive advantages, from the educational or artistic point of view, confers at least this economical benefit.[2]

Malthus gets a similar result by applying to wages his favourite idea of the golden mean. The "funds destined to pay wages" may, he says, be increased either by high prices or by great production at low prices,—increased value without increased quantity, or increased quantity without increased value. The latter is the more secure way, but it lies on the road to "glut." The most desirable plan is the union

[1] Ricardo, *Pol. Econ. and Taxation*, ch. xxi. p. 176 (MacCull.'s ed.). Mill (*Elements*, pp. 193 ft., 194) is more rigid.

[2] *Essay*, 7th ed., IV. xiii. 473.

of the two. "There is somewhere a happy mean, where, under the actual resources of a country, both the increase of wealth and the demand for labour may be a maximum. A taste for conveniences and comforts not only tends to create a more steady demand for labour than a taste for personal services, but by cheapening manufactures and the products of foreign commerce, including many of the necessaries of the labouring classes, it actually enlarges the limits of the effectual demand for labour, and renders it for a longer time effective."[1] If any one had urged against this, in the words of Mill, that a demand for goods is not a demand for labour, but simply gives labour a new direction, Malthus would probably have answered that the new direction was all important, because the trade begun in it might be a trade in goods more widely used, and might therefore last longer and more steadily than the old trade.

We see that in his views of this subject, expounded tediously enough, and at unnecessary length, Malthus had constant thought of the relations of production and distribution to consumption as well as to each other, for the condition of the people was always more important to him than the state of the articles concerned. But he never yielded to his feelings so far as to adopt Sismondi's reactionary ideas on the effects of machinery on the workmen. He never wrote any

[1] *Pol. Econ.* (1836), ch. iv. sect. iii. p. 239, slightly altered from 1st ed., 1820, ch. iv. sect. iii. p. 266.

[2] Sismondi, *Nouveaux Principes de l'Écon. Pol.*, 1819. See Malthus, *Pol. Econ.* (1820), p. 420, (1836) pp. 325 n., 366 n. Cf. on the other hand *Essay*, III. xiii. 372-3 and n.

description of the evils of division of labour at all so strong as Adam Smith's.[1] He goes little farther than Ricardo, who says in a well-known passage:—"The same cause which may increase the nett revenue of the country may at the same time render the population redundant and deteriorate the condition of the labourer," for all the increase may possibly be devoted to fixed and not circulating capital, to machinery and buildings instead of wages.[2] Ricardo's admission, that he was wrong in not recognizing this sooner, makes us wonder (as men were even then doing in Germany over similar confessions of their philosophers) whether his demonstrations are more accurate than ordinary reasonings. His brother economists never claimed infallibility. Adam Smith gave up his defence of Usury Laws.[3] Malthus amended his first views on population, to say nothing of the measure of value.[4] Mill gave up the Wages Fund. It was only the minor economists who proudly remained at the end where they were at the beginning. James Mill refused to follow Ricardo in allowing that food could be over-produced, and MacCulloch refused to go with him in the admission above quoted, that increase of wealth might go to fixed capital instead of wages.[5]

[1] *Wealth of Nations*, V. i. art. ii. pp. 350—353 (ed. MacC.). He is outrivalled by Ferguson, *Civil Society*, parts iv. and v. (ed. 1773).

[2] 3rd ed. of *Pol. Ec. and Tax.* (1821), ch. xxxi. pp. 468-9, ed. MacCull., pp. 235-6. Cf. below (Critics). It is the position of Marx.

[3] If we believe Bowring, *Life of Bentham* (ed. 1843), p. 176.

[4] "Supposing that his opinions have not altered within the last twelve months."—*De Quincey*, vol. iv. p. 231.

[5] James Mill, *Elements*, pp. 193, 194. MacCull., *Pol. Ec.*, p. 207. Cf. the tract *Mordecai Mullion* (1826).

Orthodox economy became most abstract when on the death of Ricardo in 1823 its doctrines passed into the hands of the Minor Prophets.

In the last ten years of his life Malthus made no serious change in his economical views, and approached no nearer to the Ricardians. They were years when economists and political reformers had not learned to work together so harmoniously as they were to do after his death. Huskisson's changes in commercial policy were preparing the way in high quarters for free trade. The sliding scale of corn duties introduced in 1826 pointed on the whole in the same direction. But the agitation of the humbler classes for political freedom, made solid as it was by an appreciable progress in popular education,[1] and kept within bounds of law by the influence of Cobbett,[2] went on in a way apart; and it will be remembered how Chartism stood aloof from the Anti-Corn-Law League. A man might be an advanced economist and social reformer and a reactionary in politics. In 1824, when trades unions were for the first time allowed by law and the Factory Acts were still too imperfect to give the weak a fair chance against the strong, the "natural state of things," free development of individual and national faculties, did not exist; and Malthus, who missed them keenly, would have been much amazed to hear that his doctrines were, like Ricardo's, a vindication of things

[1] Especially by Sunday Schools, according to the testimony of Samuel Bamford.—*Radical*, vol. i. p. 7 (1844).

[2] We have his counterparts in our own day.

as they are. Not only the notorious fact of his opposition to Ricardo, but his views on commercial policy are against the notion.[1] At the Peace there were many fallacies current about wages. The new Corn Law of 1815 had inaugurated the aggressive policy of the agricultural interest, who frankly endeavoured, by forms of law, to convert an occasional scarcity into a permanent one, and keep prices at 80*s.* a quarter. Not a few false friends of the working man recommended him to countenance the law and let his bread be made dear, for then, said they, his wages would be made high. Many manufacturers, on the other hand, were declaring the interest of the country to be low wages, and, unto that end, cheap food and a great population. Malthus was with neither. His partial approval of the new Corn Law was no doubt based on erroneous grounds; but he held no such mistaken views of wages. His opinion, if not sufficiently obvious from his general views of population, was laid down explicitly in all his writings. He says, for example: "If a country can only be rich, by running a successful race for low wages, I should be disposed to say at once 'Perish such riches!'"[2] "It is most desirable that the labouring classes should be well paid, for a much more important reason than any that can relate to wealth, namely, the happiness of the great mass of society."[3] Being asked, "In a national point of view, even if it were admitted that the low rate of wages

[1] See below, Bk. III., for disproof of the charge that he was reactionary in his politics, like many economical optimists.

[2] *Pol. Econ.*, 1820, p. 236.

[3] *l. c.* p. 472.

was an advantage to the capitalist, do you think it fitting that labour should be kept permanently in a state bordering on distress, to avoid the injury that might accrue to the national wealth from diminishing the rate of profit?" he answered, "I should say, by no means fitting; I consider the labouring classes as forming the largest part of the nation, and therefore that their general condition is the most important of all."[1]

He thinks, however, that the change from low to high wages might quite possibly so reduce profits as to make trade unprofitable. We might need to sacrifice something of our commercial prosperity. He cannot rise to the conception of a society in which the entire body of workmen as consumers would be a sufficient market for the same body as producers. He cannot rid himself of the idea that a body of unproductive consumers is a social necessity, to give a stimulus to production by developing the wants which the manufactures are to satisfy. It seems easy to answer that those unproductive consumers can only pay for the manufactures by means of other products, whencesoever obtained, and there seems no reason why their producers should not obtain them.[2] If the workmen themselves had the wants and supplied them by their own labour, all the results that Malthus desires would be obtained without invidious

[1] *Emigr. Comm.* (1827), p. 317, qu. 3281.

[2] Some such view is suggested by Malthus himself, *Essay*, IV. xiii. p. 473 (cf. *Pol. Ec.*, 1820, p. 475), a passage which it is hard to reconcile with the passages in the *Quarterly* and in the *Pol. Ec.* that speak of the necessity of a special class of unproductive consumers.

distinctions of classes, and with distinct improvement in the condition of the workmen. His aims, at least, were good. The indispensable leisure would be secured if the hours of labour were shortened, as he desired them to be. "I have always thought and felt that many among the labouring classes in this country work too hard for their health, happiness, and intellectual improvement."[1] The general wealth therefore, if need be, must be sacrificed to the general happiness. Factory Acts that would prevent children from labouring too young or too long[2] he thoroughly approves, though such Factory Acts as would interfere with adult labour he considers an injustice to the work-people themselves, and a hopeless interference with "the principles of competition, one of the most general principles by which the business of society is carried on."[3] The salvation of the labouring classes must come from themselves, from their own "simultaneous resolution to work fewer hours in the day." But trades unions, as we now know them, had not then come into being; and he talks of a future improvement of the working classes in knowledge, comfort, and self-restraint,[4] with much hesitation.

We have seen that the economics of Malthus, whether in relation to the landlords, the employers,

[1] *Pol. Econ.* (1820), ch. vii. sect. ix. p. 473. Cf. *Tract on Rent*, p. 48 n.

[2] *Essay on Pop.*, III. iii. p. 282 (in relation to Robert Owen). Cf. the whole ch. xiii. of Book III., where he treats of "Increasing Wealth as it affects the Condition of the Poor."

[3] *Pol. Econ.*, l. c. p. 474.

[4] *Ibid.*, l. c. pp. 474-5.

or the workmen, are by no means identical with the economics of Ricardo and his school, which have been the ruling and orthodox doctrine for the first half of the nineteenth century.

It would be neither complimentary nor true to ascribe the difference to the logic of sentiment; but it is true that the acute sensitiveness of Malthus to the evils of poverty kept constantly before him large classes of facts which Ricardo seemed willing to forget, and the path that he took, though long ago obscured and forgotten, led him in some important points away from *laissez faire* to doctrines of our own day, in which society acting through its Government is allowed an originative and not merely a regulative action in the matter of industry and wealth.

Resuming the thread of the essay, we shall find that the relation of society to its destitute poor is not to Malthus, as to Ricardo, a question of taxation and finance, but a problem of morals and politics, which could only be solved by a clear view of the relation of the citizen to the commonwealth.

CHAPTER IV.

THE BEGGAR.

Arrangement of the Essay—Nature's Mighty Feast—Tract on *High Price of Provisions*—I cannot, therefore I ought not—Poor Laws condemned—Frederick the Great's Army—Mitigation of Bad Effects of Poor Law—Step towards Abolition—New Poor Law.

IN the foregoing brief review of the economical doctrines of Malthus, the chapters on commercial policy and the Corn Laws,[1] in the third book of the *Essay on Population*, have been already noticed. As the First and Second books of the essay were supposed to deal with the state of population in past and in present times, the Third is supposed to deal with the "different systems of expedients which have been proposed or have prevailed in society" for curing the evils arising from the principle of population, while the Fourth relates to the future prospects of society, and the possibility of removing the evils in question. This division of the subject could not be maintained very strictly. The "systems proposed" no doubt were in most cases mere theories and could be considered

[1] See above, pp. 245 *seq.* and 252.

by themselves; but the "systems that prevailed" included such laws as the Corn Laws and Poor Laws, which directly affected the present habits and wealth of the people, and might fairly have been considered in the second book. The fourth book might quite logically have been part of the third, for it simply adds to the "systems proposed" the proposal of Malthus himself. The arrangement is not in itself so perfect or so closely respected by its author that we need have any remorse for disregarding it. The earliest chapters of the third book (i. and ii.) are substantially the refutation of Godwin, Wallace, Condorcet, as it appeared in 1798, with a postscript (ch. iii.) on Owen and Spence, which will be best considered in another place.[1] In point of style they are probably the best in the book.

After a chapter (iv.) on Emigration[2] come three chapters on the Poor Laws, to be viewed with ch. viii. of the fourth book, which deals with Plans for their Abolition. Of all the applications of the doctrines of Malthus, their application to pauperism was probably, at the time, of the greatest public interest. Even the first essay had distinct bearing on Pitt's Poor Bill; the next writing of the author was on a question of parish relief; and these three chapters in the later *Essay on Population* have influenced public opinion and legislation about the destitute poor almost as powerfully as the *Wealth of Nations* has influenced commercial policy. Malthus is the father

[1] See below, Bk. IV., and cf. above, p. 208.

[2] See above, p. 142.

not only of the new Poor Law, but of all our latter-day societies for the organization of charity.

The subject is best introduced in the words of a celebrated parable, which Malthus having used once was never afterwards allowed to forget:[1]—"A man who is born into a world already possessed, if he cannot get subsistence from his parents, on whom he has a just demand, and if the society do not want his labour, has no claim of *right* to the smallest portion of food, and, in fact, has no business to be where he is. At nature's mighty feast there is no vacant cover for him. She tells him to be gone, and will quickly execute her own orders, if he do not work upon the compassion of some of her guests. If these guests get up and make room for him, other intruders immediately appear demanding the same favour. The report of a provision for all that come, fills the hall with numerous claimants. The order and harmony of the feast is disturbed, the plenty that before reigned is changed into scarcity; and the happiness of the guests is destroyed by the spectacle of misery and dependence in every part of the hall, and by the clamorous importunity of those, who are justly enraged at not finding the provision which they had been taught to expect. The guests learn too late their error, in counteracting those strict orders to all intruders, issued by the great mistress of the feast, who, wishing that all her guests should have plenty, and knowing that she could not provide for unlimited

[1] The passage is quoted in full because by recent critics it is much garbled; *e. g.* in *Progress and Poverty*, VII. i. 304 n.

numbers, humanely refused to admit fresh comers when her table was already full."[1]

Our neighbours' misfortunes have seldom been made so picturesque. The figure itself was no new one. Lucretius had written :—

> "Cur non, ut plenus vitæ conviva, recedis?"[2]

and Fenton, in Pope's[3] familiar lines :—

> "From Nature's temperate feast rose satisfied,
> Thanked heaven that he had lived and that he died."

But the new application took hold on the public fancy. Sir William Pulteney and Windham are said to have been, beyond others, delighted with its conservative moral.[4] Malthus may have got the hint of it from a passage in Paley's *Moral and Political Philosophy*. Paley was criticizing a justification of private property, which founded it on every man's right to take what he wants of the things God made for the use of all, just as, when an entertainment is given to the freeholders (as the free and independent electors?) of a county, we see them coming in and eating and drinking each what he chooses, without asking the consent of the other guests. The simile, says Paley, is not perfect, for in a freeholder's feast nobody is allowed to fill his pockets or to throw anything away, "especially if by

[1] *Essay*, 2nd ed., IV. vi. 531.

[2] Lucretius, iii. 951. Cicero's simile of the theatre open to all comers, but giving each man his own seat, had special application to Property (*De Finibus*, iii. 20).

[3] Epitaph on Fenton.

[4] James Grahame's *Population* (1816), p. 34. Cf. *Quarterly Rev.*, Dec. 1812, p. 327; Hazlitt, *Spirit of the Age*, 'Malthus,' end.

so doing he pinched the guests at the lower end of the table." [1]

Even the friends of Malthus thought the passage too gloomy; and, as every one noticed,[2] it was not retained after 1803. It contains, however, at least two positions that were never retracted:—that the poor cannot claim relief as a right, but only as a favour, and that poor relief can only raise one man by depressing another. The latter position may be illustrated from the tract written in 1800 on the *High Price of Provisions.* The main aim of the tract was to show that the price was too extravagantly high to be due to the deficiency, which was admittedly only one-fourth. But the author throws light on his own general doctrines.[3] He argues, in substance, that to give relief in money is to enable the relieved persons to retain their ordinary rate of consumption at the expense of the rest. To this the reply is obvious:—the sufficiency of the stock is not so finely calculated, neither is the amount of it so fixed that it cannot be increased from home or foreign stores,—and to withdraw money from the rich for the poor, and increase the country's total expenditure on necessaries, might be simply to divert the stream of importation into the channel of necessaries, and lead to a larger use of food other than bread. Under the

[1] Book III. Part I. ch. iv. (1785).

[2] *E. g.* Godwin, *Population* (1820), I. iii. 17. The withdrawal was probably due to Sumner. See Otter, Life of Malthus in *Pol. Ec.* (1836), p. lii.

[3] Cf. *Essay*, 2nd ed., pp. 400, 401, and nn.; 7th ed., p. 298 n. Cf. pp. 295 and 297 n. Cf. also Tooke, above quoted, p. 291.

conditions of the time, however, the author's views were not unnatural. On his return from Sweden in 1800 he found scarcity prevailing in England as elsewhere, but with prices much higher than in other countries. These were the days when Chief Justice Kenyon and a jury enforced the antiquated laws against forestalling and regrating.[1] Malthus had not read his Adam Smith to so little purpose that he could approve such proceedings; much of his pamphlet was simply an application, to one particular case, of the principles of the *Wealth of Nations* (Book IV. chap. v.).[2] Neither could he agree with the notion that the paper currency had done it all.[3] Settling down to his parish work in Surrey, he watched the course of events. What happened, he said, there and presumably elsewhere was as follows:—In progress of the scarcity the poor complained to the justices that their wages were too low to buy bread at present prices; the justices thereupon inquired at what, as the lowest wages, they would have been able to buy it, and then "very humanely, and I am far from saying improperly," gave parish relief accordingly.[4] But, like the water from the mouth of Tantalus, the corn slipped from the grasp of the poor; prices rose a step further, and the relief had to follow the prices.

The rates accordingly rose in many places from

[1] Cf. above, p. 220.

[2] On Bounties and the Corn Trade. Cf. *High Price of Provisions*, p. 3.

[3] *l. c.* p. 23. See above, p. 289. Also *Corn Law Catechism*, 1839, qu. 244.

[4] *l. c.* pp. 9—11. Cf. the "make up" and "bread money" mentioned in *Report of Poor Law Commission*, 1834, p. 27.

four to fourteen shillings in the pound. By the double burden of dear food and high rates, perhaps five or six millions of the richer classes were certainly made to feel the pinch of the scarcity, which would otherwise have been borne, say by two millions of the poorest, who would have died under it.[1] In this instance the Poor Laws did the country a distinct service. But it was done by taking from the first guests to give to the importunate intruders, and could not justify a general eulogy of the Poor Laws. The whole drift of the *Essay on Population* had gone against such institutions; and "two years' reflection," says the writer of the *Essay*, "have served strongly to convince me of the truth of the principle there advanced, and of its being the real cause of the continued depression and poverty of the lower classes of society, of the total inadequacy of all the present establishments in their favour to relieve them, and of the [certainty of] periodical returns of such seasons of distress as we have of late experienced."[2] In the first essay he had spoken strongly not only against Pitt's new Poor Bill, but against all legal relief, and amongst other reasons precisely on the ground that it caused food to rise in price beyond the point to which scarcity would have raised it apart from interference.[3]

The second was a stronger reason;—in the language of Kant, the claim allowed (with little qualification[4]) by the English Poor Laws was a claim that could not

[1] *High Price*, &c. pp. 19, 20. [2] *l. c.* p. 27. Cf. above, p. 43.
[3] 1st ed., pp. 82, 83; 7th ed., pp. 302-3.
[4] *Essay*, 7th ed., Appendix, p. 493.

be made universal without contradiction. If every one exercised the supposed right of demanding relief, no community could fulfil the supposed duty of granting it.[1] If it could have been fulfilled, Malthus thinks, the obligation would have held; and, instead of declaring "I cannot, therefore I ought not," he would have confessed, "I can, therefore I ought."[2] As the case stands, he agrees with Sir Frederick Eden in thinking the giving of legal relief impracticable, and therefore no duty, and also that, "upon the whole, the sum of good to be expected from a compulsory maintenance of the poor will be far outbalanced by the sum of evil which it will inevitably create."[3] It relieved individual suffering at the cost of making the suffering general. It created the poor which it maintained, for it led men to marry with the certainty of parish assistance. It thereby increased the population without increasing the food of the country, and it has to a large extent broken down the ancient spirit of independence. "Hard as it may appear in individual instances, dependent poverty ought to be held disgraceful."[4] High wages and independence and moral restraint are better than low wages with a parish supplement and a pauper family. "I feel persuaded that if the Poor Laws had never existed in this country, though there might have been a few more instances of very severe distress,

[1] He borrows, as he himself says, the language of Sir Frederick Eden on the *State of the Poor* (1797). See *Essay on Population*, 2nd ed., p. 417 n.; 7th ed., p. 308 n.

[2] *Letter to Whitbread* (1807), pp. 12, 13; cf. *Essay*, p. 445 ft.

[3] Quoted, *Essay*, III. vi. 308 n. [4] 7th ed., III. vi. 303; 1st ed., p. 365.

the aggregate mass of happiness among the common people would have been much greater than it is at present."[1] This was his belief to the end.[2]

An allegory of these things may be found in Dr. John Moore's description of the army of Frederick the Great. Dr. Moore saw a man caned for being a few seconds late in replacing his ramrod; and the officers told him that, since they could not distinguish wilful blunders from accidental, they punished all alike, and the result, they said, was excellent; all the men were on the alert, and fewer blunders were committed on the whole. It used to be common on field days for dragoons to have their hats blown off and to be thrown from their horses. At last a general gave orders to punish every man to whom either of these accidents happened; since then hardly anybody lost his hat or fell from his horse. Dr. Moore heard of a poor hussar who had fallen from his horse at last review, and was to be punished for it as soon as he could leave the hospital. This seemed hard, but the King of Prussia thought he could only hope to make his army superior to others by improving its discipline, training its officers by honour and disgrace, and its privates by physical punishment; he considered that the occasional suffering of an innocent individual does less harm to an army than the toleration of negligence, which makes the negligence greater.[3] So far as legal relief goes, Malthus would

[1] III. vi. (7th ed.), p. 305.

[2] See e. g. *Emigration Committee*, 1827, qu. 3369, p. 323.

[3] Dr. John Moore's *View of Society and Manners in France, Switzerland, and Germany* (7th ed., 1789), vol. ii. pp. 144—157.

recommend the same martial severity, and try to put men on their guard against poverty by making them bear the discipline of its consequences. There are other points in which the allegory applies to the "simple system of natural liberty;" the discipline of industrial competition is certainly in some respects as severe as the discipline of an army. On the other hand, society does not consist of picked strong men, but includes the weak also, and its privates are supposed not to take their orders from a commander, but to "fend for themselves." Society under socialism may resemble an army, but not society under individualism. Malthus, therefore, would have repudiated the analogy. He does not reach his conclusions by a preconceived theory of the state, but by observing the ill results of the common preconceived theory that every citizen when destitute has a right to be supported by the state. He finds that, as a matter of fact, where material relief has been given as a duty, and claimed as a right, the effect on the recipient has been clearly bad; the Poor Law stands condemned by experience.

Yet he admits that the badness of the law has been largely counteracted by the remissness of its execution. The attempt to secure a fixed rate of wages to the labourer in all states of trade has not really been made in England as the Elizabethan Poor Law enjoined. The scantiness of the relief actually given, together with the insolence of the officials concerned in the giving of it, has disturbed the sense of complete security, which in the view of

Malthus would in such a case have been fatal. "The desire of bettering our condition and the fear of making it worse, like the *vis medicatrix naturæ* in physics, is the *vis medicatrix reipublicæ* in politics, and is continually counteracting the disorders arising from narrow human institutions." The Poor Law has been so imperfectly carried out that it has left some room still for prudential motives among the labourers; they cannot count on complete provision for their families if they marry recklessly, and some few of them still think caution needful. Moreover, from fear of the Poor Law the rich will often refuse to build cottages, lest their occupants become paupers.[1] In the third place, pauper children, like foundlings, do not live long.[2]

In his *Letter to Samuel Whitbread, M.P., on his proposed Bill for the amendment of the Poor Laws* (1807), Malthus allows that abolition must not come till public opinion is ripe for it; but he recommends legislation in the direction of abolition, to prepare the minds of all classes for the final steps, and to expose to the working classes the delusiveness of the present boon. Poor Laws, he says, are peculiar to England, and their absence in other countries does not seem to have the effects expected from their abolition here. In reply to Malthus, it might be urged that the Poor Laws are not entirely peculiar to England, but occur in Denmark and elsewhere.[3] In the second

[1] *Essay*, 7th ed., III. vi. p. 307; *Emigration Committee* (1827), qu. 3361, p. 323.

[2] *l. c.* pp. 307-8. Cf. above, p. 134.

[3] *Reports to Local Gov. Bd. on Foreign Poor Laws*, 1875, p. 7.

place, as MacCulloch argues in a letter, aimed at Malthus, to Macvey Napier,[1] Britain is peculiarly subject to fluctuations in trade, due, for example, to the changes in foreign tariffs, and therefore there are more cases of sudden and unavoidable distress, that need such a provision as the Poor Law's. In the third place, too, it is difficult to see how we can make begging unlawful if we make legal relief inaccessible,[2] any more than we can logically make education compulsory while we insist on the payment of fees. In the fourth place, an indiscriminate private charity is probably more mischievous than a discriminating public relief. Malthus, however, was not against all relief, but only against it when claimed as a right; and he was fully aware that the risks of the English working man were greater than those of his Continental brethren. All he desired was to give the workman scope for that sense of personal responsibility out of which the Poor Law was beguiling him. He knew quite well that no good end would be served by the removal of the Poor Law, unless the public had been educated out of the evil ways of it. He proposed therefore to make a gradual change, the essence of which was to be the disclaimer of any right on the part of a poor man to be supported at the public expense; children have a right to be supported by their parents, but not by the public.[3]

[1] Macvey Napier's *Correspondence*, pp. 29 *seq.* Date 30th Sept., 1821.

[2] *Report of Poor Law Comm.*, 1834; *Remedial Measures*, p. 227.

[3] *Essay on Population*, Appendix, p. 492. It was probably this disclaimer of public duty that led Coleridge to complain, "the entire tendency of the modern or Malthusian political economy is to denation-

Let a law be passed, he said, declaring that no legitimate child born from any marriage taking place a year after the law's enactment, and no illegitimate born two years thereafter, shall ever be entitled to parish relief. "And to give a more general knowledge of this law, and to enforce it more strongly on the minds of the lower classes of people, the clergyman of each parish should, previously to the solemnization of a marriage, read a short address to the parties, stating the strong obligation on every man to support his own children; the impropriety, and even immorality, of marrying without a fair prospect of being able to do this; the evils which had resulted to the poor themselves, from the attempt which had been made to assist, by public institutions, in a duty which ought to be exclusively appropriated to parents, and the absolute necessity which had at length appeared, of abandoning all such institutions, on account of their producing effects totally opposite to those which were intended. This would operate as a fair, distinct, and precise notice which no man could well mistake, and without pressing hard upon any particular individuals, would at once throw off the rising generation from their miserable and helpless dependence upon the Government and the rich."[1] Both their irritation against the upper classes and their helplessness in devising expedients in time of

alize" (*Table Talk*, p. 327). Cf. Toynbee, *Industr. Revol.*, p. 24. But it may have been simply the idea that Malthus, like Ricardo, advocated *laissez faire;* and in this case it is singular he should not have said "Ricardian" instead of "Malthusian."

[1] *Essay*, 2nd ed., IV. vii. p. 538; 7th ed., IV. viii. p. 530.

want, arise from "the wretched system of governing too much. When the poor were once taught, by the abolition of the Poor Laws, and a proper knowledge of their real situation, to depend more upon themselves, we might rest secure that they would be fruitful enough in resources, and that the evils which were absolutely irremediable they would bear with the fortitude of men and the resignation of Christians."[1] However comical may be the picture of a clergyman following up the very un-Malthusian marriage service by such a moral lecture as is here recommended, the principle of the recommendation is sober sense, and has largely influenced the benevolence of later philanthropists. Dr. Chalmers applied it in his Parochial System, which would have been an admirable substitute for the Poor Law on the (unfortunately untrue) hypothesis of an absence of sects. The Mendicity Society (dating from 1815) and the Charity Organization (from 1869) build on the same foundation.

The new Poor Law of 1834 differed from Malthus in that it did not deny the right to relief, and still kept up the fiction that the law of Elizabeth was good, and we had degenerated from it.[2] But it allowed the right only to the indigent,[3] refusing all relief in aid of wages to the merely poor and the able-bodied; and it carried out the principle that dependent poverty (in the words of Malthus) should be held disgraceful and made disagreeable. "Every penny bestowed that tends to render the condition of a pauper more eligible

[1] *Essay*, 2nd ed., p. 539. [2] E. g. *Report of Commissioners*, p. 13.
[3] *Report*, pp. 227-8.

than that of the independent labourer is a bounty on indolence and vice." "In proportion as the condition of any pauper class is elevated above the condition of independent labourers, the condition of the independent class is depressed."[1] If this meant that poor relief should run a race with the average wages of labour, keeping always one stage behind them, it might be argued that in good times a pauper would get too much comfort and in bad times too little food. But the disgrace of dependence and the discomfort of constraint are the deterrents which Malthus himself has most in mind.

Without the discussions raised by the *Essay on Population* it is very doubtful if public opinion would have been so far advanced in 1834 as to make a bill, drawn on such lines, at all likely to pass into law. The abolition of outdoor relief to the able-bodied was nothing short of a revolution. It had needed a lifetime of economical doctrine, reproof, and correction to convince our public men, and to some extent the nation, that the way of rigour was at once the way of justice, of mercy, and of self-interest. The history of the English Poor Law is ample proof that men do not instinctively follow their own interest. It was the ratepayer's interest,[2] unless he was an employer, that relief should be sparely given; and it was given lavishly. It was the poor man's interest to be thrifty and sober; and as a rule he was neither.

[1] *Report*, p. 228.

[2] Even if he were a poor ratepayer, voting a sum of which his richer neighbour would pay the larger share.

There was no hope of reform till both rich and poor learned a deeper sense of their personal responsibility for the remoter effects of their own acts, whether unwisely benevolent or heedlessly selfish. The clear consciousness of personal responsibility seems to Malthus to be the soul and centre of every healthy reform. In this sense, at least, he would say that virtue is knowledge.

His thoughts on society are connected at this point with his thoughts on man's place and duty in the world. His psychology and ethics, slightly as they are sketched, throw light on his sociology and economics, and must be considered before we can estimate his position in social philosophy. This will lead us over the greater portion of the fourth book of the essay, leaving the critical chapters till we come to deal with the Critics as a body.

Note (on p. 316).

The pulpit sometimes supported Malthus, and there is a small book recommending his doctrines in nine "Sermons preached before Friendly and Charitable Societies in the country and written chiefly with the view of illustrating the principles delivered by Mr. Malthus in his *Essay on Population*, of showing their accordance with the precepts of Christianity, and of making them familiar to the understandings of the lower orders. By a Clergyman of the Established Church" (London, Hatchard, 1820).

Internal evidence shows that the book is not by Malthus himself. Indeed the imputation in the Preface of "all the merit of originality in upholding such tenets" to Malthus alone is proof enough.

BOOK III.

MORAL AND POLITICAL PHILOSOPHY.

Cardinal Doctrines of the Malthusian Ethics—Application to Desire of Marriage—Place of Man on the Earth—Criticism of Moral Philosophy—Teleology and Utility—Benevolence and Self-love—Malthus and Paley—Greatest Happiness—Earthly Paradise—Malthus and the French Revolution—Malthus not a Political Reactionary—Not committed to *laissez faire*—His Modifications of that Doctrine—Utilitarianism *plus* Nationality—Experience as much the Riddle as the Interpretation—The State an Organism—Political Ideals before and after 1846.

THE moral philosophy of Malthus, like that of Aristotle, starts from a teleology.

Nature makes nothing in vain. Every desire has its proper place and proper gratification, if we can find them. The passions are the materials out of which happiness is made; and they are therefore to be regulated and harmonized; they are not to be extinguished, or even diminished in intensity.[1] There is a way of so gratifying the desires that they produce a general balance of consequences in favour of happiness; and there is an opposite way with opposite effects. The former is evidently the way of nature, for utility is the only guide of conduct we have apart from

[1] *Essay*, 2nd ed., p. 490; 7th ed., p. 394; cf. pp. 392 top and 396.

Scripture.[1] We must not eradicate any impulses; but we must follow none so far "as to trench upon some other law [*sic*] which equally demands our attention." What is the golden mean, and what is too much or too little, we can only know by our own and others' experience of the consequences of actions.[2] Nature shows us the wrongness of an act by bringing from it a train of painful consequences. Diseases, instead of being the "inevitable inflictions of Providence," are "indications that we have offended against some of the laws of nature. The plague at Constantinople and in other towns of the East is a constant admonition of this kind to the inhabitants. The human constitution cannot support such a state of filth and torpor; and, as dirt, squalid poverty, and indolence are in the highest degree unfavourable to happiness and virtue,[3] it seems a benevolent dispensation that such a state should by the laws of nature produce disease and death, as a beacon to others to avoid splitting on the same rock."[4] As epidemics indicate bad food, unwholesome houses, or bad drainage, and as indigestion follows over-eating, so the misery that follows on too great an increase of numbers is simply the law of nature recoiling on the law-breaker.[5] In this case it has taken a longer experience to teach

[1] *Essay*, 7th ed., IV. x. pp. 442-3; cf. p. 161.

[2] 7th ed., IV. i. p. 390. Cf. above, p. 37.

[3] Not quite logical, if the test of a virtuous action is its tendency to produce happiness.

[4] *Ibid.*, IV. i. p. 390.

[5] 2nd ed., pp. 489, 490, 501; 7th ed., pp. 390, 401. Cf. Paley, *M. and P. Phil.*, I. vi., II. iv.; Tucker, *Light of Nature* (1st ed., 1768), vol. ii. ch. xxix., esp. § 12.

men the conduct most favourable to happiness, and therefore the conduct right for them. But even the best food, best clothing, and best housing have not been taught all at once; and the principle of the lesson is clearly the same in all the cases.

To say, therefore, that the desire of marriage is to be restrained and regulated is not to treat it exceptionally or to deny its naturalness. There is a lawful and there is an irregular gratification even of hunger and thirst; and the irregular is punished both by nature and, when it takes, for example, the form of theft, by human laws. Society could give such punishment only on the ground that the action punished tended to injure the general happiness. The act of the hungry man who steals a loaf is only distinguishable from the act of the hungry man who takes a loaf of his own, by means of its consequences. If all were to steal loaves there would in the end be fewer loaves for everybody.[1] We must apply the same criterion to the irregular gratification of all other desires.

After the desire for food, the desire of marriage is the most powerful and general of our desires. "When we contemplate the constant and severe toil of the greatest part of mankind, it is impossible not to be forcibly impressed with the reflection that the sources of human happiness would be most cruelly diminished if the prospect of a good meal, a warm

[1] *Essay*, 7th ed., IV. i. 391. Kant's test of a moral law, so far as it was not purely dogmatic, was most easily illustrated, or he would have said parodied, by this Utilitarian argument.

house, and a comfortable fireside in the evening were not incitements sufficently vivid to give interest and cheerfulness to the labours and privations of the day."[1] This desire gives strength of character to a man in proportion as the animal element in it is hidden away out of sight, and in proportion as the gratification of it is won by exertion and, it may be, by waiting. To do as Jacob did for Rachel, a man must have some strength of character. Most of us, in the opinion of Malthus, owe whatever of definite plan there is in our lives to the existence of such a central object of affection.[2] Malthus himself, it will appear, did not marry till on the eve of becoming a professor at the East India College, nearly a year after these passages were written. Even in 1798 he wrote: "Perhaps there is scarcely a man who has once experienced the genuine delights of virtuous love, however great his intellectual pleasures may have been, that does not look back to the period as the sunny spot in his whole life, where his imagination loves to bask, which he recollects and contemplates with the fondest regrets, and which he would most wish to live over again."[3] Such a passage, though it disappeared, with other flowers of language, in the later editions of the essay, show us that Malthus, though wiser, was not colder than his fellow-men, and drew his facts from experience as well as observation, of the matters concerned.[4]

[1] *Essay*, 2nd ed., p. 487; 7th ed., p. 392.

[2] *Ibid.*, 2nd ed., p. 488; 7th ed., pp. 392-3; cf. p. 398.

[3] *Ibid.*, 1st ed. (1798), p. 211.

[4] The passage in *A Tale of the Tyne*, which left no trace on Miss

If we assume the intention of the Creator to replenish the earth, we can see a reason in cosmical polity for the strength of this desire of marriage. If the fertility of fertile soils had been as great as the power of population to increase, there would have been no inducement to men to cultivate the poorer soils or frequent the less attractive parts of the earth's surface; human industry and ingenuity would have wanted their first stimulus.[1] As it is, the disparity of the two powers leads to an over-spreading of the world; men are led to avoid over-crowding from fear of the evils that spring from it. Man's duties vary with his situations; and, as these are not uniform, but infinitely various, all his powers are kept in play. This language might make us doubt whether the final cause is the development of man, or simply the replenishment of the earth. If the first essay be allowed in evidence, it is clear that man (with whatever justice) is made the chief end of the earth, though his own chief end is not supposed to be realized there.[2]

The natural theology of Malthus and Paley is the foundation of their ethics. It was the English ethics of last century, not only before Kant, but before Bentham. There are signs that Malthus, in his views of metaphysics and of the "moral sentiments,"[3]

Martineau's own memory, but so faithfully expounded Malthus that he called on purpose to thank her for it (*Autobiogr.*, i. 253), is easily identified in the light of these extracts as ch. iii. p. 56 of ed. 1833.

[1] 2nd ed., pp. 491-2; 7th ed., p. 395. See above, p. 36.

[2] 2nd ed., p. 494; 7th ed., p. 397. Cf. above, p. 38.

[3] The phrase in *Essay*, 7th ed., p. 401.

preferred where he could to draw rather from Tucker than from Paley. Abraham Tucker[1] (the "Edward Search" who began the *Light of Nature* in 1756, and finished it, blind, in 1774) lived for nearly fifty years[2] at Betchworth Castle near Dorking. It is possible in those days, when near neighbours knew each other better than they care to do now, that Daniel Malthus, though the younger man, may have known Tucker. They were both of them Oxford men, small proprietors, eccentric, literary, and fond of philosophizing. Whether through his father at home or through Paley at college, it is certain that Malthus at an early date studied the *Light of Nature* and adopted much of its teaching. Before he appeared in public as an author, he had formed some settled philosophical convictions, which (whatever their value) at least left his mind free for its other work, and kept it at peace with itself as regards the problems of philosophy.

The substantial agreement of his views with the doctrines of the *Moral and Political Philosophy* no doubt helped to bring Malthus under the common prejudice against "Pigeon Paley,"[3] the defender of things as they are and preacher of contentment to starving labourers. When Paley became an open convert to the *Essay on Population*, the public would

[1] Not to be confused with his contemporary, Josiah Tucker, Dean of Gloucester, the forerunner of Adam Smith.

[2] 1727 to 1774, the year of his death. Betchworth, now absorbed in Mrs. Hope's estate of Deepdene, was on the farther side of Dorking from Albury and the Rookery.

[3] Epithet ascribed to George III referred to *M. & Pol. Phil.* III. I. I. apologue of the pigeons.

no doubt believe their suspicions confirmed. But Malthus and Paley agree not as disciple and master, but at most as disciples of the same master. Malthus tries to work out his own philosophy for himself.[1]

It is open to many criticisms. In his ethics he seems to have made no distinct analysis or classification of the passions. He takes for granted that the Passions are on one side and Reason on the other, and there is no middle term between the two except the Design of God, which is worked out by the passions of men as by external nature, and which is (we are left to infer) in some way akin to human reason, for human reason can find it out. The impulse of benevolence, for example, is said to be, like all our natural passions, "general" (by which he seems to mean vague), "and in some degree indiscriminate and blind;" and, like the impulses of love, anger, ambition, the desire of eating and drinking, or any other of our "natural propensities," it must be regulated by experience and frequently brought to the test of utility, or it will defeat its own purpose.[2] In other words, Malthus treats all human impulses as if they were appetites, co-ordinate with each other, primary and irresolvable. All desires are equally natural, and abstractedly considered equally virtuous,[3] though not equally strong, and therefore not equally fit at first sight to carry out their Creator's purpose.

The Reason of Man, therefore, must assist the Reason

[1] A point of difference has been noted above (p. 39) and below (p. 330). He differs from Bentham also, who would not gratify the passions but destroy them. See Held, *Soc. Geschichte*, p. 213.

[2] *Essay*, 7th ed., IV. x. 441.

[3] *Ibid.*, IV. i. 391.

of his Maker in carrying out the teleology of his passions, as well as the teleology of nature itself.[1] The "apparent object" (or evident final cause), for example, of the desire of marriage is the continuance of the race and the care of the weak, and not merely the happiness of the two persons most concerned.[2] To take another example, the object of the impulse of benevolence is to increase the sum of human happiness by binding the human race together.[3] Self-love is made a stronger motive than benevolence for a wise and perfectly ascertainable purpose. The ascertainment of the purpose, however, presents a difficulty. Acknowledging that we ought to do the will of God, how are we to discover it?

We are told in answer to this question, that the intention of the Creator to procure the good of His creatures is evident partly from Scripture and partly from experience; and it is that intention, so manifested, which we are bound to promote. What on God's side is teleology, on man's is utility; utility is the ruling principle of morals. Not being a passion it cannot itself lead to action; but it regulates passion, and that so powerfully, that all our most important laws and customs, such as the institution of property and the institution of marriage, are simply disguised forms of it.[4] As animals, we follow the dictates of nature, which would mean unhindered passion; but as reasonable beings we are under the strongest obliga-

[1] See above, p. 35. [2] 7th ed., p. 441 ft. [3] *Ibid.*, p. 442 top.

[4] *Essay*, III. ii. 279, explains in this way the popular prejudice which, in one case at least, visits the same sin more severely in a woman than in a man.

tions to attend to the consequences of our acts, and, if they be evil to ourselves or others, we may justly infer that such a mode of indulging those passions is "not suited to our state or conformable to the will of God." As moral agents, therefore, it is clearly our duty to restrain the indulgence of our passions in those particular directions, that by thus carefully examining their consequences, and by frequently bringing them to the test of utility, we may gradually acquire a habit of gratifying them only in the way which, being unattended with evil, will clearly "add to the sum of human happiness, and fulfil the apparent purpose of the Creator."[1] All the moral codes which have laid down the subjection of the passions to reason have been really (thinks Malthus) built on this foundation, whether their promulgators were aware of it or not. "It is the test alone by which we can know independently of the revealed will of God whether a passion ought or ought not to be indulged, and is therefore the surest criterion of modern rules which can be collected from the light of nature." In other words, our theological postulates lead us to control our passions so as to secure not merely our own individual happiness, but "the greatest sum of human happiness." And the tendency of an action to promote or diminish the general happiness is our only criterion of its morality.[2]

From this it directly follows that, because the free

[1] *Essay*, 7th ed., IV. x. 442.

[2] *Ibid.*, IV. ii. 401. Cf. Paley, *Moral Philos.*, Vol. I. Book II. ch. iv. p. 65, there quoted, and Tucker, *L. of N.* (1st ed.), vol. ii. ch. xxix., especially §§ 5-7 and 12.

and indiscriminate indulgence of benevolence leads to the reverse of general happiness, we ought to practise a discriminating charity which blesses him that gives and him that takes. There is what Bastiat would call a harmony between the two.

In this case, indeed, nature reinforces utility by making the passion of self-love stronger in men than the passion of benevolence. Every man pursues his own happiness first as his primary object, and it is best that he should do so. It is best that every man should, in the first instance, work out his own salvation, and have a sense of his own responsibility. Not only charity but moral reformation must begin at home. Benevolence apart from wisdom is even more mischievous than mere self-love, which is not to be identified with the "odious vice of selfishness," but simply with personal ambition, the person to whom it is personal including as a rule children and parents, and in fact a whole world besides the single atom or "dividual self."[2] If the desire of giving to others had been as ardent as the desire of giving to ourselves, the human race would not have been equal to the task of providing for all its possible members. But because it is impossible for it to provide for all, there is a tendency in all to provide for themselves first; and, though we consider that the selfish element in this feeling ought to grow less in a man in proportion as he becomes richer and less embarrassed by his own

[1] *Essay*, 7th ed., IV. x. 443, 444 ft.

[2] *Ibid.*, IV. viii. 432, 433, compared with 492.

wants, we must recognize that its existence has been due to a wise provision for the general happiness.[1] Malthus does not deny at the same time that benevolence is always the weaker motive, and needs continually to be strengthened by doctrine, reproof, and correction. It ought always to be thought a "great moral duty" to assist our fellow-creatures in distress.[2]

With these ethical views, it was easy for Malthus to meet the objection that the general adoption of the moral restraint recommended in his *Essay on Population* would diminish the numbers of the people too far. He (or his spokesman) answers[3] that we might as well fear to teach benevolence lest we should make men too careless of their private interests. "There is in such a case a mean point of perfection, which it is our duty to be constantly aiming at; and the circumstance of this point being surrounded on all sides with dangers is only according to the analogy of all ethical experience." There is as much danger of making men too generous or too compassionate, as there is of "depopulating the world by making them too much the creatures of reason, and giving prudence too great a mastery over the natural passions and affections. The prevailing error in the game of life is, not that we miss the prizes through excess of timidity,

[1] *Essay*, 7th ed., App. pp. 492-3. Cf. 7th ed., p. 280: "Self-love is the mainspring of the great machine."

[2] III. vii. 311.

[3] *Edin. Rev.*, 1810 (Aug.), an article on Ingram's *Disquisitions on Population*, and [Hazlitt's] *Letters in Reply to Malthus*. As the relations of Malthus to the *Review* were close at this time, and as the arguments and the style are remarkably like our author's, there is at least a strong probability that he wrote the article, Jeffrey after his custom providing it with a head and tail to disguise the authorship. Cf. Cockburn's *Life of Jeffrey*, Vol. I. 301, 302, cf. 285.

but that we overlook the true state of the chances in our eager and sanguine expectations of winning them.[1] Of all the objections that were ever made to a moralist who offered to arm men against the passions that are everywhere seducing them into misery, the most flattering, but undoubtedly the most chimerical, is that his reasons are so strong that, if he were allowed to diffuse them, passion would be extinguished altogether, and the activity as well as the enjoyments of man annihilated along with his vices."[2]

In his view of the passions and of the moral sentiments, Malthus is clearly a man of the eighteenth century, and on the whole is more nearly at one with Paley than with any moralist after Tucker. There are points of divergence. He could not, in view of his cosmology, have fully approved Paley's definition of virtue, "doing good to mankind in obedience to the will of God and for the sake of everlasting happiness."[3] He may have seen how it followed that a solitary man had no duties, that a pagan had no power to do right, that the moral imperative was hypothetical, and that it had no force for any who abjured their future bliss. At least he contents himself with agreeing that "the will of God is plainly general happiness, as we discover both by Scripture and the light of nature;"[4] and, "provided we discover it, it matters nothing by what means;"—

[1] Cf. *Wealth of Nations*, I. x. 48, 49.

[2] *Edin. Rev.*, 1810 (Aug.), p. 475.

[3] Paley, *Mor. and Pol. Phil.*, I. vii. 9; cf. Malthus, *Essay*, IV. ii. 397, &c. Cf. above, p. 39.

[4] Paley, *ibid.*, I. iv. 14.

there are clear marks of design in the world showing that its Maker willed the happiness of His creatures; and what He willed they should will.

In other words, the ethical system of both is a utilitarianism which is narrow and personal in its motive (the private happiness of the individual in another world), but broad and catholic in its end (the general happiness of human beings in the present world). It is as if God induced us to promote other people's happiness now, by telling us that He would in return promote our own by-and-by. There are signs that Malthus took a larger view, and thought rather of the development of the human faculties[1] than of mere satisfaction of desires, both in this world and in the next; but he nowhere distinctly breaks with Paley, and his division of passions into self-love (or prudence) and benevolence is taken straight from that theologian.[2]

By the vagueness of their phraseology when they spoke of the general sum of happiness, the older utilitarians avoided some of the difficulties that encounter their successors. Apart from the hardness of defining happiness and a sum of happiness,[3] there is a difficulty in fixing the precise extent of the generality. The tendency of utilitarianism in the hands of Bentham was towards equality and the

[1] See above, p. 37. The passages there cited completely refute Held's assertion that "Malthus appealed to Utility in the teeth of his belief in the Bible" (*Sociale Geschichte Englands*, Book I. ch. ii. p. 234).

[2] *Mor. and Pol. Phil.*, vii. 10.

[3] "Any condition may be denominated 'happy' in which the amount or aggregate of pleasure exceeds that of pain."—Paley, *M. and P. Ph.*, I. vi.

removal of privilege; every one to count as one, no one as more than one. But both with him and with the older school it may be doubted whether the doctrine did not tend to benefit the majority at the expense of the minority.

We find Malthus thinking[1] that, had the Poor Laws never existed, there "might have been a few more instances of very severe distress," but "the aggregate mass of happiness among the common people would have been much greater than it is at present." In other words, what he wanted was the "greatest amount of happiness" on the whole, whatever an "amount" of happiness may mean. Malthus would probably have refused to use the formula of Bentham, "the greatest happiness of the greatest number"; he would have counted the first item, the happiness, out of all proportion more important than the second.[2] He had refused something like it at the hands of Paley. "I cannot agree with Archdeacon Paley, who says that the quantity of happiness in any country is best measured by the number of its people. Increasing population is the most certain possible sign of the happiness and prosperity of a state; but the actual population may be only a sign of the happiness that is past."[3] Malthus would not, for example, have wished to see the highlands of Scotland brought back to their ancient condition, in which they had greater numbers

[1] *Essay*, 7th ed., III. vi. 305.
[2] See Mr. Sidgwick's *Method of Ethics*, p. 385 ft.
[3] Quoted from *The Crisis*, by Empson, *Edin. Rev.*, Jan. 1837, p. 482.

than now living in rude comfort, but also greater numbers exposed to precarious indigence.[1]

On the other hand, it is certain (in spite of a common prejudice) that Malthus desired the great numbers as well as the great happiness, and was indeed quite naturally led by his theological views to prefer a little happiness for each of many individuals to a great deal for each of a few. He "desires a great actual population and a state of society in which abject poverty and dependence are comparatively but little known,"[2]—two perfectly compatible requirements, which if realized together would lead to what may be called Malthus' secondary or earthly paradise, which is not above mundane criticism.

This earthly paradise is, even in our author's opinion, the end most visibly concerned in our schemes of reform. His idea of it as a society where moral restraint is perfect, invites the remark that the chief end of society cannot be the mere removal of evil; it must be the establishment of some good, the former being at the utmost an essential condition *sine quâ non* of the latter. Moreover, moral restraint is not the removal of every but only of one evil; and it kills only one cause of poverty. A complete reformation must not only remove all the evils, but must positively amend and transform all the three branches of social economy,—the making, the sharing, and the using of wealth,—not one or even two of them alone. Every Utopian scheme should be tested by

[1] *Report of the Crofters Commission*, 1884, p. 9.
[2] *Essay*, IV. iii. 407.

the question: Does it reform all three, or only one, or two, of the three? Neglect of any might spoil all. A scheme which affects all three, however, must have something like a Religion in it. With these reservations Malthus' picture of the good time coming has much value and interest.[1]

Unlike Godwin, he relies on the ordinary motives of men, which he regards as forms of an enlightened self-love. Self-love is the mainspring of the social machine;[2] but self-love, when the self is so expanded as to include other selves, is not a low motive. Commercial ambition, encouraged by political liberty, and unhampered by Poor Laws, leads naturally to prosperity.[3] The happiness of the whole is to result from the happiness of individuals, and to begin first with them. He "sees in all forms of thought and work the life and death struggles of separate human beings."[4] "No co-operation is required. Every step tells. He who performs his duty faithfully will reap the full fruits of it, whatever may be the number of others who fail. This duty is intelligible to the humblest capacity. It is merely that he is not to bring beings into the world for whom he cannot find the means of support. When once this subject is cleared from the obscurity thrown over it by parochial laws and private benevolence, every man

[1] It would help the social reformer to learn, *e.g.* from clergymen, guardians of the poor, and police magistrates, what exact proportion of the destitution within their experience has been due, (*a*) to the fault of the victim, (*b*) to the fault of his parents, (*c*) to the fraud or oppression of others, and (*d*) to the mere accidents of trade.

[2] 7th ed., p. 280. [3] III. ii. 434. [4] *Scenes of Clerical Life*, p. 250.

must feel the strongest conviction of such an obligation. If he cannot support his children, they must starve; and, if he marry in the face of a fair probability that he will not be able to support his children, he is guilty of all the evils which he thus brings upon himself, his wife, and his offspring. It is clearly his interest, and will tend greatly to promote his happiness, to defer marrying till by industry and economy he is in a capacity to support the children that he may reasonably expect from his marriage; and, as he cannot in the mean time gratify his passions without violating an express command of God, and running a great risk of injuring himself or some of his fellow-creatures, considerations of his own interest and happiness will dictate to him the strong obligation to a moral conduct while he remains unmarried."[1] Supposing passion to be thus controlled, we should see a very different scene from the present. "The period of delayed gratification would be passed in saving the earnings which were above the wants of a single man." Savings Banks and Friendly Societies would have their perfect work; and "in a natural state of society such institutions, with the aid of private charity well directed, would probably be all the means necessary to produce the best practicable effects."[2] The people's numbers would be constantly within the limits of the food, though constantly following its increase; the real value of wages would be raised, in

[1] 7th ed., p. 404.

[2] p. 464, 1817. As early as 1803 (*Essay*, 2nd ed., IV. xi. 589) Malthus had recommended Savings Banks.

the most permanent way possible; "all abject poverty would be removed from society, or would at least be confined to a very few who had fallen into misfortunes against which no prudence or foresight could provide."[1] It must be brought home to the poor that "they are themselves the cause of their own poverty."[2] While Malthus insists against Godwin that it is not institutions and laws but ourselves that are to blame, he still shares, with Godwin, the desire to lessen the number of institutions; and, as a first reform, would repeal at least one obnoxious law.

The relation of Malthus to the French Revolution and its English partisans is indeed not to be expressed in a sentence. It has been said that he cannot be justly described as being a reactionary;[3] and, in truth, besides being a critic of Godwin and of Condorcet, he is influenced to some extent by the same ideas that influenced them. The *Essay on Population* is coloured throughout by a tacit or open reference to the Rights of Man, a watchword borrowed from France by the American Republic, to be restored again at the Revolution. Paine's book on the *Rights of Man*, in reply to Burke's *Reflections on the French Revolution*, had been widely read before it was suppressed by the English Government; and Godwin and Mackintosh[4] were not silenced. Malthus himself,

[1] 7th ed., p. 397. Cf. p. 407, &c.

[2] 7th ed., p. 405. To make the whole picture complete we must add what is said above (ch. i.) on the place of man on the earth, and also (Bk. III. chs. ii. and iii.) on industrial society as it might be.

[3] See above, p. 298.

[4] Mackintosh changed but repented of it. See Macaulay's *Essays*.

as a Whig, does not disparage the rights of man when they meant political freedom and equality, but only when they included the right to be supported by one's neighbour, as had been asserted by the Abbé Raynal and some other writers of the Revolution.[1] As the same assertion was practically made by the English Poor Law, which had venerable conservative prejudice on its side, our author's opposition to it was no proof that his politics were reactionary. His economical antecedents and his political views bound him to the French Revolution. In his range of ideas and his habitual categories he could not depart far from the French Economists, who had helped to prepare the way for the Jacobins. Adam Smith himself had felt their influence. Though he had criticized the noble savage and the state of nature,[2] he had himself a lingering preference for agriculture over manufacture; and he himself spoke of a "natural" price, a "natural" progress of opulence, a "natural" rate of wages, and "natural liberty." To him as to the French writers, Nature[3] meant what would grow of itself if men did not interfere,—the difficulty being that the interference seems also to grow of itself, and it is impossible to separate the necessary protection from the mischievous interference. Malthus retains the phraseology with an even nearer approach to personification. Nature points out to us certain courses of conduct.[4] If we

[1] *Essay*, 7th ed., IV. vi. 420-1.
[2] *W. of N.*, I. i.
[3] More strictly, what grows of itself is natural; what makes it grow of itself is Nature.
[4] See e. g. *Essay*, p. 390.

break Nature's laws, she will punish us. At Nature's mighty feast there is no cover laid for the superfluous new-comer. The Poor Laws offend against Nature; they interfere with human action in a case where it would spontaneously right itself by ordinary motives of self-interest; if men knew they could not count on parish relief, they would probably help themselves. Be the argument worth much or little, its strength is not the greater because of this figure; and his use of it shows that Malthus had not risen above the metaphysical superstitions of his age. But the charge sometimes made against him is that he was not merely not before his age but positively behind it; and this is certainly false.

In politics he was as little of a reactionary as his opponent, who if "in principle a Republican was in practice a Whig."[1] He followed Fox rather than Burke, and lost neither his head nor his temper over the Revolution. "Malthus will prove a peace-monger," wrote Southey in 1808.[2] He was a steady friend of Catholic Emancipation. He saw the folly of attributing with Godwin and Paine all evil to the Government, and with Cobbett all evil to taxation and the funds;[3] but he is one with them all in dislike of standing armies, and is more alarmed at the overbearing measures of the Government against sedition than at the alleged sedition itself. One of

[1] *Life of Godwin*, ii. 266.

[2] Southey wished some "Crusader" like Rickman to write economical articles for the *Quarterly* and keep out Malthus (*Life and Letters*, vol. iii. p. 188).

[3] *Essay*, III. vii. 318: written in 1817.

the most remarkable chapters in the second edition of the essay[1] is on "the effects of the knowledge of the principal cause of poverty on civil liberty." Its main argument is, that, where there is much distress and destitution, there will be much discontent and sedition, and, where there is much of the two last, there will be much coercion and despotism. A knowledge of the chief cause of poverty by taking away the distress would leave Government at least no excuse for tyranny. "The pressure of distress on the lower classes of people, together with the habit of attributing this distress to their rulers, appears to me to be the rock of defence, the castle, the guardian spirit of despotism. It affords to the tyrant the fatal and unanswerable plea of necessity. It is the reason why every free Government tends constantly to destruction, and that its appointed guardians become daily less jealous of the encroachments of power."[2] The French people had been told that their unhappiness was due to their rulers; they overthrew their rulers, and, finding their distress not removed, they sacrificed the new rulers; and this process would have continued indefinitely if despotism had not been found preferable to anarchy. In England "the Government of the last twenty years[3] has shown no great love of peace or liberty," and the country gentlemen have

[1] 2nd ed., IV. vi.; 7th ed., IV. vi. and vii. He must have remembered, when he wrote these words, the imprisonment of his poor tutor Gilbert Wakefield for a seditious pamphlet (1799-1800). See below, Bk. V.

[2] 7th ed., p. 417.

[3] 7th ed., p. 426: written in 1817. For the tendency of the French before the Revolution to look to Government for everything, see *e. g.* Dyer's *Modern Europe*, vol. iv. ch. lii. p. 304.

apparently surrendered themselves to Government on condition of being protected from the mob.[1] A few more scarcities like 1800 might cause such convulsions and lead to such sternness of repression that the British constitution would end as Hume foretold,[2] in "absolute monarchy, the easiest death, the true *euthanasia* of the British constitution." The "tendency of mobs to produce tyranny" can only be counteracted by the subversion, not of the tyrants, but of the mobs. The result would be a lean and wiry people, weak for offence, but strong for defence; there would be freedom at home and peace abroad.[3]

Of course the "knowledge of the principal cause of poverty" is not conceived by Malthus as the only lesson worth learning. He shares the growing enthusiasm of all friends of the people for popular education,[4] and thinks the Tory arguments against instructing the poorer classes "not only illiberal, but to the last degree feeble, if not really disingenuous."[5] "An instructed and well-informed people would be much less likely to be led away by inflammatory writings, and much better able to detect the false declamation of interested and am-

[1] 7th ed., p. 418.

[2] *Essays Moral and Political*, vol. i. p. 49: 'The British Parliament.'

[3] Malthus, *Essay*, 2nd ed., p. 502; 7th ed., p. 402. Cf. a striking passage in the review of Newenham, *Edin. Rev.*, July 1808, pp. 348-9.

[4] *E. g.* 7th ed., pp. 438-9 and 478. Cf. above, p. 56. Horner's letter to Malthus 8th Feb. 1812 (*Mem. of Horner*, vol. ii. pp. 109-10) shows it was an active sympathy. Malthus agreed to act as a "steward" at one of Lancaster's meetings in London.

[5] 2nd ed., pp. 556-7: opponents "may fairly be suspected of a wish to encourage their ignorance as a pretext for tyranny."

bitious demagogues than an ignorant people."[1] These words were written in 1803, four years before Whitbread made his motion on Schools and Savings Banks, and thirteen years before Brougham's Committee on Education.[2] Malthus in fact was in politics an advanced Whig, ahead of his party in ideas of social reform. This may be seen from the following passage, which is only one out of many, that show his large view of his subject. He says that in most countries among the poor there seems to be something like "a standard of wretchedness, a point below which they will not continue to marry." "This standard is different in different countries, and is formed by various concurring circumstances of soil, climate, government, degree of knowledge, civilization, &c." It is raised by liberty, security of property, the diffusion of knowledge, and a taste for the conveniences and the comforts of life. It is lowered by despotism and ignorance. "In an attempt to better the condition of the labouring classes of society, our object should be to raise this standard as high as possible by cultivating a spirit of independence, a decent pride, and a taste for cleanliness and comfort. The effect of a good Government in increasing the prudential habits and personal respectability of the lower classes of society has already been insisted on; but certainly this effect will always be incomplete without a good system of education, and indeed it may be said that no Government can approach to perfection that

[1] 7th ed., p. 439; 2nd ed., pp. 555-6.
[2] Miss Martineau, *Hist. of Peace*, I. vii. 117-18.

does not provide for the instruction of the people. The benefits derived from education are among those which may be enjoyed without restriction of numbers; and, as it is in the power of Governments to confer these benefits, it is undoubtedly their duty to do it."[1]

Our author's historical sense saved him from Ricardian presumptions in favour of *laissez faire*. Writers go too far, however, in declaring unlimited competition to be against the spirit of his work, and asserting that he undervalued the influence of institutions, only that he might save his country's institutions from hasty reform.[2] He knew that society did not grow up on economical principles; instead of beginning with non-interference, and extending interference by degrees where it was found imperative, it began with interference everywhere, and relaxed the interference by degrees where it was found possible and thought desirable. We have begun with status and paternal government, and have made our way towards contract and *laissez faire;* but we have never reached them, because, as men now are, we cannot go on without damage to the common weal. But it seemed to Malthus that experience had shown the need as clearly as the dangers of natural liberty;—history, for example, had clearly proved that the material relief of the poor, which had never been abandoned by the Government, might best have been left to private action. The extreme view would have been that it was not every one's duty in general, but every one's in particular, a responsibility of which no

[1] *Essay*, 7th ed., IV. ix. 440, 441. [2] Held, *Soc. Gesch.*, p. 215.

one could divest himself. But, though Malthus often speaks as if the burden ought to lie specially on a man's relatives and private friends, he does not share Adam Smith's antipathy to associations, and would probably have recognized division of labour to be as necessary in charity as in industry. Still, even as administered by an organization of men specially fitted for the work by nature and choice, the distribution of material relief never seems to him a case where society can help the poor without in some degree injuring their independence and their strength of character. In the matter of charity he is clearly on the side of natural liberty and individualism.

But, in other directions, he has made admissions which seriously modify the unlimited competition of natural liberty. He admits, first of all, that the struggle for existence when it is the struggle for bare life does not lead to progress;[1] and he admits, therefore, in the second place, that the state should interfere with the "system of natural liberty," positively, to educate the citizens,[2] and to grant medical aid to the poor,[3] to assist emigration,[4] and even to give direct relief in money to men that have a family of more than six children,[5]—as well as negatively, to restrict foreign trade when it causes more harm to the public than good to the traders,[6] and to restrict the home trade where children's labour is concerned.[7]

[1] See above, pp. 95, 96, &c.
[2] See above, p. 340.
[3] *Essay*, 7th ed., IV. x. 446-7.
[4] Emigr. Comm. (1827), qu. 3310.
[5] IV. xiii. 474. Potatoes are a godsend to such, he says in another place (*Edin. Rev.*, July 1808, p. 344).
[6] See above, Bk. II. ch. i.
[7] See above, p. 301.

A critic might ask on what principle he justifies these admissions; or might hint that he makes them on no conscious principle at all, but in the spirit of a judge, who is administering a law that he knows to be bad, but prefers to make continual exceptions rather than suggest a new law;—otherwise could any rule stand the test of so many exceptions?

It might be replied that Malthus nowhere writes a treatise on political philosophy, and his views must be inferred from scattered hints, but it does not follow that he was not, consciously or unconsciously, possessed of a guiding principle. His several admissions have a certain logical connection. It is more doubtful whether their connecting principle will seem adequate to a modern reader whose questions in political philosophy have been stated for him by Comte and the latter-day socialists.

The first of the admissions is the more significant, as Malthus, while making it, refuses to approve of the means then actually adopted (by the Poor Law) for raising the level of the weakest citizens, and so fitting them for their struggle. If the absence of provision was an evil, the existing provision was hardly a less one. It was bad for society to give help by giving bread and butter, for that was a gift to full-grown men and women, not really weak, but quite ready to be indolent. A gift of education, on the other hand, is given, he considers, to those who are really incapable of helping themselves and really ignorant of their powers.[1] It makes the weak

[1] E. g. *Essay*, IV. ix. 439.

strong, and tends to remove indolence, not create it.[1] In the same way Factory Acts assist the weak and not the indolent, while the (rare) interference with free trade, the granting of medical relief, the special aid in case of large families, and the aid to Irish peasants, are all of them special remedies in cases where the sufferers could not be expected to foresee and provide against the distress, and were therefore sufferers from circumstances rather than from indolence. Malthus continually takes the view that security is a greater blessing than wealth itself, and insecurity a worse evil than poverty. The circumstances that cause insecurity were therefore in his view the most distressing; they baffled individual effort.

His critics might have answered: "In all the cases mentioned by you as justifying interference, a perfectly enlightened self-interest would have provided against the mishap; and relief of any kind would be in the end equivalent to relief in bread and butter, for, as far as it goes, it allows the more to be left over either to the man or his parents for bread and butter, and thereby it is a relief that fosters indolence." He could rejoin, however, that (even if we grant the practical possibility of such a perfect enlightenment) direct relief appeals far more to indolence than indirect,[2] and the good of the indirect can often, the

[1] In Germany poor scholars from the country are often, when attending the University, billeted for bread and butter on the well-to-do citizens; and learning proves on the whole so inconsistent with laziness, that the practice does not make them unwilling to earn their own living afterwards.

[2] A protective duty is indirect relief of the protected industry, but as a rule the protected are secured against indolence by their own domestic

good of the direct very seldom, outweigh the evil. He would have added that even the direct relief in bread and butter was not opposed by him on any theory, but on the ground of its known tendency to evil,—and, if it had been possible from the nature of men and things to keep the promises of the Poor Law, he would have given his voice for it. He was committed to free trade itself only because and only so far as experience was in its favour. His only axiom in political philosophy was that the end of politics is the greatest happiness of the great body of the people; and his only rule for securing that end was the observation of what, as a matter of experience, actually did secure it.

On the other hand, nothing is clearer from his own writings than that the language of experience owes much of its meaning to its interpreter; and we ask "What were his principles of interpretation?"

The answer is, that, in spite of the affinity between utilitarianism in morals and individualism in politics, he tried to retain the first without the second. He understood moral goodness to consist in the tendency of actions to produce a balance of pleasures over pains; but his utility when examined turned out, as we have seen, to be much nearer the notion of self-development than simply a sum of pleasures irrespective of their quality. At this point the strong grasp which family life held on his fancy lifted him above the notion that the chief end could be the

competition; and the fault of protection lies elsewhere than in encouragement of indolence.

individual happiness of isolated units, and showed him that the real unit was a group. The state to Malthus, as to Aristotle, is an aggregate of families, though he recognizes very clearly that, besides the connection of householder with householder by the common subjection to the laws, there is the common bond of nationality, a community of feeling, a partnership of past traditions, present privileges, and future hopes.[1] It is one of the plainest facts of experience that men are often led by their attachment to their country and countrymen to run counter to their worldly interests.[2]

The nation is a little world within the great world, and on the analogy of the great world it is the scene where difficulties generate talents and bring out the character.[3] From this point of view it is not far from the truth to parody a well-known description of modern Judaism, and describe the political philosophy of Malthus as Utilitarianism *plus* a Nationality. The individualism of Malthus is limited by the particular institutions and particular interests of the English nation.[4] In his intellectual history a strong emphasis on the state preceded the emphasis on the individual; and even in his mature view the state is limited in its interference with the citizens only by its powers of doing good to them. But he holds with Adam Smith and the other economists that its powers of doing good to them are very much

[1] Renan, *Qu'est ce-qu'une Nation?*

[2] Cf. above, p. 225.

[3] Cf. p. 36.

[4] The reaction against Rousseau and Godwin may partly account for the absence of Cosmopolitanism.

narrower than on the old conception of the state, as a kind of family. The duties of a state to the citizens are narrower than those of a father to his children, because what the father can and must do for his children the state cannot do for its citizens with equal safety to their independence. It remains, however, true that the relation of state to citizen is not the commercial relation of one contracting party with another; it is a relation prior to the commercial, and gives to all contracts whatever validity they have.

If Malthus himself had been asked to reconcile his departure from the general principle of natural liberty with his general adherence to it, he would have made some such answer as the following: "From the first, when I wrote in 1798, it appeared to me that the action of Government could neither have so uniformly bad an effect as Godwin supposed, nor so uniformly good as Pitt's Bill implied. If, as Godwin desires, there were no Government, but only a chastened *laissez faire*, unsophisticated human nature would be quite enough to bring back misery and sin.[1] But the chastening of the *laissez faire* could not in my opinion take place without the Government, for it is one of the most proper functions of Government, not adequately dischargeable by individuals, to provide for the people the education that is supposed to chasten. Even when that provision has been made, the education will not do its perfect work if it has not included the particular

[1] See above, ch. i.

doctrines which it has fallen to me more than any man to bring home to the public mind. With such an education there will be hope for better things. Things as they are and the struggle for existence as it now is among the helpless classes can please me as little as Godwin. It is a struggle which leads to no progress. But, unlike Godwin, I do not regard Government as necessarily creating the distress; and I certainly regard it as the necessary engine for removing the distress by education in the end, and toning down its effects by restrictions for the present. If only as an engine of education, paternal government must be a permanent factor of society. Where a public necessity has been well supplied by individual action, I should leave it in the hands of individuals; but not otherwise. I did not object to the Poor Law on the broad ground that it took the place of private action, but because its own action was mischievous. I should try every case on its merits, and be guided to interfere or not interfere by the known results of the existing policies."

In so speaking, Malthus would no doubt have justified his own consistency. But the modern reader might justly reply to Malthus, that we have often to judge tendencies as well as results, and experience becomes then an uncertain guide; he might complain that Malthus himself is sometimes led to judge both of them by a half-acknowledged supplementary principle of the balance of classes and safety of the mean, which can be applied in a way very unfavourable to popular rights. He might urge that the apparent success of an institution might have been due to a concurrent cause that cancelled its defects, and we cannot always pronounce on its merits from experience of it. How can experience help us unless we have the key to its interpretation? Without such a key nothing would be so false as facts except figures. In human politics mere survival is seldom the test of fitness.

If we compare the state to an organism and convert our simile into a rule of judgment, we may say that, when each part has its function and contributes to the efficiency of the whole, the body politic is well; when any part fails us, there is need of the doctor or surgeon. This figure seems to give us a key for the interpretation of social experience; but unhappily the figure itself needs an interpreter.[1] If we interpret organism as the ideal union of members in one body, it ceases to be a simile, for the body politic is not merely like this union,—it is the best example of it. For in the body politic the general life is the source of all individual energy, and at the same time the individual members are continually paying back the debt, by an active sympathy and conscious union with the commonwealth, to which the commonwealth in its turn owes all its collective energy; the citizen is nothing without his state, or the state without its citizens. This is to make the figure useful, by making it change places with the thing prefigured. So long

[1] Some one has said, "Was man nicht definiren kann, zieht man als Organismus an;" and we had been told, long before, that a simile is either "idem per idem" or "idem per aliud," either of them a logical fallacy.

as the same idea is grasped in both, their relation in rhetoric need not affect us.

Such an idea of the state would lead us beyond the admissions of Malthus to some such demands as the following:—For his every possession, the citizen must be able to show some service rendered to his countrymen, and must be taught and expected to hold his property in trust for the common good, that so the body politic may have no useless member. In proportion as private possession involves monopoly, its use should be jealously restricted in the public interest, which in the extreme cases would lead to the withdrawing of it, with as little friction as might be, from the private owner to the state. Education acts, sanitary laws, and factory acts should be strictly and universally enforced, not for the sake of the parents, guardians, and employers, or even altogether for the sake of the sufferers themselves, but for the sake of the community, in order that in the struggle for existence every competitor should "start fair" as an efficient citizen, with full possession of his powers of mind and body. For the rest, security and order should be the watchword of the state, free course being allowed to commercial and industrial enterprise, scientific inquiry, and speculative discussion, in order that progress may be made in the surest of all ways, by the moral and intellectual development of the individual citizens, which will soon express itself in their institutions. With these postulates, half from the old economists and half from the new reformers, on the way to be realized, and with industrial co-operation in prospect, we need not despair of the future of man on our part of the earth.

Tried by such a standard Malthus certainly fails to give us a perfect political philosophy, and seems little farther advanced than his master Adam Smith, who taught that the state was profitable only for defence, for justice, and for such public works as could not be so well done by individuals. With all his regard for the nation, Malthus looks at social problems too much from the individual's point of view. He speaks much, for example, of the good effect, on the individual man, of the domestic ideal, and of the ideals of personal prosperity in the world, both built on security of property and liberty of action. He speaks little of the duty of the citizen to the community, and of the return he owes it for his security and liberty. The citizen in his picture of him seems to have nothing but duties to his family and nothing but claims on the state. The citizen is lost in the householder. He is content to be let alone, and does not positively and actively recognize his identity with the legislative power, and his obligation to repay service with service. Later political philosophy would press the counter-claims of the community on the citizen. It would demand, for example, that he shall neither leave his lands waste nor preserve his game, if either practice is contrary to the public good. It would keep in mind that the holders of large fortunes owe more to the public for protection of them than the holders of small, and should bear a heavier burden of taxes. It would not leave men to do as they willed with their own.[1]

In regard to the lowest classes that are hardly to be called citizens, for they are struggling in hopeless weakness for mere bread, Malthus never seems to see that his own acknowledgment of their powerlessness to rise must justify much more than the mere establishment of compulsory education for their children or even mechanics' institutes for themselves. It would justify the adoption of such measures as will make their surroundings likely to give and preserve to them a higher standard of living. It would sanction measures of "local option" to keep away from them the infection of dangerous moral diseases; and it would enforce the obligation on the owners of houses to make them habitable and healthy. It would give town and country tenants secure tenure by law, where an insecure tenure of custom had induced them to spend labour on their holdings.

The older economists had the just idea that security in possession was the first condition of industrial progress; but they did not see that this very principle would justify very large restrictions on the use of property, and that the restrictions would increase in largeness as the property approached the nature of a monopoly; they did not see that for the public interest it may be as necessary to prohibit deer forests as to pull down unsanitary dwellings or enforce vaccination.

[1] *Essay*, Bk. IV. ch. x. p. 445. "Every man has a right to do what he will with his own." But the question is :—What is his own?

The reason was that for a long time in England it was a hard enough task for reformers to secure the negative freedom of being let alone, the freedom of trade and of the press and of local government, with the abolition of privileges. Cobden's attempt to resolve Politics into Economics was well-timed and fruitful in its generation; and the Manchester school has still a part to play in our own time. But the special work of political reform in the future is to achieve the positive freedom, "the maximum of power, for all members of human society alike, to make the best of themselves."[1] Of this programme neither Malthus nor any writer of his day had any clear conception. He himself had no claim to a seer's vision; and the horizon of his opponents was never wider than his own.

It is time to go back to the *Essay* and confront its opponents. We have now a sufficient knowledge of the economics and philosophy of Malthus to be able to sympathize with him under misconception, or at least to understand what appearance an objection would wear to his mind. Not that we have a complete picture of the man, or even a view of his entire mental furniture, which is more than this *curta supellex;* but we see enough to judge the cause of the *Essay* on its merits, not prejudiced, favourably or unfavourably, by the life and character of the author.

[1] Professor T. H. Green, *Liberal Legislation and Freedom of Contract*, Oxford, 1881.

BOOK IV.

THE CRITICS.

Three Questions for the Critics—Parr and *Thoughts on Parr*—Pulpit Philosophy—Godwin's Blessing in 1801—The Cursing in 1820—Theology—The Command to Noah—The Ratios—Population "fitful"—S. T. Coleridge among the Economists—James Grahame—Empson's Classification of Critics—Weyland and Arthur Young—"Cannot, therefore ought not"—Spence's *Plan* and Owen's—*Progress and Poverty*—*Das Kapital*—Herbert Spencer—Classification of Critics—Ethics of the Hearth and of the World—End and Means of Malthus.

THE critics of Malthus had three questions before them: Do the conclusions of Malthus follow from his premises? Does he himself draw them? Are they true as a matter of fact? The answers will be best given by a short survey of the principal critics with whom Malthus contended in his lifetime, and those who have most formidably contended with his followers since his death.

There is a sense in which the *Essay on Population* begins and ends with Godwin, for it begins and ends with the question of human perfectibility. The relations of Malthus and Godwin are as it were the tale on which the play is founded.

Godwin's *Political Justice* was written in 1793, his

Enquirer in 1797, and Malthus' *Essay* in 1798. Others kept the ball a-rolling. On the Easter Tuesday of 1800 Dr. Samuel Parr preached an anniversary sermon in Christ's Hospital before the Corporation of London. He chose his text from Galatians vi. 10: "As we have therefore opportunity, let us do good unto all men, especially unto them who are of the household of faith." Like Butler's sermons in the Rolls Chapel, the discourse was really a treatise on moral philosophy. It began by contrasting the selfish and the benevolent system of ethics, pronouncing both of them faulty. If the one has done less harm, the other has done less good than might have been expected, for it has been connected with the new doctrine of universal philanthropy. The new doctrine is false because local neighbourhood of all men is impossible, *vi terminorum*, and a widening out of the feelings that usually prevail between local neighbours would only make those feelings thin and watery.[1] Man's obligations cannot be stretched beyond his powers; he has no power, and therefore no obligation to do good unto all men.[2] Love of the universe, in the intense sense of the word love, can only belong to the omnipotent Being who has the care of the universe upon Him. We, being men, must only see to it that our benevolence is of His quality, extending, like His, to the unthankful and to the evil. But a universal philanthropist exaggerates and pampers this one particular form of the duty of benevolence

[1] *τὴν φιλίαν ἀναγκαῖον ὑδαρῆ γίνεσθαι.* *Ar. Pol.*, II. ii.

[2] See above, p. 310.

at the expense of the rest, and forgets duties that lie near to him, towards kindred and friends and neighbours; he neglects common duties of life in favour of the uncommon and fanciful. Very different is "the calm desire of general happiness," which draws those that are near still nearer, and makes us value and assist the benevolent institutions, like Christ's Hospital, which are at our own doors.

The hearers of the sermon could have no doubt at whom it was aimed; and the footnotes of the published version of it contained large quotations from the *Essay on Population* and large direct commendations of its author, which made the sermon's oblique censure of Godwin the more stinging.

Pulpit philosophizing was not rare in those times; it had been practised since Butler's days by Dr. Ezra Styles[1] in 1761; and Dr. Richard Price had used a dissenter's pulpit to utter his enthusiastic views on the future improvement of mankind (1787) and the love of our country (1789).[2] Burke had denounced him for this in his *Reflections*;[3] but, if Parr could do the same thing on the other side a few years afterwards, it cannot have been any great singularity. Parr's sermon was the subject of Sydney Smith's first paper in the *Edinburgh Review* (Oct. 1802); but its economical interest is due to its effect on Godwin. Godwin had been assailed shortly before by Sir James Mackintosh, a former friend and political

[1] *Discourse on the Christian Union.* See *Essay on Population*, 7th ed., p. 254 n.; Price, *Observations*, p. 206 n.

[2] From Matth. vi. 10, and Psal. cxxii. 2 *seq.*

[3] See esp. pp. 12—18, and 20 (4th ed., 1790).

ally, in his *Discourse on the Law of Nature and Nations*, delivered in Lincoln's Inn Hall, 1799; but Dr. Parr's censures were more severe. Parr may have been alienated by an offensive description in the *Enquirer*[1] of the clergy, as characterized by "a perennial stationariness of understanding, abortive learning, artificial manners, infantine prejudices, and arrogant infallibility." As all the other professions were equally well abused, the censure need not have been taken to heart. The letter of Malthus to Godwin, written after the publication of the *Enquirer*, is full of courtesy. At that time, and indeed for a few years afterwards, there was nothing but good-will between the two writers. When Godwin in 1801 made his letters to his three critics into a book,[2] under the title, *Thoughts on Dr. Parr's Spital Sermon*, with remarks on Mackintosh and the writer of the *Essay on Population*, he was bitter only against the two former. He was surprised at the "overbearing scornfulness" of Mackintosh, and at the "venom" of Dr. Parr. If he had changed some of his views it was not in deference to their criticism. Of the *Essay on Population*, "and the spirit in which it is written," he "can never speak but with unfeigned respect;" contending only that it is meant to attack his conclusions and not his premises.[3] Parr had hailed it as a complete demonstration that Godwin's scheme of equality

[1] Pt. II. Essay V. pp. 228 *seq.* *Life*, ii. 292. Cf. ii. 64.

[2] *Life*, ii. 64.

[3] *Thoughts*, p. 10 and n. Cf. pp. 43, 45. In *Progress and Poverty* (p. 93, ed. 1881) we are told that Godwin "until his old age disdained a reply" to Malthus.

would not work, and many better men had felt their mouths shut, and had begged Godwin to speak for them. Godwin consents in these *Thoughts*. If he was sincere in saying, "I confess I could not see that the essay had any very practical bearing on my own hopes" (p. 55), he must have been in the state which the *Enquirer* ascribes to the clergyman: "He lives in the midst of evidence and is insensible to it. He is in daily contemplation of contradictions and finds them consistent. He listens to arguments that would impress conviction upon every impartial hearer and is astonished at their futility. He never dares trust himself to one unprejudiced contemplation. He starts with impatience and terror from its possible result." Malthus, on the other hand, though in orders, has behaved very unlike the clergyman of the *Enquirer*, for we are told by Godwin himself, "he has neither laboured to excite hatred nor contempt against me and my tenets; he has argued the questions between us just as if they had never been made a theme for political party and the intrigues of faction; he has argued just as if he had no end in view but the investigation of evidence and the development of truth" (p. 55 ft.). Moreover, he has "made as unquestionable an addition to the theory of political economy as any writer for a century past. The grand propositions and outlines of his work will, I believe, be found not less conclusive and certain than they are new. For myself, I cannot refuse to take some pride in so far as by my writings I gave the occasion and furnished an incentive to the producing so valuable a treatise" (p. 56). Surely concession could no further go. Godwin even admits the arithmetical and geometrical ratios.[1] His criticisms are all on the checks, which (be it remembered) were only the checks of the first essay, vice, misery, and the fear of them. Are Governments henceforward to prevent the evils of an excessive population by encouraging these unsightly counter-agents? and is every scheme for the amelioration of man's lot foredoomed? No, the "author of the essay" has too small an idea of the resources of the human mind; it is no conclusive argument against a scheme to say that when it is realized it will probably not last.[2] He does not attach sufficient weight to the fact that in England, for example, "prudence and pride" prevent early marriages, and from late ones come smaller families. In a state of universal improvement there would be not less but more of these feelings, and a similar effect would follow in a greater degree.[3]

That there was force in this reasoning appears from the way in which Malthus received it when stated to him by letter a few months after the publication of the first essay. He replied that the "prudence" in question, if existing in Godwin's new society, would mean an eye to the main chance; it would mean that one man is strengthening his position and getting to himself more than the minimum of necessaries; if you prevent this, what becomes of your freedom? if you do not, what becomes of your equality and wealth? Secondly, the effect of the prudence would

[1] *Thoughts*, p. 61. [2] *Ibid.*, p. 67. [3] *Ibid.*, pp. 72-3.

be that the population would not be the greatest possible, but considerably within the limits of the food; and yet you object to present society, that its arrangements prevent the "greatest practicable population." In all our political theories, if we would trace to particular institutions the evil that is really due to them, we must deduct the evil that is known to be due to other causes. "The very admission of the necessity of prudence to prevent the misery from an overcharged population, removes the blame from public institutions to the conduct of individuals. And certain it is, that almost under the worst form of government, where there was any tolerable freedom of competition, the race of labourers, by not marrying, and consequently decreasing their numbers, might immediately better their condition, and under the very best form of government, by marrying and greatly increasing their numbers they would immediately make their condition worse." [1]

This was no doubt a point against Godwin, but it was also a point against Malthus himself. The essay in its first form had not made sufficient allowance for "prudence"; and the introduction of moral restraint in the second edition might very plausibly have been ascribed by Godwin's friends to Godwin himself, in spite of the elaborate reply to the *Thoughts* in a chapter afterwards dropped.[2] Godwin said to him afterwards that he had no right to introduce a new element into his solution of the problem, and pretend

[1] Letter of M. to G., Album Aug. 1798. *Life of Godwin*, I. 324. They had met in London (Ibid. 321).

[2] See above, p. 208 n. In the 5th edition he turns his back on Godwin and adresses Owen.

that it was the same solution as before;[1] if he altered his premises he ought to alter his conclusion. To which Malthus might have answered, that, though his conclusion is altered, it retains its value as an argument against Godwin. At first the tendency of numbers to increase up to the food was described as an obstacle fatal to progress; now it is indeed an obstacle which must be faced and overcome, but it is fatal not to progress, but only to equality. Godwin himself had at first considered it an entirely imaginary obstacle which might be ignored for the present by reformers; and his very doctrine of prudence amounts to an admission that his view of it had changed.

Godwin himself was not conscious of his change of front; as the seventh of thirteen children he may have thought the matter personal; and whatever concessions he had made in 1801 he withdrew in 1820. In that year, with David Booth, the patient author of the *English Analytical Dictionary*, to arrange his statistics and vouch for his calculations, he published an elaborate reply to the *Essay on Population*. The politicians, the political economists, the bulk of the press, and the public had accepted the Malthusian doctrines, though the conversion of the public was no deeper than it was on Free Trade, and the statesmen with a few exceptions were not sorry to make capital out of the "odiousness" of the doctrines whenever the "acknowledged truth" of them would

[1] So Coleridge (MS. note to p. vii of his quarto copy of the essay): "And of course you wholly confute your former pamphlet, and might have spared yourself the trouble of *making up* the present quarto."

not serve their turn. Still it seemed true that time had declared for Malthus, and Godwin had fallen out of notice. Sydney Smith's assertion,[1] "Malthus took the trouble of refuting him, and we hear no more of Mr. Godwin," is not very far from the truth. Malthus had survived his refutation, and Godwin his reputation. Pitt, Paley, and Copleston were with Malthus; he had gained over Hallam among historians, James Mill, Senior, and Ricardo among economists, Brougham, Mackintosh, and even Whitbread among politicians. Southey, Hazlitt, and Cobbett were not a sufficient make-weight. Hazlitt in his *Reply* to the *Essay on Population* (in letters of which some appeared in Cobbett's *Pol. Register*, 1807) acknowledges the popularity, though he predicts its decay.[2] It seems clear that in educated circles at least the view of Malthus was as early as 1820 what it was in 1829, "the popular view,"[3] which is quite compatible, as Darwin long experienced, with great unpopularity in particular quarters. No better evidence could be given of this popularity than the unwilling testimony given by Godwin himself in his new book.[4] At the end of 1819 Brougham had referred in the House of Commons to the principle of Malthus as "one of the soundest principles of political economy," and said it was melancholy to observe how the press scouted it and abused its defenders.[5] The press, however, was

[1] *Edin. Rev.*, 1802, on Dr. Rennel's *Discourses*, Syd. Sm., *Works*, i. p. 8.
[2] p. 18. Compare De Quincey's answer to Hazlitt in *London Magazine*, 1823 (vol. viii. pp. 349, 459, 569, 586).
[3] Senior, *Lect. on Pop.*, p. 35. [4] *Population*, I. iv. p. 27 (1820).
[5] Cf. also speech on 9th April, 1816. Hansard, *sub dato*, p. 1109.

divided. The *Edinburgh Review* from the first had sided with Malthus. The *Quarterly* had begun by strong hostility (Dec. 1812, pp. 320 *seq.*); had softened its tone as time went on (Dec. 1813, pp. 157 *seq.*, and Oct. 1814, pp. 154-5); had spoken with hesitation and doubtfulness (Oct. 1816, pp. 50 *seq.*); and had at last completely surrendered (July 1817, pp. 369 *seq.*), confessing it to be "much easier to disbelieve Mr. Malthus than to refute him" (p. 396), thereafter utilizing his doctrine for the support of things as they are, only regretting that Malthus himself would not do the same a little more stoutly (pp. 402-3). Finally, as we have seen, Malthus, after having contributed to the *Edinburgh*, became a contributor to the *Quarterly*. The change of public opinion, illustrated by the conversion of the *Quarterly*, gave greater bitterness to the attacks of the enemies that remained unconverted. But it gave them no new arguments.

In Godwin's *Enquiry concerning Population* (when we neglect mere epigrams such as "a man is surer that he has ancestors than that he will have posterity") there are substantially four arguments:—Malthus has changed his position; the world is not peopled; the ratios are not as he represents; and experience is against him. We have already discussed the first. The use of the second implies a misunderstanding of the Malthusian position, for it ignores distinction between actual and possible supplies of food, and does not allow that a man is "confined" by four walls unless he touches them.[1]

[1] See above, p. 75. Cf. also above, pp. 142 *seq.*, on Emigration.

Godwin does not mend the argument by comparing it to the objection brought against Christianity—"the world is not yet Christianized"; still less by appealing to Christianity itself, and taunting Malthus with the texts, "Increase and multiply," "Happy is the man that hath his quiver full of them," "made a little lower than the angels," "forty sons and thirty grandsons, which rode on threescore and ten ass colts," "In the last days some shall depart from the faith, forbidding to marry."[1] Malthus had been attacked in 1807 by a Puritan or Covenanting pamphlet entitled, 'A summons of Wakening, or the evil tendency and danger of Speculative Philosophy, exemplified in Mr. [Sir John] Leslie's *Enquiry into the Nature of Heat*, and Mr. Malthus' *Essay on Population*, and in that speculative system of common law which is at present administered in these kingdoms.'[2] The body of this book had been even more remarkable than its title, for it had proved Malthus guilty not merely of heterodoxy, but of atheism. "It is evident to any one who attentively reads the *Essay on Population* that its author does not believe in the existence of God, but substitutes for Him sometimes the principle of Population, sometimes that of Necessity." Sadler many years later declared in the same spirit that "the insults the theory of Malthus levels at God, and the injuries it meditates inflicting upon man, will be endured by neither."[3]

Once for all, let Parson Malthus explain his con-

[1] Godwin, *Popn.*, I. xiii. 106. Cf. I. iv. 22, II. ii. 142, VI. vi. 585.
[2] Hawick, 1807, especially p. 84. [3] Sadler, *Popn.*, I. i. 15 (1830).

sistency with the religious text-book of his Church. Prior to the injunction given to men to increase and multiply, come, says Malthus, all the moral and physical laws without which they cannot increase or multiply. Suppose the command had been to increase and multiply not men but vegetables; this could not mean, "Sow the seed broadcast, in the air, over the sea, on stony ground," but, "Take all the means made necessary, by pre-existing laws, to secure the best growth of vegetables." That man would best obey the command, who should prepare the soil, and provide for the watering and tilling of it, where those things were wanting before. So he will best obey the command to increase and multiply Men, who prepares food for men where there was none before, and not he who brings them recklessly into the world without any such provision. "I believe it is the intention of the Creator that the earth should be replenished, but certainly with a healthy, virtuous, and happy population, not an unhealthy, vicious, and miserable one. And, if, in endeavouring to obey the command to increase and multiply, we people it only with beings of the latter description and suffer accordingly, we have no right to impeach the justice of the command, but our irrational mode of executing it." He might have added, that to give any other interpretation of the passage in Genesis is to forget the circumstances in which the words were spoken. The Deluge had just swept away all the earth's inhabitants except one family, expressly on the score of wickedness; and, if

[1] Append. to 3rd ed., 1806; 7th ed., p. 485; cf. pp. 395, 446, and al.

a wicked replenishing were not desirable, an unhappy or a poor one would be at the best only one degree less so. Regarding the question then purely from the outside, we cannot find anything in the writings of Parson Malthus inconsistent with his ecclesiastical orthodoxy; and we can hardly believe that freethinking Godwin was very serious in the objection.

Malthus himself replies to it as a charge commonly brought against him by others, with no reference to Godwin in particular. For the most part he ignores Godwin's book on Population, as mere rhetoric and scurrility.[1] Godwin, however, had given more than two years of hard labour to the writing of it;[2] and his biographer regards it as the last work of his best days. He employed his son William and his friend Henry Blanch Rosser to help him, in addition to Booth. His whole mind was occupied with Booth's calculations and his own deductions from them. He himself "could not pursue a calculation for an hour without being sick to the lowest ebb."[3] If Booth lagged behind him he was miserable. He rose in early morning to note down an idea and was ill for the rest of the day after it. He is satisfied, however, with the result of his labours. He thinks his chapter on the Geometrical Ratio will delight his friends and astonish his foes. In any case his comfort is that "truth" will prevail, and, whether through him or another, "the system of Malthus can never rise again, and the world is delivered from this accursed apology in

[1] See Appendix to ed. 1825, 7th ed., p. 527. [2] *Life*, ii. 271.
[3] *l. c.* p. 259.

favour of vice and misery and hard-heartedness and oppression,"[1] and the world will see that there is "no need of any remedies," for the numbers of mankind never did and never can increase in the ways described by Malthus.[2] A few of his younger friends[3] believed him successful; and the book was mentioned in the House of Commons as a conclusive refutation of Malthus, especially in regard to the ratios.[4] But the fact remains not only that poor Godwin made no bread and butter by it,[5] but that he converted no one whose opinion in such a matter was of any weight. Mackintosh, though at peace again with his old friend, when he writes to him in September 1821,[6] cannot praise his work; even thinks its tone intolerant; and will only say that he sees nothing in the Malthusian doctrines inconsistent with perfectibility. He takes pains at the same time to disclaim the authorship of the notice in the *Edinburgh Review* for July 1821, which was lacking in the courtesy due to Godwin, though it did not reproduce the scurrility of the earliest review of him.[7] The inconclusiveness of the book, even in the view of Malthus' opponents, appears from the stream of new refutations, which made no pause.

Even the question of the ratios was not settled. Godwin had counted his discussion of them the most important part of his book. It gives us his third

[1] *Life*, ii. 259, 260. Cf. what Godwin writes to Sir John Sinclair, July 1821 (Sinclair's *Correspondence*, i. 393). [2] *l. c.* p. 271.
[3] Morgan and Rosser, *e. g.* See *Life*, ii. 272-5; cf. p. 280.
[4] *Edin. Rev.*, July 1821, p. 364. [5] *Life of Godwin*, ii. 274.
[6] *Ibid.*, pp. 274-5. [7] No. 1, Oct. 1802, esp. p. 26.

substantial argument against Malthus. Godwin takes up,[1] what seems to have been a common charge, that the essayist had written a quarto volume to prove that population increases in a geometrical and food in an arithmetical ratio. The essayist had answered, as long ago as 1806,[2] that the first proposition was proved as soon as the facts about America were authenticated, and the second was self-evident; his book was meant less to prove the ratios than to trace their effects. His authorities, as he told Godwin afterwards,[3] were Dr. Price, Styles, Benjamin Franklin, Euler, and Sir William Petty, supplemented, for figures, by Short and Süssmilch and the censuses of the United States and England, and, for principles, by Adam Smith and Hume. We have already seen[4] how far the simile of geometrical and arithmetical ratios was meant to be pressed. Godwin thinks he exposes it by arguing that the increase of population can never be quite exactly geometrical[5] (which Malthus would admit),—that America was an exception[6] (in face of the maxim that the exception tests the rule),—that, in order to suppose population doubling itself in the United States, we must suppose it, as regards births, doing the same in the Old World (in other words, fact is the same as tendency),

[1] *Population*, I. i.
[2] Appendix to 3rd ed., p. 520 n.; 7th ed., p. 491 n.
[3] See his Letter to Godwin, dated October 1818, and quoted in Godwin's *Population*, Bk. II. ch. i. pp. 116—123, with comments.
[4] See above, p. 66.
[5] *Population*, II. x. 244-7.
[6] *E. g.* II. xi. 274, 282, but especially I. iv. 25, and for the third argument, pp. 29, 30, cf. pp. 43—50, &c. Cf. also Godwin to Sinclair in Sinclair's *Correspondence*, i. 393.

—that the normal increase is not that of America but that of Sweden,[1] in which case (Malthus would answer) the normal increase must be one that takes place in face of very severe restrictions. To the charge of damaging the borrowed kettle the old Irishwoman had three answers:—It was cracked when I got it; it was whole when I returned it; I never had it. So Godwin's views of the American colonies vacillated between three inconsistent propositions: the great increase of the numbers is natural (or spontaneous), but that of the food is greater still;[2] the great increase is not natural, but due to immigration;[3] there has been no great increase at all.[4] The reader has three alternative arguments presented to him, and it matters little whereby he is convinced, if only in the end he is persuaded to believe with Godwin, that population requires no checks at all,[5] and is a fitful principle.[6] In history, says Godwin, it seems to operate by fits and starts; and such irregular effects cannot have a uniform cause. It might be replied that in the same sense gravitation is fitful, for we seem to break it by walking upstairs as well as down, by using a siphon as well as a water-jug, or by drying up a drop of ink with blotting-paper instead of letting it sink down into the paper. Yet in these cases the fitfulness is never imputed to the absence of a cause, but to the presence of more

[1] Population tends to double in a hundred years, and there is no risk of over-population except in occasional times of dull trade (Letter of Godwin to Sinclair, Sinclair's *Correspondence*, l. c.). A notable exception.

[2] *Population*, II. xi. 251-2. [3] IV. i. [4] II. ii. 127, and cf. above.

[5] II. xi. 287, &c., &c. [6] III. iii. 327 *seq*.

causes than one. To believe, as Godwin seems to do, in occult laws which vary with the circumstances is to believe in no laws at all. The only constancy would be the constant probability of miracles.[1] Free-thinkers had not as yet identified themselves with the party of order in physics; and perhaps Godwin was simply carrying out his dislike of law one step farther. Having applied it to politics (1793) and to style (1797), he now applied it to nature (1820). He deliberately placed a whole army of facts out of the range of science. It was fortunate for himself that he appeared no more in the character of an economist, but left Booth the task of replying to the Edinburgh reviewer.[2]

If economical criticism was weak with Godwin, the political philosopher, it was still weaker with Coleridge, the philosophizing poet. The main criticisms of Coleridge[3] are contained in manuscript marginal comments with pen and pencil written on his copy of the second (quarto) edition of the Essay (1803), now in the British Museum. When Malthus writes (in Preface, p. vi) that if he had confined himself to general views, his main principle was so incontrovertible that he could have entrenched himself in an impregnable fortress, Coleridge breaks in: "If by the main principle the author means both

[1] *Coups d'état* in nature. Paul Bert, *L'Enseignement Primaire*, 1880, p. xxviii.

[2] *Edinburgh Review*, July 1821. Cf. Letter to the Rev. T. R. Malthus by David Booth (1823), who had assumed Malthus to be the reviewer. See Ricardo's Letters to Malthus 11th Oct. 1821, p. 198.

[3] Others, in *Table Talk* and *Biogr. Literaria*, are chiefly declamation.

the *Fact*[1] (i. e. that population unrestrained should infinitely outrun food) and the deduction from the fact, *i. e.* that the human race is *therefore* not indefinitely improvable, a pop-gun would batter down the impregnable Fortress. If only the Fact be meant, the assertion is quite nugatory, in the former case vapouring, in the latter a vapour." (And on p. vii :) "Are we now to have a quarto to teach us that great misery and great vice arise from poverty, and that there must be poverty in its worst shape wherever there are more mouths than loaves and more Heads than Brains!"

This may be taken as simply the argument of Hazlitt, who "did not see what there was to be proved;" — the principle of Malthus is a truism. Even when commenting on the statement of the Ratios (on p. 8), after some denunciation of the "verbiage and senseless repetition" of the essay, Coleridge goes on to agree with it. He would restate the whole so as to substitute "a proportion which no one in his senses would consider as other than axiomatic, viz. : Suppose that the human race amount to a thousand millions. Divide the square acres of food-producing surface by 500,000,000, that is to say, so much to each married couple. Estimate this quotum as high as you like, and, if you will, even at a thousand or even at ten thousand acres to each family. Suppose population without check, and take the average increase from two families at five (which is

[1] In these quotations the capitals are in the original, and the italics correspond to underlinings.

irrationally small, supposing the human race healthy, and each man married at twenty-one to a woman of eighteen), and in twelve generations the increase would be 48,828,125. Now as to any conceivable increase in the production or improvement in the productiveness of the thousand or ten thousand acres, it is ridiculous even to think of production at all, inasmuch as it is demonstrable that either already in this twelfth generation, or *certainly* in a few generations more (I leave the exact statement to schoolboys, not having Cocker's Arithmetic by me, and having forgotten the number of square feet in an acre), the quotum of land would not furnish standing room to the descendants of the first agrarian proprietors. Best do the sum at once. Find out the number of square acres on the globe (of land), and divide the number by 500,000. I have myself been uselessly prolix, and in grappling with the man have caught his itch of verbiage." He goes on to say that if every man were to marry and have a family, and each of his children were to do the same, their posterity would soon want standing room, and, if *all* checks were removed, this would of course happen much faster. "Any schoolboy who has learned arithmetic as far as compound interest may astonish his younger sister both by the fact and by the exact number of years in which it would take place. On the other hand, let the productiveness of the earth be increased beyond the hopes of the most visionary agriculturist, still the productions take up room. If the present crop of turnips occupy one-fifth of the space of the turnip field, the increase can never be more than quintupled, and, if you suppose two planted for one, the increase still cannot exceed ten; so that, supposing a little island of a single acre, and its productions occupying one-fifth of its absolute space, and sufficient to maintain two men and two women, four generations would outrun its *possible* power of furnishing them with food; and we may boldly affirm that a truth so self-evident as this was never overlooked or even by implication contradicted. What proof has Mr. Malthus brought? What proof can he bring that any writer or theorist has overlooked this fact, which would not apply (with reverence be it spoken) to the Almighty Himself when He pronounced the awful command, 'Increase and multiply'?"

From some of the phrases dropped in the course of these comments, we should infer they were the preparation for a formal review of the book by Coleridge himself. It is therefore extremely puzzling to find the whole comments printed almost word for word and letter for letter in a review[1] hitherto considered by every one (Southey included) to be Southey's. This applies to the subsequent MS. notes, which are happily briefer. Coleridge finds fault with Malthus (p. 11) for using the words virtue and vice without defining them, apparently overlooking the footnote under his very eyes (p.

[1] Arthur Aikin's *Annual Review*, vol. ii. (for 1803) pp. 292 *seq.* Cf. Southey's *Life and Correspondence* (ed. 1850), vol. ii. p. 251, 20th Jan. 1804: "Yesterday Malthus received, I trust, a mortal wound from my hand;" cf. vol. vi. p. 399, and vol. ii. p. 294. There is no hint of obligation to Coleridge.

11 n.) which says, "The general consequence of vice is misery, and this consequence is the precise reason why an action is termed vicious."[1] Coleridge says, in relation to the list of irregularities given in the last paragraph but one of the page (11): "That these and all these are vices in the present state of society, who doubt? So was Celibacy in the patriarchal ages. Vice and Virtue subsist in the agreement of the habits of a man with his reason and conscience, and these can have but one moral guide, Utility, or the Virtue[2] and Happiness of Rational beings. We mention this not under the miserable notion that any state of society will render those actions capable of being performed with conscience and virtue, but to expose the utter unguardedness of this speculation." Then after some remarks on New Malthusians (as they would be now called) he goes on: "All that follows to the three hundred and fifty-fifth page[3] may be an entertaining farrago of quotations from books of travels, &c., but surely very impertinent in a philosophical work. Bless me, three hundred and forty pages—for what purpose! A philosophical work can have no legitimate purpose but proof and illustration, and three hundred and fifty pages to prove an axiom! to illustrate a self-evident truth! It is neither more nor less than book-making!" He thinks, however, that what Malthus wrote of Condorcet applies to himself;—though his

[1] Cf. above, ch. iii. pp. 81 *seq.*, and Bk. III.
[2] *Sic*, though it explains a thing by itself.
[3] He probably meant 353rd, but his numbers are careless.

paradox is very absurd, it must be refuted, or he will think the toleration of his contemporaries due to their mental inferiority and his own sublimity of intellect.[1] The remaining marginal notes are chiefly of an interjectional character,[2] many of them not very refined. Malthus himself never falls into coarseness; but his opponents seldom avoid it, and Coleridge (or Southey) is no exception to the rule. Except for the interest attaching even to the foolish words of a great man, it would not have been worth while to revive his *obiter scripta* on a matter beyond his ken.

A few words are necessary in regard to Grahame and Weyland, who form the chief subject of the long second appendix of later editions of the essay. Grahame's charges were such as owed all their force to the general ignorance of the actual writings of Malthus himself.[4] Mr. Malthus regards famine as nature's benevolent remedy for want of food; Mr. Malthus believes that nature teaches men to invent (p. 100) diseases in order to prevent over-population; Mr. Malthus, regarding vice and misery generally as benevolent remedies for over-population, thinks that they are rather to be encouraged than otherwise

[1] On margin of p. 364, 2nd paragr.: "Quote and apply to himself."

[2] *E. g.* on p. 65 opposite to lines 5, 6, "Ass!" a monosyllabic refinement omitted in Southey's review.

[3] First in 1817, 7th ed., pp. 509 *seq.*

[4] One of the charges (p. 18: that Malthus recommends the same remedies as Condorcet) is sufficient to stamp the character of the book—*An Inquiry into the Principle of Population*, &c., by James Grahame. Its Introduction gives a useful list of writers on both sides; see p. 71. (Edin., 1816.) Simonin repeats Grahame's charges, with more mistakes of his own. See his *Hist. de la Psychologie* (1879), pp. 397-9.

(p. 100). Malthus, for his part, deploring the fact that this last charge has been current "in various quarters for fourteen years" (or since his quarto essay of 1803), thinks he may well pass it by. "Vice and misery, and these alone, are the evils which it has been my great object to contend against. I have expressly proposed moral restraint as their rational and proper remedy," a sufficient proof that he regarded them as the disease.[1] Grahame himself does not deny the tendency to increase beyond food (p. 102), but thinks emigration a sufficient remedy (p. 104).

Empson,[2] playfully classifying the opponents of Malthus, says there are some who will not comprehend "out of sheer stupidity, like Mr. Grahame," or out of sentimental horror, like Southey,[3] Coleridge, and Bishop Huntingford;[4] or because, like Sadler[5] and Godwin, who followed Price and Muret,[6] they imagine the law of population to vary with the circumstances; or else because they invent laws of their own, like Anderson, Owen, and Poulett Scrope;[7]

[1] 7th ed., p. 511. Cf. above, p. 52, and the reply to Godwin's Reply, *Essay*, 2nd ed., III. iii. 384.

[2] *Edinburgh Review*, Jan. 1837.

[3] *Life and Correspondence of Southey*, vol. iii. pp. 21-2, and p. 188.

[4] Bishop of Gloucester and later of Hereford. *Theolog. Works* (1832).

[5] "The prolificness of human things, otherwise similarly circumstanced, varies inversely as their numbers."—Sadler, *Popn.*, vol. iii. p. 352 (1830). Reviewed somewhat caustically by Macaulay in *Edin. Rev.*, July 1830. See Trevelyan's *Life of Macaulay*, vol. i. p. 126. Cf. Sadler's 'Reply' to *Edin. Rev.* His weakest point was his use of "inversely."

[6] Malthus, *Essay*, II. v. (7th ed.), pp. 164, 166; cf. p. 485.

[7] G. P. Scrope, M.P., *Pol. Econ.*, 1833, &c. Malthus, *Essay*, III. iii. (7th ed.), 282-6 (Owen), IV. xii. 457 (Owen), III. xiv. 380 n. (Anderson).

or because, like Weyland,[1] they deny the premises of Malthus as well as the conclusion. Weyland, like Grahame, has the honour of a special refutation from Malthus. He allows that Malthus in his essay has raised his subject from the level of desultory academical discussion to that of scientific inquiry, and his book is the point from which every later investigation must start. He allows that his order is lucid and his reasoning fair, and that he enables an opponent at once to discuss the question on its merits. Granting his premises, says Weyland, we cannot deny his conclusion; but that premise of his is false which assumes that the highest known rate of increase in a particular state of society is the natural or spontaneous rate in all;[2] we cannot take the height of Chang or of the Hale Child as the natural standard of the height of all. To this Malthus answers, that, if we had observed in any country that all the people who were short carried weights upon their heads, and the people who were tall did not, we should infer that the weights had something to do with the height,—and so, when we find that the increase of a people is fast or slow in proportion as the pressure of certain checks on increase is heavy or light, we cannot but believe that the rate would be at its fastest if there were no checks at all. To say with Weyland, in the terms

[1] John Weyland, junr., F.R.S. *The Principles of Population and Production as they are affected by the Progress of Society with a view to Moral and Political Consequences*, 1816.

[2] So Arnold Toynbee, *Industrial Revolution*, p. 107.

of his first cardinal proposition,[1] that "population has a natural tendency to keep within the powers of the soil to afford it subsistence in every gradation through which society passes," is to say "that every man has a natural tendency to remain in prison who is necessarily confined to it by four strong walls." One might as well infer that the pine of the crowded Norwegian forest has no tendency to have lateral branches, because as a matter of fact there is no room for it to have any.[2]

Weyland thinks that, without any moral restraint, population will keep within limits of the food, in proportion as it reaches a high state of morality, religion, and political liberty.[3] Malthus, on the contrary, would say that, without moral restraint, even morality, religion, and political liberty will not save a people from wretchedness;[4] and, for his part, the design always uppermost in his mind when writing has been "to improve the condition and increase the happiness of the lower classes of society."

One argument of Weyland's[6] has some weight in it. With a rich soil, high farming, and abundant food, the bulk of the people of a country might by the natural division of labour be employed in manufacture, and their unhealthy manner of life in towns might so check population that it might be far from keeping up to the level of the food. Malthus replies

[1] Ch. iii. p. 21. He adds, as his second: "This tendency can never be destroyed."

[2] *Essay*, Appendix, p. 517.

[3] Propos. iii. and iv.

[4] *Essay*, l. c. p. 521, a very strong passage.

[5] Append. p. 526.

[6] *Pop. and Prod.*, pp. 82 *seq.*

that this case is rare, for our town populations have increased rapidly,—but, such as it is, he has allowed for it in the second clause of his second proposition: "Population invariably increases where the means of subsistence increase, *unless prevented by some very powerful and obvious checks*."[1]

There are two other critics to whom Malthus replies in some detail, one the visionary Owen, who is embraced in Empson's classification, the other the practical man Arthur Young, who cannot so easily be classified. "I mean," says the latter, "to deal in facts alone, happy when I can discover them pure and unalloyed with prejudice."[2] As this was his practice as well as his profession, it may easily be believed that in his voluminous records of fifty years' travelling and experimenting[3] he has spun rope enough to hang himself. It ought to be added that, like Godwin, he claims the privilege of being inconsistent. Nothing could be more clear than his recognition in his *Travels in France* of the evils of over-population.[4] Yet in 1800, in his *Question of Scarcity plainly stated and Remedies considered*, he recommends as his remedy that each country labourer who has three children be provided with a cow and half an acre of potato ground.[5] In other words, he would reduce the English standard of living to the common Irish one, milk and potatoes.

[1] 7th ed., I. ii. 12 n.; 2nd ed., p. 16.

[2] *Tour in Southern Counties of England*, 1767, p. 342.

[3] Between 1767 and 1820. Cf. above p. 216.

[4] *Travels in France*, pp. 408-9 (ed. 1792) and al.

[5] *Essay on Pop.*, 7th ed., pp. 449, 451 *seq.*; *Annals of Agriculture*, no. 239, pp. 219 *seq.* (quoted in *Essay*, App. pp. 496-7). Young had reproached Malthus for denying the right to relief.

Malthus replies by giving reasons why people should "live dear," and by reminding Arthur Young of his own comments on the proceedings of the National Assembly. Recognizing their duty to grant relief, but wishing to avoid an English Poor Law, the National Assembly set aside fifty millions of francs a year for support of the poor. If it had been really a duty, wrote Arthur Young (in his *Travels*), necessity might have occasioned them to extend the relief to one hundred, two hundred, or three hundred millions, and so on, "in the same miserable progression that has taken place in England."[1] Malthus hardly needed to go back to the *Travels*, as Young himself confessed in his later writings that his plan did not apply to large cities, and though he still held by the claim of right, he confessed that his faith must be without works; in other words, he claimed the right to be inconsistent. But he continued to question Malthus' axiom that what cannot be ought not to be; and he thinks that, if a man marries without the means to keep a family, he may justly blame society for not providing him with the means He argues, too, that Malthus for the success of his scheme assumes perfect chastity in the unmarried. Malthus really assumed only that the evils, which on an average in a civilized country attend the prudential check, are less than the evils of premature mortality and other miseries entailed by the opposite course; he declares himself not against but in favour of schemes that improve the condition of the poor

[1] *Travels in France*, ed. 1792, pp. 438-9.

even on a limited scale; and he only asks that every such scheme be tested not by its first success, for hardly any scheme of the kind is unsuccessful at first, but by its effect on a new generation.[1]

This test might be applied to schemes like Owen's and later ones on the same model. Malthus perhaps deals too peremptorily with them. Speaking of Owen's system of the community of labour and goods, and of Spence's *Plan for Parochial Partnerships in the Land*[2] ("the only remedy for the distresses and oppressions of the people," the land to be "the people's farm"), he answers that there are two "decisive arguments against systems of equality": first, the inability of a state of equality to furnish adequate motives for exertion, the goad of necessity being absent,—and, second, the tendency of population to increase faster than subsistence. In reply it must be said that there might be socialism without communism; there might even be communism without an absolute equality, such as would put idle and industrious on the same footing; there might be an approximation of the social extremes, bringing poor and rich nearer, and giving the former not weaker but stronger motives to exertion; finally, it is not at

[1] App. to *Essay*, pp. 499, 500. It is not true that "Owen was right *as against Malthus* when he regarded a certain amount of comfort as the indispensable condition of a moral life, and thought that a considerable increase of man's powers of production was possible" (Held, *Soc. Gesch. Englands*, pp. 351-2). Malthus himself did both.

[2] The *Plan* is quoted by Cobbett, *Pol. Reg.*, Dec. 14, 1816. Malthus (*Pol. Ec.* (1820), pp. 434, 435, (1836) p. 378) thinks that "co-proprietorship" of Government with the landlords, after the scheme of the Economistes and on the analogy of Oriental "sole proprietorship," might become too ready an engine of taxation for a military despotism.

all inconceivable that at least one-half of this result might come, as Godwin wished, by the act of the rich themselves, which means also as Malthus wished, for it would come from a strong sense of personal obligation. It cannot be denied that Malthus, in using the argument in question, seems to forget his own admission, that the goad of necessity does not act with effect either on the lowest or on the highest classes.[1] Moreover, he allows, there have been cases, *e. g.* among the Moravian communities, where industry and community of goods have existed side by side. "It may be said that, allowing the stimulus of inequality of conditions to have been necessary in order to raise man from the indolence and apathy of the savage to the activity and intelligence of civilized life, it does not follow that the continuance of the same stimulus should be necessary when this activity and energy of mind has been once gained."[2]

The second of his arguments against Owen is of course his more cogent and characteristic one. As we have seen, it is not deprived of its point by the inclusion of moral restraint among the checks to population. It was argued against him that his own ideal of a society where moral restraint universally prevailed would involve precisely what is necessary to make such systems as Godwin's and Owen's permanently possible.[3] There is an air of conclusiveness in the remark that, in proportion

[1] See above, pp. 87, 112, &c. [2] *Essay*, 7th ed., p. 284.

[3] *E. g.* by Bagehot, *Econ. Stud.* (1880), pp. 135 *seq.*, and by Southey in Aikin's *Annual Review* above quoted.

as moral restraint prevails in the world, Malthus approximates to Godwin. But Malthus believes that equality and community would destroy the motive for moral restraint. The passions would still be present, and no man would be in a position where there seemed any need to restrain them; the restraint would be the interest of the whole society, but not of the individual himself, for the effects were to be borne not by himself, but by the whole society. No doubt the good of the whole society ought to be a sufficient reason; but it would be so in a very few men now; and, unless it were in all men then, the result would be an expansion of population, with the results Malthus described. Owen is aware of this, and suggests artificial checks, allowing men to gratify desire without the usual consequences, and dispensing with any effort of will. Malthus, on the other hand, would throw all the responsibility and burden on the individual, which he thinks it impossible to do without allowing the individual his private property.[1] No further justification of things as they are is to be found in Malthus; and, so far from being reactionary, his principles (with all their qualifications) were probably the most advanced individualism that was ever preached in these days. They are adopted in full view of the facts that have been again vividly brought before the public mind in our day by writers who are to our generation what Godwin, Spence, and Owen were to theirs.

[1] III. iii. 286. This and the rest of his argument (even its application to Civil Liberty) is to be found in Aristotle, *Politics*, ii. 3 and 4, but esp. 5. δεῖ δὲ μηδὲ τοῦτο λανθάνειν, &c.

Malthus seems to believe, with Dugald Stewart, that Utopian schemes are like the tunes of a barrel-organ, recurring at melancholy intervals from age to age with damnable iteration.[1] But, unless society itself has moved in a circle, the Utopias will resemble each other no more and no less than do the states of society which they would replace. Our own socialists, therefore, can hardly be dismissed by the stroke of the pen, that classifies them with people so curiously unlike them and each other as Plato, Ball, More, the Fifth Monarchy men, the Levellers, Godwin and Spence and Owen. Malthus does not, in fact, so dismiss them. Besides bringing forward his own argument, he examines Owen's attempt to deal with it.[2]

Since Malthus, every complete reform has needed to face in some way or other the question which he treated ; but he left little for others to do. Of the two most prominent schemes of our own day for the reconstruction of society, one, that of Mr. Henry George, involves an unconscious recourse to the old weapons of Godwin, Sadler, and other opponents of Malthus ; *Progress and Poverty* does not contain any argument not to be found in these writers. The conjecture about a "fixed quantity of human life on the earth" (ed. 1881, p. 97) is hardly an argument. It may be compared with what is stated by St. G. Mivart[3] to be the basis of Darwinism. "Every individual has to endure a very severe struggle for existence owing to the tendency to geometrical

[1] *Essay on Pop.*, 7th ed., p. 282. [2] See above, p. 24.
[3] *Genesis of Species*, 2nd ed., 1871, p. 5.

increase of all kinds of animals and plants, while the total animal and vegetable population (man and his agency excepted) remains almost stationary." Mr. Mivart's reason for excepting man seems to be Mr. George's reason for including him. The latter's more direct arguments against Malthus are as follows:—first, the difficulty is in the future (p. 85);—second, Malthus shifts the responsibility from man to the Creator (p. 87);—third, Malthus justifies the *status quo* and parries the demand for reform (p. 88);—fourth, Malthus ascribes excessive increase of numbers to a general tendency of human nature, while it is really due to the badness of our institutions in old countries, as in India and Ireland (pp. 101—114), or the very thinness of population in new (p. 92);—fifth, Malthus does not distinguish between tendency to increase and actual increase, and is therefore refuted by the fact that the world is not yet peopled (p. 94). In the sixth place, we are told, if there had been such a law as the Malthusian, it would have been sooner and more widely recognized (p. 98);—that families often become extinct (p. 99), and it is more certain that we have ancestors than that we shall have descendants;[1]—that better industry would keep a larger population (p. 107);—Malthus says that vice and misery are necessary (p. 109);—Malthus does not

[1] The puzzling effect of counting up one's great-grandfathers and great-grandmothers up to the twentieth degree or so is described by Blackstone as quoted by Godwin (*Popn.*) and re-quoted by Hazlitt (*Spirit of the Age*, 1825, p. 273, 'Godwin'). The puzzle is less if we remember that our remote ancestors must have married into each other's families, or rather were scions in the end of the same families. We cannot go back to a single pair except through the "prohibited degrees."

see that vegetables and animals increase faster than population (p. 115),—or that the increase of man involves the increase of his food (p. 116), for a division of labour makes man produce more than he consumes (p. 126), and so the most populous countries are always the most wealthy (p. 128);—Malthus forgets that the world is wide (p. 119),—and that the tendency to increase is checked by development of intellect,[1]—and by the elevation of the standard of comfort (pp. 121, 123);—he forgets that "the power of population to produce the necessaries of life is not to be measured by the necessaries of life" it actually produces, but by its powers to produce wealth in all forms (p. 127);—Malthus will not see that twenty men where nature is niggardly (*e.g.* on a bare rock?) will produce more than twenty times what one man will where nature is bountiful (p. 134);—and the Malthusian theory "attributes want to the decrease of productive power" (p. 134);—finally Malthus does not know "the real law of population," which is that "the tendency to increase, instead of being always uniform, is strong where a greater population would give increased comfort, and where the perpetuity of the race is threatened by the mortality induced by adverse conditions, but weakens just as the higher development of the individual becomes possible, and the perpetuity of the race is assured" (p. 123). What is right in this view of

[1] We are to understand, therefore, that Malthus and the author agree *that* population needs a check, and are simply not agreed *what* the checks are to be.

the real law of population is common to Mr. George with Mr. Herbert Spencer;[1] what is wrong is common to him with Godwin.[2]

The view of Karl Marx,[3] the prophet of the International and of modern economic Socialism, is built on much more solid foundations. It is a corollary of his view of capital. The general law of the accumulation of capital, in these days of large manufactories and machinery, involves not only a progressive addition to the quantity of capital, which is all that Adam Smith contemplated, but a qualitative change in the proportion between fixed capital, such as machinery, and the circulating which is paid in wages. To use the author's words, the progress of accumulation brings with it a relative decrease of the variable component of capital and a relative increase of its constant component. New machinery is constantly supplanting labour without any real compensation in increased demand, either at once or in the long run. The constant element increases at the cost of the variable; and this can only result in the progressive production of a population which, in relation to capital, is a surplus or superfluity, an over-population;—the cause which increases the net

[1] See below, p. 393.

[2] See above, p. 370. The sixteen positions not touched in their own place will be met by a reference to the following places in this book: i. to p. 20, add *Essay*, 2nd ed. Bk. III. ch. iii. p. 383, ii. to p. 37, iii. to p. 338, iv. to pp. 51, 78, v. to p. 80, vi. to p. 83, viii. to p. 113, ix. to p. 376, x. to p. 67, xi. to pp. 231, 297, see *Essay*, 7th ed. p. 381, xii. to pp. 70, 75, 91, xiii. to p. 393, xiv. to pp. 91, 270, xv. to p. 294, xvi. to p. 69, and xvii. to p. 75.

[3] *Das Kapital*, 7ter Abschn. 23tes Kap. pp. 653 *seq.* (ed. 1872); cf. 646 *seq.*

revenue of the country at the same time renders the population redundant and deteriorates the condition of the labourer.[1] So far from deploring the existence of this redundant class, the capitalists depend on it,[2] as the reserve of their army. They trust to its cheap labour to save them from the depression which in our days (though never before) appears with unfailing regularity after brisk trade and a crisis. If the hands were not always there for them to employ, they would not at once be able to seize the happy moment of a reviving demand for their goods. "Malthus with his narrow views understands the surplus population to be superfluous absolutely in itself, and not merely in relation to capital; but even he recognizes that over-population is a necessity of modern industry."[3] In proof of these statements he quotes the words of Malthus (*Pol. Econ.*, ed. 1836, pp. 215,[4] 319, 320):—"Prudential habits with regard to marriage carried to a considerable extent among the labouring classes, of a country mainly depending upon manufactures and commerce, might injure it." . . . "From the nature of a population, an increase of labourers cannot be brought into [the] market, in consequence of a particular demand, till after the lapse of sixteen or eighteen years; and the conversion of revenue into capital, by saving, may

[1] The language of Ricardo, ch. xxxi. p. 236 (quoted by Marx, p. 656 n.). Cf. above, p. 297. Cf. also Marx, pp. 427 foll.

[2] Cf. what Prof. Rogers says in *Six Centuries*, p. 229, of the attempt made in the fifteenth century to increase the "residuum" of agricultural labour for the benefit of the farmers and landlords. Also above, p. 164 n.

[3] Marx, *ibid.*, p. 659.

[4] Misprinted in Marx as 254.

take place much more rapidly; a country is always liable to an increase in the quantity of the funds for the maintenance of labour faster than the increase of population."

To these charges the answer is, first, that Malthus always recognized that over-population was relative, relative to the actual food;[1] second, that he did *not* recognize the over-population as necessary; it took place as a matter of fact, but he believed that, if working men did as he wished them, it would disappear;[2]—and in the third place, the first sentence quoted by Marx from the *Political Economy* is explained by a second, which he does not quote: "In a country of fertile land such habits would be the greatest of all conceivable blessings." Malthus is comparing Commercial with Agricultural countries, not pronouncing on the general question of wages; and other passages in his writings[3] show that he regarded the high wages, resulting from prudential habits, as a public gain, more than compensating the capitalists' loss of profits. Even Marx himself grudgingly allows that Malthus was more humane than Ricardo in regard to the hours of labour desirable for the workmen.[4] In the fourth place, the latter half of the quotation (beginning with the words, "From the nature of a population") first states an obvious fact which a child could have pointed out, and then a disputable proposition which predicts not an over-population but the reverse of it.

[1] See above, pp. 137, 188, &c.
[2] See above, p. 335.
[3] See above, pp. 299, 335, &c.
[4] *Das Kap.*, p. 549 n.

Marx is seeking to demonstrate the hopelessness of the labourer's position; and he is too acute not to know that his demonstration would be seriously weakened if he admitted the truth of the Malthusian doctrine and the bare possibility of the adoption of prudential habits by the labourers. This is the real reason of his bitter attacks on the Essay. He says of it:[1] "When I say Eden's work on the Poor was the only important writing by a disciple of Adam Smith in the eighteenth century, I may be reminded of the essay of Malthus. But this book in its first form (and the later editions did nothing but add and adapt borrowed materials) is nothing but a plagiarism from Sir James Steuart, Townsend, Franklin, Wallace, full of schoolboy superficiality and clerical declamation, and not containing a single original sentence. By the way, although Malthus was a clergyman of the Church of England, he had taken the monastic oath of celibacy [!], for this is one of the conditions of a fellowship at the Protestant University of Cambridge. 'Socios collegiorum maritos esse non permittimus, sed statim postquam quis uxorem duxerit, socius collegii desinat esse' (*Reports of Cambridge University Commission*, p. 172). By this circumstance Malthus is favourably distinguished from the other Protestant clergy, who have cast off the Catholic rule of celibacy. . .[2] With exception of Ortes[3] the Venetian monk, an original and clever

[1] *Das Kap. I.* p. 641 n.
[2] The passage omitted is neither true nor decent.
[3] G. M. Ortes *Reflessioni sulla popolazione* (1790).

writer, most of the writers on Population are Protestant clergymen," a contrast, he goes on, to the days when political economists were all philosophers. Marx adopts[1] the common view that Malthus being a clergyman was the bond-slave of Toryism and the ruling classes, and therefore ready to adopt a principle that attributed over-population to the eternal laws of nature rather than to the historical laws (also natural) of the capitalists' production. Marx does not see that the "eternal laws" in question do not lead to over-population except when the precepts of Malthus are neglected; and never shows how, apart from these precepts, over-population will be prevented in the renovated society itself, which has nationalized not only the land but all the instruments of production. Would the habits of men be so changed by this stroke of nationalization that the want of ordinary commercial motives would not be felt?[2] Would not the millennium of the Socialist, like that of the Christian, postulate a religious conversion on the largest scale for its first introduction, to say nothing of its continuance? Productive Co-operation, depending on the spontaneous action of the labourers for its creation, and on their intelligence and prudence for its success, would nationalize capital more surely; and it would not make the impossible postulate of Socialism, that a passionless unselfishness, which not one in a hundred thousand in our day exhibits at any time, shall at once become the

[1] *Das Kap.*, p. 549 n.

[2] Cf. above, p. 382, and Malthus, *Essay*, 2nd ed. III. iii. 386, where he says that Duty and Interest must work together.

invariable daily rule of all without exception. But Co operation, if it neglects Malthus, will find its work no sooner done than undone.

It may be thought that there are causes at work which will remove over-population among the working classes even under the present system of separated capital and labour. It is a doctrine of the "finer wits," founded on striking biological analogies, that the general development of intellect in the race will weaken the passion for marriage and supersede the necessity for any checks on it;[1]—the exercise of the energies of concentration or "individuation" developes these energies at the expense of those of diffusion or "genesis;"—the individual is made strong in himself, at the expense of his power of creating new individuals. Quite apart from the disagreeable fact that this principle would lessen the pressure most in those classes where lessening is at present least needed, and least where it is most needed, Malthus would probably have pointed out, first, that, unless the appetite is absolutely killed, no physiological check can supersede some control of the will over the passion,—and, second, that intellectual development will more certainly check population by making men alive to their responsibilities and strengthening their power of restraint than by weakening the passion to be restrained. The expounder of the theory is of all people the least likely to teach men that they may

[1] 'Theory of Population,' in *Westminster Rev.*, April 1852, copied by the German Professor Trall in 1877 (*Eine neue Bevölkerungstheorie*), and substantially maintained by its author (Mr. Herbert Spencer) in *Principles of Biology*, Vol. II. Part vi., 'Laws of Multiplication.'

become civilized by the progress of their race without the trouble of civilizing themselves individually. But his theory admits the misapplication; and, if it be said by the misappliers that we ought to tell the truth without fear of consequences, we must answer that in this case the consequences are part of the truth. On the other hand, to theorists like W. R. Greg, who suggest unknown physiological laws that may act as a spontaneous check, Malthus would have replied as to Condorcet:[1]

"What can we reason but from what we know?"

This brief survey of typical critics and commentators may be completed by a classification of the former, which, among other advantages, will give a bird's-eye view of the chief points in discussion. Empson classified the opponents of Malthus by their motives,[2] a proceeding hardly fair either to them or to the essay itself. It is not fair to them, for as a rule the critics appeal to argument, and must be judged by what they adduce, not by their good or ill will, wisdom or folly, in adducing it; and not fair to the essay, because few books have owed so much to their reviewers.

The positions of the critics may be classified as follows:—

I. Some say the doctrine of the essay is a truism.[3]

II. Others admit that it is unanswerable, but

[1] *Essay*, 7th ed. 269. [2] Above, p. 377.
[3] *E.g.* Hazlitt, *Reply to Essay on Population*, p. 20.

retain a philosophical faith in the future discovery of some contrary principle.[1]

III. Others find fault with the details of the doctrine, either (*a*) in regard to the ratios of increase, asserting that no tendency to a geometrical increase of population has been proved, but something much less rapid, even (a few say) a decreasing ratio,[2]—and that no mere arithmetical increase of food has been proved, but something much more rapid,[3]—or (*b*) in regard to the checks on population, asserting that no checks are necessary,[4]—that vice and misery sometimes add to population instead of checking it,[5]—that to include moral restraint is to stultify the original doctrine,[6]—that moral restraint sometimes involves as great evil as excessive numbers, both from the personal practice of it and from the preaching of it to others,[7]—that important checks have been omitted, the chief being misgovernment,[8] bad laws,[9]

[1] W. R. Greg, *Enigmas of Life*, 8th ed., 1874, pp. 58 *seq.* This was nearly Godwin's position in his first reply.

[2] Sadler on *Population*, and Reply to *Edinburgh Review*. Godwin, *Population*, Bk. VI. ch. ii., &c.

[3] Carey (H. C.), *Princ. of Social Science* (1858), vol. i. ch. xiv. ; cf. above, p. 74 *seq.* H. George, *Progress and Poverty*, pp. 115, 116. Sadler, p. 70, &c.

[4] Godwin, Sadler, &c.

[5] Sadler, pp. 354-5, &c. Cf. Adam Smith, *W. of N.*, I. viii. 36. See above, pp. 82, 83.

[6] Godwin, see above, p. 361. Southey, *Life and Corresp.*, III. 188. Bagehot, *Econ. Studies*, pp. 133 *seq.* Cf. George, II. ii. 94. Above, pp. 362, 381.

[7] Besant, *Law of Population*, ch. iii. Cf. Malthus, pp. 407 *seq.* (IV. iv.) ; Cobbett, *Taking Leave of his Countrymen* (1817), p. 6 , *Political Register*, 4th Jan. 1817, p. 26, &c., &c. Above, p. 329.

[8] Godwin, *Population*, passim. George, II. ii. 102, 109. Above, pp. 111, 112.

[9] Godwin, *ibid.;* George, pp. 138, 259, &c., &c.; Coleridge, MS. note to

high feeding,[1] intellectual development,[2] and those of Owen.[3]

There is, besides, an *a priori* criticism, which is either (I.) ecclesiastical,[4] alleging that Malthus contradicts the Bible or some other authority,—(II.) theological,[5] that he denies Providence,—or (III.) doctrinaire,[6] that he denies natural rights and the pre-established harmony of moral and economical laws, and the instinct of equality,—or (IV.) ethical and popular,[7] that he runs counter to the moral sense and the natural benevolence of men and cosmopolitan morality. These arguments have been already considered. The fourth of them has, in its last branch, an appearance of truth, because Malthus has certainly said less for the cosmopolitan than for the domestic and civic virtues. He wishes to lay the foundations solidly and leave the building to others. Cosmopolitan morality can rarely be the foundation. In the Empire, Christianity may have raised the people, and Stoicism the philosophers, to the wider morality without the training of the narrower,

p. 358 (of *Essay*, 2nd ed.), where for "physical constitution of our nature" he would read, "in the existing system of society." So verbatim Southey in Aikin's *Ann. Rev.* l. c.

[1] Doubleday, *True Law of Population* (1841). Above, p. 65. See Herbert Spencer, *Biology*, Vol. II. pt. vi. ch. xii. pp. 455, 480, &c. The physiologists have amply refuted Doubleday.

[2] Herbert Spencer. See above, p. 393. W. R. Greg, *Enigmas*. Above, p. 394.

[3] New Malthusians. See above, p. 24.

[4] See above, pp. 365 *seq.* The orthodoxy of Malthus is proved not by a few orthodox sentences which can be gleaned from him (as from Bacon), or even by the discovery of flaws in the received doctrine, but by the whole logic of the essay.

[5] See above, pp. 365 *seq.*

[6] See above, p. 336.

[7] See above, p. 328.

so that the converts were made better members of their own small communities by becoming members of the commonwealth of the saints and citizens of the great world. But it seems to Malthus that, in the world of to-day, the many conditions of a steady moral progress are best secured if the domestic and civic virtues precede the cosmopolitan. We must not legislate for a world of heroes, but for men as we know them to be; and a comfortable domestic life (βίος τέλειος) must be the common highway to goodness in a society of ordinary men. If poverty were no evil, churlishness would be no vice. But extreme poverty [1] is a real hindrance to goodness. In the apparent exceptions, as in the voluntary poverty of St. Francis, the greatest evil is absent, for there is no struggle for bare life. To abolish that struggle, and help men to comfort, is in some degree to help men to goodness; and it was the end for which Malthus laboured. The most sure and solid way of reaching it lay, as he thought, in impressing every man with a strong sense of his responsibility for his acts and of his power over his own destiny. To reform a nation, we must reform the members of it, who, if they are good at first in spite of their institutions, will at last conform their institutions to the model of their own goodness. To hold men the creatures of society, and make society responsible for their character, was, he thought, to mistake the order of nature. Society can feel its responsibility only in its individual members; and no member of it can free his own

[1] See above, p. 96.

soul by the purity of a collective or representative conscience.

The doctrine of Malthus is, therefore, a strong appeal to personal responsibility. He would make men strong in will, to subdue their animal wants to their notion of personal good and personal goodness, which, he believed, could never fail to develope into the common good and goodness of all. Believers in the omnipotence of outward circumstances and the powerlessness of the human will, to alter them or the human character, may put Malthus beyond the pale of sympathy. But all can enter into the mind of Malthus and understand his work, who know the hardness of the struggle between the flesh and the spirit, and yet believe in the power of ideas to change the lives of men, and have faith not only in the rigour of natural laws, but in man's power to conquer nature by obeying her.

Note (on p. 374 n[1]).

The difficulty of distinguishing what is of Southey and what of Coleridge was largely removed by the late Sir Richard Garnett of the British Museum, who kindly looked over the annotations for the purpose. He pointed out that on the last two of the annotated pages the handwriting is Southey's (pp. 358 and 364); Coleridge was writing for Southey's benefit. The matter was raised in the *Academy* of 7th November, 1885; and is rather of literary than of speculative interest.

BOOK V.

BIOGRAPHY.

Ancestors—Father's Life, Character and Activities—Son's Early Education—Graves and Wakefield—Jesus College, Cambridge—Studies and Achievements there—Alleged Defect of Speech—Curacy—First Pamphlet—Essay of 1798—Journey to Norway and Sweden—Tract on High Price of Provisions—Pitt at Cambridge—Professorship and Marriage—Writings—Friendship with Ricardo—Alleged Lack of Advancement—Condition of East India College—Inverarity's Notes—Opposition to the College, Malthus in Reply—Personal Touches—Portrait—Epitaph.

THE family of Malthus has been traced by the late John Orlebar Payne (in his "History" of it, privately printed in 4to, 1890) as far back as the fifteenth and sixteenth centuries. There were ancestors frequently at odds with the prevailing religion and government, a sign of strength of mind and conviction. One was an author. Thomas Malthus wrote on artillery: "A treatise of artificial fireworks both for warres and recreation (with a treatise of Arithmetike) newly written in French, and Englished by the Author" (printed by R. Hawkins, 1629), and "Pratique de la Guerre contenant l'usage de l'Artillerie, &c. Par le Sieur Malthus, gentilhomme Anglois, Commissaire général des feux et Artifices de l'Artillerie de France," &c. (Paris, 1681). The name is also given as Francis (Payne, p. 69, &c), His place in the family tree has not been quite certainly determined, or that of the publisher of the *History of the Bucaniers*, 1684; the *Merchant's Dayly Companion*, 1684; *Vindication of the late John Owen by a friendly scrutiny into Richard Baxter* [*Anon.*], 1684—all printed for Thomas Malthus at the Sun in the Poultry. More certainly an ancestor is Robert Malthus, the forty-fifth vicar of Northolt in Middlesex. He was put in under the Parliament, left in (despite remonstrances) by Cromwell, and dispossessed on St. Bartholomew's day, 1662 (Payne, pp. 78, 82). His second son Daniel, who died in 1717, was "apothecary to the very learned Dr Sydenham, on which account he caused his son to be named Sydenham; and was afterwards apothecary to King William and Queen Anne" (quoted by Payne, p. 88). The eldest son of Sydenham Malthus was Daniel. Daniel's second son was Thomas Robert, the economist, second son in a family of eight children, two sons and six daughters (Payne, family tree facing p. 154).

The authorities open to a biographer in 1885 were mainly two. Bishop Otter's preface to the 2nd ed. of Malthus' *Political Economy*, published posthumously by Pickering in 1836, was the first. Otter, Bishop of Chichester,[1] had been the college companion and lifelong friend of Malthus. The other was Prof. Empson's review of the said book in the *Edinburgh Review* of January 1837. Empson was a colleague of Malthus at Haileybury. His authorship of the article is proved by the "Selection from the Correspondence of the late MacVey Napier, Esq," 1879,

[1] First Principal of King's College, London.

p. 187, and note; that of the Preface by Empson's article, p. 472.

The kindness of the late Col. Sydenham Malthus, C.B.,[1] made possible the publication of the Letters of Ricardo to Malthus, 1810-1823 (Clarendon Press, 1887), which helped to revive interest in the two classical economists. It was followed by the Letters of Ricardo to MacCulloch (American Economic Association, 1895) and to Trower (Clarendon Press, 1899), as well as by Prof. Hollander's *Life of Ricardo* (Johns Hopkins Press, 1911). The kindness of Col. Malthus, which furnished the Letters of Ricardo, made it possible at the same time, had any opportunity occurred, to use the originals of the early letters quoted by Otter (*l.c.* xxv. *seq*). It is done now, and we have at last a nearly complete picture of the surroundings in which Malthus grew up.

Daniel, his father, was born in 1730 and died in January 1800, his wife, Henrietta Graham (granddaughter of a king's apothecary), following him in April 1800 (Payne, p. 99, and family tree). She was three years younger. Daniel matriculated at Oxford at Easter 1747, and entered Queen's College, a few months after Adam Smith had left Balliol for home (Rae's *Life*, p. 28). He got greater enjoyment there than Adam Smith, though he too had his reservations: "I used to think Oxford none the less pleasant and certainly not the less useful for being disburthened of some of its society; I imagine you will say the same of Cambridge," he wrote to

[1] Who died in 1916.

Robert on 13th January, 1786. "I have always wished, my dear boy, that you should have a love of letters, that you should be made independent of mean and trifling amusements and feel a better support than that of the next man who is idle enough to offer you his company" (Otter, *l. c.* xxv., 16th June, 1787).

Like his father Sydenham, Daniel was called to the Bar in Lincoln's Inn (1749, Payne, p. 24); married (1752) and settled down to a country life and the study of science, especially botany. He was acquainted with Rousseau. Family tradition says that Rousseau visited the neighbourhood (1766 or 1767), Miss Burney that he found an asylum in Daniel's house (*Correspondence of Madame D'Arblay*, iii. 469) in 1766 or 1767. They had in common the love of botany. Daniel in his Will leaves "to Mistress Jane Dalton all my botanical books in which the name of Rousseau is written and a box of plants given me by Mons[ieur] Rousseau" (Payne, p. 100). The private letters speak of Miss Dalton as one of the household (*e. g.* 1780). Mrs. may be old-fashioned for Miss. She was relative and ward of Daniel, and fond of books, and acted as housekeeper. She owned The Cottage, Albury, and left it to Sydenham, elder brother of Robert. Daniel is said to have corresponded with Voltaire, and to have been literary executor of Rousseau; tradition adds that after the death of the testator a lady (surely not Miss Jane Dalton) into whose hands the letters came gave them to the flames. They may certainly have contained something beyond botany.

Daniel lived first at Hadstock, Essex. In 1759 he built the Rookery (originally Chertgate Farm) outside Dorking, Surrey, on the road to Albury. After some wanderings, he settled, in 1787, at Albury in Schaw's house, now pulled down ("Recollections" of Miss Louisa Bray, granddaughter). Sydenham, his eldest son, was born in 1754; he was grandfather of Colonel Malthus. The second son, Thomas Robert (both old family names), was born at the Rookery on 14th Feb., 1766. There were six sisters, two married, one (Mrs. Bray) having a family of eleven (Payne, tree). Daniel loved a quiet life, with regular exercise, which included shooting. By his own acount (in above letter of 16th June, 1787) he was becoming a little frail at fifty-seven; "little else left but my bed and my arm-chair." Besides his science, he had studied Greek and Latin, and (we may believe) German, or the translation of Werther would hardly have been set down to him.[1] He held the "Allegro" to be the highest flight of poetry (letter of 27th Nov., 1783), a significant choice.

Among his occasional relaxations the drama, with Mrs. Siddons and Kemble to play, was evidently a favourite, as it was with his son Robert. He was always, in his science, looking to practice rather than theory. The neighbours thought him an amiable and clever man who was an ornament to his parish, but eccentric, making few friends and fondest of his own and his children's company (*Gentleman's*

[1] See the letter of his son, 19th Feb., 1800, quoted by Otter (*Pol. Ec.*, 1836, xxii.), in denial of the allegation; his father was too original to be a mere translator. See also above, p. 7.

Magazine, obituary, Jan. 1800, p. 86, and Feb. 1800, p. 177, Otter, *l. c.* xxvi.). We have his son's authority for saying that he wrote no translations but many "pieces," very good and always anonymous. With much of his son's talent, he seems to have had no power like his son's of sustained intellectual effort. That he had no ambition is no trait of unlikeness to his son, who had greatness thrust upon him. The son, like the father, though social, much enjoyed occasional solitude (letter to Daniel, 18th Jan., 1786.).

Of his mother, only a few touches are recorded. She appears from the private letters to have been the oracle of the household in practical matters. There is one letter of Robert to her written on 11th Dec., 1783, in which familiarity and affection and respect are properly blended. From a letter of Daniel to Robert (21st April, 1784), it appears that she did not want Robert to go to either of the two great Universities. "I have myself" (adds his father) "a partiality for your taking degrees, and I prefer Cambridge," he having been himself at Oxford and taken no degree.

Neither of the boys was sent to a public school. Like Sydenham, Robert was sent to his father's old friend, Richard Graves, Rector of Claverton near Bath (1779), to be taught Latin and good behaviour, along with a few other boys, most of them older than himself. "Don Roberto, who, though most peaceably inclined, and who seems rather to give up even his just rights than to dispute with any man, yet, paradox as it may seem, loves fighting for fighting's sake and delights in bruising. Yet he and his antagonist are soon the best of friends" (Graves to Daniel, 10th Aug., 1780).

Graves had been a friend of Shenstone the poet (who died in 1763). They had been together at Pembroke College, Oxford. From Graves' novel, *The Spiritual Quixote* (a satire on the Methodists, published 1772) we should not fancy him the best of guides for ingenuous youth. But the two letters from him in the collection of the Malthus family make a more favourable impression; and he seems to have taught Robert to appreciate Terence and to write tolerable Latin.

From Graves he passed in 1782 into the hands of a stronger man, Gilbert Wakefield, whose sole pupil he was till he went to Cambridge. Wakefield, still known to all students of Conington's *Virgil*, was a clergyman who had rebelled against the Thirty-nine Articles, turned dissenter, and founded an academy at Warrington (1779–1783) "to provide a course of liberal education for the sons of dissenters, and particularly for dissenting ministers" (Wakefield, *Life*, 1804, Vol. I. p. 214). About a third of the boys, however, were sons of members of the Church of England, like Daniel Malthus, liberal in their opinions. Wakefield's views were in keeping with the *Émile* of Rousseau, and presumably with Daniel's ideas. "The greatest service of tuition," he wrote (*Life*, I. 344), "to any youth is to teach him the exercise of his own powers, to conduct him to the hill of knowledge by that gradual process in which he sees and secures his own way, and rejoices in a consciousness of his own faculties and his own proficiency." The tutor is to point the pupil to the best authors and give him advice, not lectures, when he needs it. In 1782 Robert was with him a few months at Warrington, and went with him in 1783 from Warrington to Bramcote, near Nottingham. The other pupils did not at once follow him thither (see the private letters, Daniel to Robert, 27th Nov., 1783; Robert to Daniel, 26th April, 1782, 20th Nov., 1783).

Robert admired Wakefield, and to have his sole attention was to Robert's advantage. He writes to his father (15th April, 1784):[1] "I think I shall never repent having been this little time at Bramcot before my going to college, for I have, if I am not deceived, got into a more steady and regular way of study." In March (16th) he comments on current politics: "Mr. Fox and his party have, it seems, at last given up the struggle, and by the account of the papers Mr. Pitt is quite elated with his success. I really think he will ruin himself and will not be able to stand it after all, for the rest of the Ministry have but very little ability. He will never be so great a man as if he had shown a little more condescension and less ambition. It appears almost ridiculous that so young a man should hold the highest offices in the State." His father did not

[1] The letter, like the next, is dated 1783, but Pitt did not accept office till December of that year. The docket repeats 1783 mechanically.

agree: "Thank you for your politics" (he writes on 7th April, 1784), "but I am not of your mind with regard to young ministers. They may have a little liberty and a little of the fine enthusiasm caught from Athens, Lacedæmon, and Rome, which Sir Robert Walpole used to say cost him a year or two to rid some obstinate boys of. I am afraid that . . . old men buy their political experience with the loss of too many virtues." Robert held his ground (15th April, 1784): "I am by no means against young ministers, but I think that general enthusiasm of youth which you mention is seldom found separated from a kind of modesty and diffidence in their own abilities. This, from the accounts I have always heard, seems to be by no means the case with young Pitt, who has taken upon himself the sole management of the State without any single person of any ability to associate in the arduous undertaking."

Wakefield, once (1776) Fellow of Jesus College, Cambridge, procured admission for Robert there as a pensioner or ordinary commoner, 1784, and he began residence in the winter term.[1] He writes on 14th Nov., 1784, to his father: "I am now pretty well settled in my rooms"—he had come on the 3rd. "The lectures begin to-morrow; and, as I had time last week to look over my mathematics a little, I was, upon examination yesterday, found prepared to read with the year above me, though I believe I shall attend a few lectures at the same time with those of my own year. We begin with mechanics and

[1] Otter's dates have been corrected by the letters.

Maclaurin, Newton, and Keill's *Physics*. We shall also have lectures on Mondays and Fridays in Duncan's *Logick*, and in Tacitus's *Life of Agricola* on Wednesdays and Saturdays. I have subscribed to a bookseller who has supplied me with all the books necessary. We have some clever men at college, and I think it seems rather the fashion to read. The chief study is mathematics, for all honour in taking a degree depends upon that Science, and the great aim of most of the men is to take an honourable degree. At the same time I believe we have some good classics. I am acquainted with two, one of them of this year, who is indeed an exceedingly clever man and will stand a very good chance for the classical prize if he does not neglect himself.— I have read in chapel twice. It seems that it is the custom when the readers are absent that the two juniors should read the lessons, and I believe I am the junior of my year." On 29th Dec., 1784, he writes that the term's "bill is 44 pounds, 16 of which is the income of my room, and 7 tuition and other articles for the two quarters, Midsummer and Michælmas, which I did not reside" [*sic*]. His father thought £100 a year a reasonable figure for the University expenses of ordinary folk; else certainly the clergy, for example, could not go on sending their sons to college; abroad at Leipzig it could be done for £25 (letter to Robert, 15th May, 1785). Wakefield was a little inclined to be extravagant. There is certainly no sign that Robert was so. His pleasures and amusements were of the simplest character, the favourite in winter being skating on the fens. He was on his guard against running into debt (letter to Daniel, 29th Jan., 1785).

He did not narrowly confine himself to mathematics, nor did he show what his father conceived to be the Cambridge failing, the worship of pure theory and neglect of applications.[1] He says he was "remarked in college for talking of what actually exists in nature or may be put to real practical use" rather than for abstract speculations. He took frequent refuge in literature, English and French. He took prizes for Latin, Greek and English declamations. We do not hear of Italian, which he certainly knew afterwards.[2]

Long before Cambridge he had thought of taking orders, and in the middle of his Cambridge course he consulted the head of the college, Dr. Beadon, on the subject, and writes to Daniel, 19th April, 1786: "He seemed at first rather to advise against orders, upon the idea that the defect in my speech would be an obstacle to my rising in the Church, and he thought it a pity that a young man of some abilities should enter into a profession without at least some hope of being at the top of it. When, however, I afterwards told him that the utmost of my wishes was a retired living in the country, he said he did not imagine that my speech would be much objection in that case, that, for his own part, when I read or declaimed in

[1] Otter quotes him as saying, "I hate to see a girl working curious stitches upon a piece of rag" (*Pol. Ec.*, I.c. xxvi.). The original has "curious stitches upon a rag" (13th Jan., 1786).

[2] About 1832 he gave a dainty Metastasio to a little girl (Mary Ballantyne, afterwards Mrs. Hector MacKenzie), then staying with her uncle, Col. Michael, in the College.

chapel he scarcely ever lost a single word. As to the business of getting into orders, he did not conceive there was any legal objection, but the Bishops had it so entirely in their power to ordain whom they pleased that it was impossible to say how they would act; he thought there were some who might refuse, but that the generality would not." It was a hereditary defect, and is said, in a Petition of certain parishioners of Northolt, to have characterised Robert Malthus, left there by Cromwell. "The said Mr. Malthus is one who hath not only a low voice but a very great impediment in his utterance" (Payne, p. 80). In our hero's case the defect is remarked by Miss Martineau (*Autobiography*, I. 327–8; *cf.* above, p. 58) and by Sydney Smith (*Life*, by Holland, II. 326), palliated by the one and exaggerated by the other. It seems unlikely that it entered into his calculations.[1] What he got when he left Cambridge was probably just what he wanted, not a living but a curacy, and time to think and study (See D. to R., 20th March and 25th April, 1789). He seems to have been of good physical health and strength. Once or twice we hear of rheumatism which his father reproaches him for misspelling: "Don't say *rhumatism*, but consider the derivation, and that no man should have a disorder which he can't spell, especially a man of Jesus" (D. to R., March 1786). There is some fatherly advice, in the private letters, about plans of study—Daniel eventually, like a wise man, giving way: "I won't

[1] The late Mr. Jowett, Master of Balliol, had met Henry, the son, and remarked no defect of this sort.

dispute with you about your plan of study. Whate'er is best administered is best" (D. to R., 31st Jan., 1786). He had reluctantly parted with the illusion natural to all fathers, the belief that their sons are at a given age exactly what they themselves were at the said age: "I thought I foresaw in you, from the memory of my own youth, the same tendency to lose the steps you had gained, with the same disposition to self-reproach, and I wished to make my unfortunate experience of some use to you. It was indeed but little that you wanted it, which made me the more eager to give it you, and I wrote to you with more tenderness of heart than I would in general pretend to, and committed myself in a certain manner, which made your answer a rough disappointment to me, and it drove me back into myself. You have, as you say, worn out that impression, and you have a good right to have done it, for I have seen in you the most unexceptionable character, the sweetest manners, the most sensible and the kindest conduct, always above *throwing little stones into my garden*, which you know I don't well[1] forgive, and uniformly making everybody easy and amused about you. Nothing can have been wanting to what, if I were the most fretful and fastidious,[2] I would[3] have required in a companion" (D. to R.; prob. 1788. Letter addressed to Rev. Mr. R. M. Otter, xxviii).

Malthus was fortunate in his father. He was also fortunate in his tutor, William Frend. Frend was afterwards to be removed from his fellowship because

[1] So MS. Otter "easily." [2] Written "fastigious." [3] Otter "could."

of his *Thoughts on Subscription to Religious Tests* (1789) and from the University because of his book on *Peace and Union* (1793). Otter, Fellow of Jesus since 1790, voted against prosecution. Malthus became Fellow only in that year (1793), and is not mentioned (*Proceedings against Frend*, 1793, p. xxiii, etc.; *Dict. Nat. Biogr.*, "Malthus," by Leslie Stephen).

Malthus finished his course with credit, as ninth Wrangler, 1788. He had thought himself lucky if he became a Wrangler at all (letter to D., 4th Nov., 1787, in anticipation), but he had "kept an act" (defended a thesis) in the schools with some credit, and probably no one else was surprised at his place. He was the only Jesus man among the Wranglers. He writes on 17th April, 1788, after the event: "I have laid aside my chemistry for a while and am at present endeavouring to get some knowledge of general history and geography. I have been lately reading Gibbon's *Decline of the Roman Empire*. He gives one some useful information concerning the origin and progress of those nations of barbarians which now form the polished States of Europe, and throws some light upon the beginning of that dark period which so long overwhelmed the world, and which cannot, I think, but excite one's curiosity. He is a very entertaining writer in my opinion; his style is sometimes really sublime, everywhere interesting and agreeable, though perhaps it may in general be call'd rather too florid for history. I shall like much to see his next volumes." He was soon to have his wish. Volumes IV., V. and VI. of the *Decline and Fall* were published in that very year, 1788,[1] containing the second half of the entire work, and carrying it to its conclusion. There are many "Malthusian" passages in the *Decline and Fall*.

Malthus seems to have taken orders immediately after the Wranglership (see address on letter above, and on letter of 5th June, 1790). He became M.A. in 1791. About 1796 he ceased residence and was curate at Albury, Surrey, to which address his father wrote from Bath when Robert had written his first pamphlet, *The Crisis*,[2] and had in vain tried to get Debrett to print it. Daniel puts only 14th April, without the year; but the date 1796 is clear from docket and postmark. "The truth is that the market overflows, and, if there is not some particular abuse or known name, the booksellers are not willing to risk their money. I would give very little for Debret[t]'s judgment with regard to the pamphlet, but I believe that what he said to you was a pretty true picture of the farce of publick affairs. If any warning voice can awake us from this apathy there never was a time when it was more wanted. What you have done appears to me to be extremely[3] well done and to be perfectly adapted to the occasion. The bills only make a part of the general subject, and, if they are now to be considered as puppets that have just passed in the procession, upon my life it is not worth while to write seriously about anything." "I can't reconcile

[1] The Preface (in Vol. IV.) is dated 1st May, 1788, Downing St.
[2] See above, pp. 7, 30; extract, p. 332.
[3] Written "extreamly."

myself to your not publishing your pamphlet. I am sure it will never do you discredit, though I cannot answer that it will get you a Deanery."[1]

The private letters do not help us in the interval between *The Crisis* and the Essay; the discussions between Daniel and Robert took place by word of mouth. The account given above (chs. i. and ii.) represents probably all we can hope to find. It is, of course, clear that Malthus had been reading Godwin. It is clear from the Preface to the Essay of 1798 that he had been forming his opinions on political economy: "The most important argument that I shall adduce is certainly not new. The principles on which it depends have been explained in part by Hume and more at large by Dr. Adam Smith" (p. 8). He feels his judgment sufficiently mature to warrant him in criticizing the latter drastically enough (ch. xvi. p. 303 *seq.*).

After the Essay we have, in a private letter,[2] an interesting list of books which Malthus would like to get: Süssmilch's *Göttliche Ordnung*, Vol. I, 3rd ed. "If it should be in German, it will be of no use to me"; perhaps there is a French or English translation. Memoir of Mr. Wargenten [*sic*] in the *Mémoires abrégés de l'académie Royale de Sciences de Stockholm*, printed at Paris, 1772. Muret's *Memoir on Population in the Pays de Vaud*, Berne, 1766. Dr. Haygarth on the population and diseases of Chester (Chester, 1774). Kerseboom on the

[1] Otter, *l. c.*, is quite astray here.
[2] R. to D. from Albury, 4th Feb., 1799.

number of the people in Holland. Dr. Styles' *Discourse on Christian Union*.[1] Also *The Interest of Gt. Britain considered with regard to her Colonies, together with Observations concerning the Increase of Mankind, Peopling of Countries, etc.*, 2nd ed., London, 1761. He is glad to have received Sir F. M. Eden. His book "tends very much to confirm my opinion of the inefficiency of all regular establishments for the poor."

When he is on his journey (see above, p. 48) with Clarke and the rest to Sweden and Norway, he writes to his father (unhappily the last letter of the collection) from Stockholm, 18th Aug., 1799, doubtful if the party will be allowed to enter Russia, "as the Emperor [Paul I.] is so extraordinarily fearful of admitting strangers into his dominions. We hear that the last Englishman that went from Stockholm was allowed with some difficulty to pass the frontiers, but his servant and baggage were sent back and he was only allowed to take a couple of shirts with him. The loss of a wardrobe is of less consequence in entering Russia than anywhere else, as we understand that none of the common fashions of Europe are admitted, and that even in the morning you must wear a coat with a standing collar and long flaps to your waistcoat." "The town and environs of Stockholm are very agreeable and in parts beautiful, but we do not find the people very sociable. I inquired of a statistical professor, who ought to know, about the mortality you mentioned, but he had not heard

[1] "Hard to get," he adds.

of it. The *rubus arcticus* was not ripe when we were in our most northern latitude; but we even doubt whether we have seen the plant, though we have looked for it with much care. The white and red deals are the spruce and Scotch, the *pinus abies* and the *pinus silvestris*; but the *pinus silvestris* varies very much in the colour. Those who talk English in Norway call the *pinus silvestris* the fir, and the *pinus abies* the white wood." The party of four broke up at Halby on Wener Lake (midway but nearer Christiania than Stockholm), at the end of June, Malthus and Otter then crossing to Norway, leaving the eccentric and adventurous Clarke with his pupil Cripps to go by themselves to Tornea at the north end of the Gulf of Bothnia, on the way to Lapland, associated with Maupertuis and Celsius.[1] Otter and Malthus, says Clarke, "had they been lads of sufficient enterprise, might have undertaken a journey full as extensive as ours with very little addition of time or expense. It is not certain that I shall not be at Drontheim even now before they arrive. I intend to launch a balloon at the capital of Torneå, Lapmark, in order to attract the natives together"[2] (*Life of E. D. Clarke*, by Otter, 4to ed., 1824, p. 352; letter to Tyrwhit, dated 9th July, 1799). Clarke speaks of Malthus as the best sailor of the four, and with plenty of fun in him (*l. c.* pp. 384, 418).

[1] *La figure de la terre determinée*, etc. (1738), par M. Maupertuis, publ. 1738.

[2] Apparently he actually did it. See letter to Malthus same date, p. 355. He had done the same in the quadrangle of Jesus College in 1783. See *Life*, p. 54.

Malthus returned in the beginning of November 1799 (*High Pr.*, p. 8, *Clarke's Travels*, vol. ix., Preface (ed. 1824)).

His sense of humour helped to lengthen his days and made him by general vote a pleasant companion and host. The signs of it departed from his writings, with the early lightness of touch, after 1798 or at least after 1800. He had found the work of his life, to set one neglected truth before the world, and he devoted himself to this task, pushing his inquiries in all ways possible to him, study, conversation, travel among the chief. In 1806 he was in Wales with Francis Horner, a warm admirer (*Life of H.*, I., pp. 436, 437); in 1817 in Kerry and Westmeath (see above, p. 195); in 1825 in France[1] "for the sake of Mrs. Malthus" on the death of his daughter (at seventeen; Otter, *l. c.* xxxvii–xxxviii); in 1826 with Henry Cockburn in the Highlands (*Letters of C. to Kennedy*, 1874, p. 148). He was visited by Dr. Thomas Chalmers in 1822 (*Life*, by Hanna, ii., p. 358), and of course by Ricardo frequently till Ricardo's death in 1823. A. H. Everett, an American critic (*New Ideas of Population*, 1823), was charmed with his personality. Dismal and he were many miles asunder.

In his view of life and the prospects of humanity he passed from pessimism to a moderate optimism, and was never too old in spirit to confess a fault. His diction became perhaps too Johnsonian, a weakness

[1] Maria Edgeworth met them in Paris in 1820. *Life and Letters* (1894), I. 292, cf. 302, 303.

of his times. The composition is bald and sometimes diffuse. But the meaning of each sentence is always clear, and, when we are learning a single truth in its full bearing, the repetition of the same phrases in different connections is unavoidable, in proportion to the thoroughness of the discussion. The abundant metaphors of the first Essay had led to many misunderstandings. It may be said, however, that his own command of metaphor and consciousness of its drawbacks made him quick to turn the edge of an opponent's metaphor; for example, Weyland's Giant, Musket-ball, and Swaddling Clothes (in Essay, Appendix, 7th ed., pp. 514–21).

His first published writing, after the Essay was still anonymous (see above, pp. 49, 308), though the authorship was generally known (see above, p. 43). The bright and pleasant letter printed by Prof. Foxwell in the *Economic Journal*, 1897, p. 270, gives welcome details. It is addressed to the Rev. George Turner, Wickham Market, and dated 28th Nov. [1800]: "Your letter was sent to me to Bath, where I have been on a visit to a family of pretty cousins and could not therefore look down long enough to write a letter." The family was probably that of the Eckersalls at Claverton; Malthus married Harriet Eckersall in 1804. "In my ride to Town, an idea with regard to the present high prices of provisions struck me so strongly that in the day or two that I remained in Town previous to my Bath expedition I determined to write down a few thoughts on the subject. I send you the result, which would have come to you sooner but from a mistake of Johnson's [the publisher]. I sat up till two o'clock the evening before I went to Bath to finish it, that it might come out before the meeting of Parliament.[1] You will see that it was written in a hurry; but, such as it is, it has obtained some little notice. A friend of mine gave it to the Chancellor, who called it the best that had appeared on the subject and immediately sent it to Mr. Pitt. I know not the opinion of the latter about it; but, whether from that or from some other source, you will see that in the first report of the committee of the House of Commons, now just published, much of the same kind of reasoning has been adopted. I expect your thanks as a farmer; and, if I am ducked by the mob, I hope the monopolizers and forestallers will give me some dry clothes. The circulation of this pamphlet and the prevailing conversation about the population of the country has [*sic*] caused inquiries to be made about the *Essay*, which is now nowhere to be bought. This, I hope, will animate me to proceed in another edition, though, to say truth, I feel at present very idle about it." Something of the breeziness of this letter remains in the Tract. It has signs too of his profiting by his journey. Swedish scarcity was greater than ours, but prices did not increase so greatly (*High Price*, p. 3). He describes what took place in his own neighbourhood (*ibid*, p. 10). It was a real scarcity, and high prices were neither due to

[1] Tuesday, 11th Nov., *Ann. Reg.*, 1800 (p. 122), an autumn session held expressly because of the scarcity.

forestalling (pp. 4, 14, 21) nor paper currency (p. 23). Unfortunate as the measures were, they were perhaps unavoidable if free imports are not enough (pp. 20, 21). (See above, p. 307.) He was unprejudiced, as "an individual with a small fixed income" (p. 4).

The economic arguments, elementary though they be, are handled with a skill and clearness which he did not always reach in his later tracts. Pitt may really have been struck with these merits. Pitt was at Cambridge (says Otter in his *Life of Clarke*, 4to ed., 1824, p. 538 n.) on a sort of canvassing visit in December 1800. It was after the dissolution that preceded the first united Parliament of Great Britain and Ireland. He went to "a supper at Jesus Lodge, where, in the company of some young travellers, particularly Mr. Malthus, &c., he was induced to unbend in a very easy conversation respecting Sir Sidney Smith, the massacre at Jaffa, the Pacha of Acre, Clarke, Carlisle, &c." He thought some of Carlisle's translations from the Arabic beautiful, and seemed to know them by heart. Being still a man of influence, he may have contributed to the appointment of Malthus as Prof. of History and Political Economy (perhaps the first professorship[1] of the latter) in the newly founded East India College at Haileybury in 1805. In view of this post Malthus married, on 13th March, 1804. Mrs. Malthus was his junior by eleven years and survived him thirty. She is said to have sided with Owen in the fireside

[1] Dugald Stewart had lectured on "Political Economy," 1800 and 1803. See his *Pol. Ec.*, I. xvii.

discussions, perhaps from politeness to her guest. A compliment paid [by Otter] (in the obituary,[1] *Athenæum*, 10th January, 1835) to Malthus, that his servants stayed long with him, justly belongs to his wife. They had three children, of whom the two eldest survived him. Lucy, the youngest (born 1808), died in 1825. The Rev. Henry Malthus lived till 1882, and Emily (Mrs. Pringle)[2] till 1885.

Malthus held this professorship for the rest of his life. There were drawbacks, but on the whole it was thoroughly congenial. *Hoc erat in votis.* The rest of his life's story is mainly a record of his writings and his friends.

The *Essay* reached its 2nd edition (4to) in 1803, 3rd in 1806 (2 vols., 8vo), 4th in 1807 (2 vols.), 5th in 1817 (3 vols.), 6th in 1826 (2 vols.), the last in his lifetime; Johnson published the first three, Murray the remainder. His other substantial book was the *Political Economy*, 1820, of which the 2nd edition appeared posthumously in 1836.

His pamphlets make a long list.[3] There were: (1) In 1800, *High Price of Provisions;* (2) 1807, *Letter to Whitbread on the Poor Laws;* (3) 1813, *Letter to Grenville on the East India College;* (4) 1814, *Observations on the Corn Laws;* (5) 1815, *Nature and Progress of Rent;* (6) 1815, *Grounds of an Opinion on the Policy of Restricting the Importation of Foreign Corn;* (7) 1817, *Statements*

[1] Of which that in 1836 was the expansion.
[2] Capt. John Pringle, R.E., was a Waterloo veteran.
[3] For details see Palgrave's *Dict. of Pol. Ec.*, art. "Malthus," p. 676–77.

respecting the East India College; (8) 1823, *Measure of Value;* (9) 1825 (Royal Society of Literature), *Measure of Conditions Necessary to the Supply of Commodities;* (10) 1827 (*ibidem*) on Value. The *Summary View*, 1830, and *Definitions*, 1827, are rather books than tracts. The articles in the *Edinburgh Review* and *Quarterly Review*, cited above, are often nearly as long as tracts and quite as important.

From 1810, the date when the Letters of Ricardo to Malthus begin, we may be certain that the debates by word of mouth and by letter with so strong a critic had great influence on his friend, were it only by way of opposition. We have comparatively few of his own letters. Prof. Hollander has printed one of the series Ricardo-Malthus in his *Letters of Ricardo to MacCulloch* (Amer. Ec. Assoc., 1895), pp. 161–167, No. XLII, dated 11th August, 1823; and Prof. Foxwell another dated 9th October, 1814, in the *Economic Journal*, 1907, pp. 272–276. The fundamental difference of opinion appears clearly in the Ricardo–Malthus letters. Ricardo thought the depression after the war was due to a scarcity of capital; Malthus, that it was due to a glut of commodities.

Short and formal letters exist in greater abundance (*e. g* to Place, Godwin, Sinclair, Cockburn). The selected correspondence with MacVey Napier included one letter of Malthus (p. 31, on the New Political Economy and on Dugald Stewart, 1821), and nine more were furnished (from the British Museum originals) to the *Economic Journal*, 1897, pp. 264–

270 (1822 to 1830), by Prof. Hollander. There are also the letters to Senior mentioned above (p. 66, cf. 41), and to Arthur Young (1818, &c.).[1]

Malthus even in his own lifetime was more often "refuted" than any other economist. He still retains the distinction, and (to parody a well-known saying) "there is a great deal of refutation in Malthus." His illustrations may have gone; but his arguments remain. They are, however, two-edged weapons of which wise controversialists make cautious and sparing use.

His contemporaries gave him a fair measure of recognition. Otter says (*Pol. Ec.*, XLI.) that he bebecame F.R.S. in 1819 and was made a Member of the French Institute and of the Berlin Royal Academy. He was certainly made Associate of the Académie des sciences morales et politiques on its reconstitution in 1833 (see Joseph Garnier, art. "Malthus" in *Dictionnaire de l'éc. pol.*, Guillaumin, Paris, 1853, Vol. II.). He was member of the Royal Society of Literature.[2]

He helped to found the Political Economy Club in 1821 and the Statistical Society in 1834. He seems to have belonged to the Geological Society, and perhaps, like Ricardo, to their dining club (*Letters to Malthus*, pp. 64, 75, date 1815). The private letters show his liking for such studies. He was present with his son Henry at the Cambridge meeting of the British Association in 1833 (*Signatures*,

[1] Brit. Mus. Add. MSS. 35126–33, kindly noted by Mr. Henry Higgs.
[2] Above, 263, and *Dict. Nat. Biogr.*

p. 36). His chief social club before the existence of the Political Economy Club was the King of Clubs, 1812, to its end in 1824 (see *Letters to Malthus*, pp. 5 and 6, and Mr. Courtney in *Pope of Holland House*, 1906, pp. 333–340).

His post was honourable though not lucrative. There is no sign that he desired more money or wanted to be more in the sun. He had perfect health, says Mackintosh (MacVey Napier, p. 33, date 1822). Some of his friends indeed wanted more for him. Brougham, writing to Napier (31st January, and 21st February, 1837, pp. 187, 188), denies the assertion of Empson that Lansdowne and Holland tried in vain to get preferment for Malthus. Sydney Smith wrote to Grey about him in 1831 without success (*Life*, by Holland, ii. 328). Sharp says Malthus might have had preferment but would not give up the college for it (*Rogers and his Contemporaries*, ii. 104). Brougham himself offered a living, but Malthus declined it with thanks, in favour of Henry (says Brougham, *l. c.*), "who got it and I believe now has it." Henry became in this way Vicar of Effingham near Leatherhead in Surrey in 1835, the year after his father's death, and of Donnington near Chichester in Sussex, 1837, a second appointment which may have been due to Empson's reproach or Otter's influence. Henry had married Otter's eldest daughter. He died in August 1882 at the age of seventy-six, and his widow survived him seven years. The combined salaries were £672, out of which he kept four curates. His father told

Gallois in 1820 that all his works till then had not brought him £1,000. Gallois repeated this to Moore, with the remark that in England poetry was better paid than useful learning. Moore had met Malthus at Haileybury in 1819 (Moore's *Memoirs*. ed. Russell, 1853, iii, 148).

The college at Haileybury[1] was an educational experiment due to the suggestion of Governor-General Wellesley, brother of the great Duke. He proposed, in a Minute of 18th August, 1800, quoted in Malthus' *Statements*, that there be a college at Fort William, Calcutta, for the general education of the Civil Servants of the East India Company as well as their special instruction in Oriental languages. The Directors divided his scheme, and at the end of 1805 voted the establishment of a college at Haileybury for the general education and for the elementary education in languages, which should be given before the cadets left England. The rest was left to Fort William. The foundation stone was laid by the College Committee of the Company on 12th August, 1806 (*Ann Register*, 1806, *Chron.*, p. 404). The course was to be of about two years, and the general education was to be on the lines of Oxford and Cambridge. The "preliminary view" given in the *East India Register and Directory* (Hatchard, 1807, pp. xxiv *seq.*) shows that the programme corresponded in substance with that of the Competitive and the Further Examinations of candidates for the

[1] For the training of I.C.S. before the existence of Haileybury College, see Kaye's *Life of Metcalfe*, I. 31 *seq.*

India Civil Service, as later conducted. Malthus claims the credit of making the test in Oriental languages a necessary condition of final appointment (*Statements*, p. 100). The Professor of "History and Political Economy" and the Professor of "General Policy and the Laws of England" were understood to cover both the general and the special parts of the programme. The other subjects were Classics, Mathematics, Natural Philosophy (Physics), and the Oriental languages. The college year had two terms of five months, February to June, August to December. The ages of the pupils on entrance varied from fifteen to twenty-two, and about forty joined every year. Malthus would seldom have a class beyond twelve or fourteen. The ordinary work of the year is described in the *Statements* (p. 47 *seq.*). The lads had each only one room to live in, which was both bedroom and sitting-room (Macaulay's Report, 1854). The general discipline was rather on the model of an unreformed Oxford college than of a public school. Sense of personal responsibility and habits of self-government were to take the place of the schoolboy's fear of punishment (*Statements*, p. 103, &c.). This idea suited well with Malthus' general notions of the requisites of good citizenship. Unhappily, before learning the new motives, the boys, like German students, too often abused the absence of the old. After the opening of the chapel on 24th August, 1815, about half of the professors did duty there, Malthus among them. We have none of his sermons; but Prof. Alfred Marshall possesses a set of notes, compiled, not without aid from others, by a student called Inverarity, of Malthus' lectures on Adam Smith delivered in 1830. They were evidently clear and well-ordered, but add nothing to the printed books. The text was an interleaved Nelson edition, 1829, of which the type was used again in 1843, and later in 1884, with Prof. Nicholson's introduction. It was set up by Thomas Nelson and Peter Brown for the Edinburgh University Press, 1829. Inverarity calls his teacher "Pop,"[1] but otherwise shows a good deal of respect for him. It is to be remembered that Malthus once thought of a book on Adam Smith (see *Letters of Ricardo to Malthus*, p. 56, 13th January, 1815, and Walter Thom's *Outlines of Pol. Ec.*, 1814, Pref.).

Jeffrey (*Life*, Vol. II. p. 339) and Harriet Martineau (*Autob.* i. 327 *seq.*) speak with rapture of the charms of the place. The latter remarks on "the subdued jests and external homage and occasional insurrections of the young men." These occasional insurrections were a thorn in the flesh of the professors. Sydney Smith, who naturally makes the most of them, writes to Lord Holland in June 1810, near the end of term, when there was talk of making Mackintosh professor at Haileybury: "The season for lapidating the professors is now at hand; keep Mackintosh quiet at Holland House till all is over"; and to Whishaw (The "Pope" of Holland House) in January 1818, when the appointment had been made: "His situation at Hertford will suit him very well,

[1] The late Prof. E. L. Lushington had often heard the epithet used.

peltings and contusions always excepted. He should stipulate for 'pebble money,' as it is technically termed, or an annual pension in case he is disabled by the pelting of the students. By the bye, might it not be advisable for the professors to learn the use of the sling (*balearis habena*)? It would give them a great advantage over the students" (*Life*, by Holland, ii. 73, 150). The lapidations were probably no worse than similar practices at English and Scotch Universities that have not yet destroyed the credit of these institutions. Sporting over the manors of the neighbouring gentry and destroying their game were amusements less likely to be long tolerated by the public (*Ann. Register*, 1808, Chron., p. 139).

The opponents of the college had other reasons than the disorders of the students. Lord Grenville complained in the House of Lords, 9th April, 1813, that the College separated the future Civil servants from the ordinary life of Englishmen, and prevented them from becoming imbued with "English manners, English attachments, English principles, and I am not ashamed to say English prejudices" (Hansard, *sub dato*, pp. 750, 751). Malthus had gone up to London to hear this speech, and at once became champion of the college, writing first a "Letter to Lord Grenville occasioned by some observations of his Lordship on the East India Co.'s establishment for the education of their Civil servants," 1813 (cf. *Edinburgh Review*, December 1816), then more elaborate "Statements respecting the East India College, with an appeal to facts in refutation of the charges lately brought against it in the Court of Proprietors," 1817. He maintained that the plan of the college was good in theory and had proved good in practice. The disorders were due to the dependence of the professors on the Company's Directors, who had, till then, withheld from them their best means of discipline, the power of expulsion. The students were as little likely to become un-English as army or navy cadets, and were much less likely to become a caste at Haileybury than if they had been sent at once to a college in India.

The difficulties of the situation were largely due to the unlike ages of the pupils. Those of the younger age were physically and mentally still schoolboys. Many were unwilling to go to India at all, and it was their parents or guardians who really dreaded their expulsion. But it was better that the unfit should be rejected in England, where they could find other openings, than in India, where they could find none. "Little other change is wanting than that an appointment should be considered in spirit and in truth, not in mere words, as a prize to be contended for, not a property already possessed, which may be lost. If the Directors were to appoint one-fifth every year beyond the number finally to go out, and the four-fifths were to be the best of the whole body, the appointments would then really be prizes to be contended for, and the effects would be admirable. Each appointment to the college would then be of less value; but they would be more in number, and the patronage would hardly suffer. A Director could not then, indeed, be able to send out an unqualified son. But is it fitting that he should? This is a fair question for the consideration of the Legislature and the British public" (*Statements*, p. **103** n.). In these matters at least Malthus was no reactionary.

The college does not die out on the pages of the India Register till the death of the Company in 1858. Its monopoly was gone some time before then. An Act of 1827 provided, theoretically, for the examination and appointment of India Civil servants who had not studied at Hertford College. In 1833 provision was made for the limited competition which Malthus had recommended. Candidates were to be nominated in groups of four, the best of the four to have an appointment (Mill and Wilson's *British India*, Vol. IX. Book III. ch. ix. p. 381). In 1855 came the end. The Company was "relieved of the obligation to keep up the college," the reign of open competition ushered in by Macaulay's Report (November 1854) brought a new order of things, and the college was only continued till those who had already joined it should finish their course. The steps may be followed in the Fourth Report of the Civil Service Commissioners, for 1858, pp. xix *seq.*, 228 *seq.* (*Cf.* also First Report for 1855.)

For posterity the Work of Malthus was not in the East India College, but in his writings. But his connection with the college was perhaps the most important of the external facts of his life, and it has helped to preserve a record of scenes and incidents revealing fine shades of character more clearly than the laudations of friends with their broad generalities and occasional misjudgments. Samuel Rogers the poet thought Mackintosh, Malthus, and Bobus Smith to be "the three acutest men" he had ever known; they all agreed in a theological tenet (the limitation of attributes)! (*Rogers and his Contemporaries*, II. 268; *Rogers and his Circle*, p. 34). It was the tenet also of J. S. Mill (*Essays on Religion*, 2nd. ed., 1874, p. 40). It is not inconsistent with the cosmology of the first Essay. But Rogers is hardly a good authority. There is a sounder and saner word from Mackintosh (quoted by Empson, *Edinburgh Review*, January 1837, p. 473): "I have known Adam Smith slightly, Ricardo well, Malthus intimately. Is it not something to say for a science that its three great masters were about the three best men I ever knew?"

Sinclair's *Correspondence* (1831, Vol. I. Autographs)[1] gives the handwriting of all three. All are legible. Adam Smith's is a large, bold, schoolboy hand; the writing of Malthus is regular without being clerkly; Ricardo's the same with even more character and firmness.

The portrait of Malthus in old age painted by John Linnell, the friend of Blake, shows him erect and cheerful. It bears out the description in the *Gentleman's Magazine* (March 1835, 324): In person "he was tall and elegantly formed." Mrs. Malthus was short. It appears from Linnell's Life (by Story, 2 volumes, 1892), Vol. II. 249, that he painted in oil from the life in 1833 both Malthus and Mrs. Malthus.

[1] Numbers 52, 68, 69.

The original oil portrait of Malthus is still with the family; there is a good copy in Jesus College. The engraving was done by the artist himself in the same year (*l.c.* 243). It is set down (in the Life of Linnell) as "14 by 11½ inches; mezzotint from the artist's own posthumous portrait, 1833; Colnaghi & Co." Copies bear the date 1st Jan., 1834; but even that is not "posthumous" as the word is now used. Perhaps 1835 was intended. Linnell lived till 1882. The engraving is the frontispiece of this book.

Malthus died suddenly of heart disease on Monday, 29th December, 1834, when on a visit to his wife's old home at Claverton. He is buried in Bath Abbey in the north aisle of the nave. The epitaph is probably by Otter. The eleventh line refers to the matter discussed above, and might well have been spared. Otherwise the epitaph is worthy of the subject, and contains little exaggeration.

[INSCRIPTION ON THE WALL—TABLET IN BATH ABBEY.]

SACRED TO THE MEMORY

OF

The Rev. Thomas Robert Malthus,

LONG KNOWN TO THE LETTERED WORLD
BY HIS ADMIRABLE WRITINGS ON THE SOCIAL BRANCHES OF
POLITICAL ECONOMY,
PARTICULARLY BY HIS "ESSAY ON POPULATION."

ONE OF THE BEST MEN AND TRUEST PHILOSOPHERS
OF ANY AGE OR COUNTRY,
RAISED BY NATIVE DIGNITY OF MIND
ABOVE THE MISREPRESENTATIONS OF THE IGNORANT
AND THE NEGLECT OF THE GREAT,
HE LIVED A SERENE AND HAPPY LIFE
DEVOTED TO THE PURSUIT AND COMMUNICATION
OF TRUTH,
SUPPORTED BY A CALM BUT FIRM CONVICTION OF THE
USEFULNESS OF HIS LABOURS,
CONTENT WITH THE APPROBATION OF THE WISE AND GOOD.

HIS WRITINGS WILL BE A LASTING MONUMENT
OF THE EXTENT AND CORRECTNESS OF HIS UNDERSTANDING.

THE SPOTLESS INTEGRITY OF HIS PRINCIPLES,
THE EQUITY AND CANDOUR OF HIS NATURE,
HIS SWEETNESS OF TEMPER, URBANITY OF MANNERS,
AND TENDERNESS OF HEART,
HIS BENEVOLENCE AND HIS PIETY,
ARE THE STILL DEARER RECOLLECTIONS OF HIS FAMILY
AND FRIENDS.

Born, Feb. 14, 1766. *Died Dec. 29, 1834.*

INDEX.